Approaches to Teaching the Novels of Nella Larsen

Approaches to Teaching World Literature

For a complete listing of titles,
see the last pages of this book.

Approaches to Teaching the Novels of Nella Larsen

Edited by

Jacquelyn Y. McLendon

The Modern Language Association of America
New York 2016

Library of Congress Cataloging-in-Publication Data

Names: McLendon, Jacquelyn Y. editor.
Title: Approaches to teaching the novels of Nella Larsen / edited by Jacquelyn Y. McLendon.
Description: New York : The Modern Language Association of America, 2016. | Series: Approaches to teaching world literature ; 138 | Includes bibliographical references and index.
Identifiers: LCCN 2016002446 | ISBN 9781603292191 (cloth : alk. paper) | ISBN 9781603292207 (pbk. : alk. paper) | ISBN 9781603292214 (EPUB) | ISBN 9781603292221 (Kindle)
Subjects: LCSH: Larsen, Nella—Study and teaching.
Classification: LCC PS3523.A7225 Z75 2016 | DDC 813/.52—dc23
LC record available at http://lccn.loc.gov/2016002446

Approaches to Teaching World Literature 138
ISSN 1059-1133

Cover illustration of the paperback and electronic editions:
Cocktails, by Archibald Motley. 1926. Courtesy of the Chicago History Museum.
© Valerie Gerrard Brown and Mara Motley, MD.

Published by The Modern Language Association of America
85 Broad Street, suite 500, New York, New York 10004-2434
www.mla.org

CONTENTS

ACKNOWLEDGMENTS

I wish to thank the Modern Language Association's editorial board and publications committee for understanding the need for and importance of this book. I especially thank Sonia Kane, former series editor, for her patience, advice, and support through all the correspondence, questions, and revisions that went into bringing this volume to fruition. Many thanks as well to Margit Longbrake who had the onerous task of taking over a project already under way.

I also extend much gratitude to the many survey participants who shared their teaching strategies and suggestions for the kinds of essays they wished to see included in this volume. And, of course, there wouldn't be a book without the contributions of those whose essays follow. I thank them first for their continued interest in Nella Larsen's work, for their patience through many months of waiting, and for their willingness to share their classroom experiments and experience with all of us who teach or would like to teach Larsen's work. A special thanks to Heidi Durrow, a wonderful author in her own right, who personally shared her story with me and my students about Larsen's importance as a model.

The encouragement and support of colleagues and friends who read and made suggestions at various stages enabled me to see this project through: the caring, the expertise, and the judiciously critical comments of those in my writing group—Gayle Murchison, Iyabo Osiapem, Hermine Pinson, Dierdre Royster, Mei Mei Sanford, and especially Kimberley Phillips, who read and made suggestions beyond our regular meetings; the wide-ranging knowledge of Nancy Gray, who often has talked me through writing dilemmas with her sage advice and patient understanding; and the high-tech skills of Chon Glover, who so patiently shared her expertise with me. I have come to rely on the keen critiques and erudition of P. Gabrielle Foreman over many years and many projects, and I'm grateful for her continued support. I am also deeply grateful to my indispensable research assistant Ashleigh Washington, for her many trips to the library, her persistence in tracking down difficult to acquire material, her computer skills that made sharing information effortless, the discussions we shared as her own interest in the subject grew, and her overall assistance in helping to put the volume together. Thanks also to Sarah Kathryn Atkinson, who was extremely helpful in filling in for Ashleigh over a summer, and to Kierstin Moses, who located valuable material for me during her short time as my newest research assistant.

During the final stages of putting the volume together, Shanay Butler, the English department's administrative assistant, provided invaluable support. Her patience, optimism, and computer skills enabled me to complete the final manuscript. The cooperation and assistance of Jeanne Smith, office manager, Department of English, as well as Hope Yelich, Mary Molineux, and others at Swem Library, the College of William and Mary, were of tremendous value as well.

Last but not least, I dedicate this book to the many students in my Harlem Renaissance courses over the years as a way to thank them for their questions, comments, and insights—and especially for their love of Larsen's work that so often equaled my own.

Part One

MATERIALS

Overview

The essays included in this volume aim to help students better understand various aspects of the literary and historical periods in which Nella Larsen's two novels, *Quicksand* and *Passing*, were written. Contributors address such issues as the ways in which the novels reflect history; the shift from Victorian ideas and ideals to modernist ones; prevailing attitudes toward women, especially black women; the art and artistry of the "New Negro" movement, subsequently called the Harlem Renaissance; the meaning of canonicity and Larsen's novels' relation to other literature; and legal issues involved with racial identities and differences. In so doing, they demonstrate how new and seasoned instructors alike might use Larsen's novels to explore a wide range of topics and themes—including the difficult and provocative issues of race, gender, class, and sexuality—across multiple disciplines.

The Novels

Quicksand and *Passing* were published by Alfred A. Knopf in March 1928 and April 1929, respectively. Through its protagonist, Helga Crane, *Quicksand* examines, among other themes and issues, the problems of being biracial in both America and Denmark. It also critiques the black elite and explores the most oppressive aspects of marriage and motherhood. *Passing* centers on two women protagonists, Irene Redfield and Clare Kendry, both light-skinned enough to pass and both confined by the psychological narrowness of black and female life. Irene physically passes on occasion, but Clare moves fully into the white world through marriage to a white man. Depicting the women as psychological doubles, Larsen shows the act of passing as both physical and emotional and, as in *Quicksand*, challenges conventional "mulatta" and "passing" narratives, as I discuss in my introduction to part 2.

Although both novels were out of print and thus little known for many years, they are currently available from a number of publishers, either separately or in a single volume, with forewords and introductions by noteworthy scholars and fiction writers. The two novels and Larsen's three short stories may be found together in Charles Larson's *An Intimation of Things Distant: The Collected Fiction of Nella Larsen* (1992), *The Complete Fiction of Nella Larsen:* Passing, Quicksand, *and the Stories* (2001), and *Short Fiction of Nella Larsen* (2010).

Some respondents to the survey sent to college and university instructors in the United States and abroad indicated that they use a number of different editions in the classroom, often depending on which are least expensive for students. Others cited the Rutgers University Press edition of *Quicksand* and *Passing* (1986), edited by Deborah McDowell; the Penguin edition of *Quicksand* (2002), edited by Thadious Davis; and the Norton Critical Edition of *Passing* (2007), edited by Carla Kaplan. *The Norton Anthology of African American*

Literature (Gates, Higginbotham, and McKay) includes *Quicksand* in its first two editions and includes *Passing* in its entirety in the third edition, and Anchor Books has published *Passing*, with an introduction by Ntozake Shange. Translations of the novels are available in at least two other languages. *Quicksand* has been translated into Italian (*Sabbie Mobili,* translated by M. Giulia Fabi) and *Passing* in French (*Passer la ligne*). E-book editions of Larsen's fiction are also available.

The Short Stories

First published under the pseudonym Allen Semi, Larsen's married name anagrammatized, two short stories, "The Wrong Man" and "Freedom," appeared in *Young's Realistic Stories* magazine in January and April 1926, respectively. These two stories do not concern themselves directly with racial issues nor are the characters identifiably black; however, both were proleptic of what was to come in the greater accomplishments of her novels. Secrets, shameful pasts, repressed upper-middle-class black life, suffocating marriages, uncontrollable fear—all surface repeatedly in Larsen's fiction.

"Sanctuary," Larsen's third and final short story, appeared in 1930 in *Forum* magazine. It is the most well-known of her short stories primarily because of the accusation of plagiarism that one of the magazine's readers leveled against Larsen. The accuser said that she recognized similarities to British writer Sheila Kaye-Smith's "Mrs. Adis," a story that had appeared earlier in *Century* magazine. After submitting a written explanation and several drafts of her story, Larsen was exonerated by *Forum*'s editors, but that did not put a stop to the controversy, which continues in current scholarship (see "Suggestions for Further Reading," below, for a list of articles about Larsen and plagiarism, and see the introduction to part 2 for a more detailed description of the controversy).

Interest in "Sanctuary" notwithstanding, Larsen's short fiction has received minimal critical attention, her biographers, Charles Larson, Thadious Davis, and George Hutchinson, and the critic Cheryl Wall (in *Women of the Harlem Renaissance*) being notable exceptions.

Other Writings

Larsen's earliest known publications appeared in *The Brownies' Book* as follows: "Playtime: Three Scandinavian Games" (June 1920) and "Playtime: Danish Fun" (July 1920). She also published review essays of Kathleen Norris's novel *Certain People of Importance*, which appeared in the *Messenger* in 1923, and Thomas Bowyer Campbell's *Black Sadie*, for *Opportunity* in 1929. For unpublished fiction discussed in Larsen's correspondence or submitted to publishers, see the biographies by Charles Larson (*Invisible Darkness*), Thadious Davis (*Nella Larsen*), and George Hutchinson (*In Search of Nella Larsen*). The James Weldon Johnson Collection at the Beinecke Library holds much of her correspondence, some of which has been published in William Bedford Clark's "The Letters of Nella Larsen to Carl Van Vechten: A Survey."

Suggestions for Further Reading

In addition to McDowell's introduction to *Quicksand* and *Passing* in the 1986 Rutgers University Press edition and Thadious Davis's introduction to *Passing* in the 2002 Penguin edition, the Norton Critical Edition of *Passing* (2007), edited by Kaplan, provides an efficient and economical way to expose students to a variety of critical interpretations, historical documents, and excerpts from similar fiction. In the Norton Critical Edition, instructors might find especially useful Mark J. Madigan's excerpt from "Miscegenation and 'The Dicta of Race and Class': The Rhinelander Case and Nella Larsen's *Passing*" and Miriam Thaggert's "Racial Etiquette: Nella Larsen's *Passing* and the Rhinelander Case." *Love on Trial: An American Scandal in Black and White*, by Earl Lewis and Heidi Ardizzone, provides the details of the *Rhinelander* case as well as an analysis in the context of the times. For a fuller discussion of the *Rhinelander* case, see the introduction to part 2.

Charles Larson's *Invisible Darkness: Jean Toomer and Nella Larsen*, Thadious Davis's *Nella Larsen: Novelist of the Harlem Renaissance: A Woman's Life Unveiled*, and George Hutchinson's *In Search of Nella Larsen: A Biography of the Color Line* are indispensable resources for information on Larsen's life and works. Hutchinson's biography corrects assumptions and inaccuracies regarding Larsen's Danish heritage as well as sheds additional light on, though it does not resolve completely, the mysteries surrounding her father, stepfather, and family circumstances.

Barbara Christian's *Black Women Novelists: The Development of a Tradition, 1892–1976* and *Black Feminist Criticism: Perspectives on Black Women Writers* and Hazel Carby's *Reconstructing Womanhood: The Emergence of the Afro-American Woman Novelist* remain good choices for placing Larsen's work in a larger African American women's literary tradition. Survey respondents cited a number of other texts as the ones they often use in preparing to teach the Harlem Renaissance and Larsen specifically: Houston Baker's *Modernism and the Harlem Renaissance*; Ann DuCille's *The Coupling Convention: Sex, Text, and Tradition in Black Women's Fiction*, especially the chapter "The Bourgeois, Wedding Bell Blues of Jessie Fauset and Nella Larsen"; Barbara Johnson's "The Quicksands of the Self: Nella Larsen and Heinz Kohut"; Judith Butler's "Passing, Queering: Nella Larsen's Psychoanalytic Challenge"; Jacquelyn Y. McLendon's "Social Nightmare in Quicksand" and "(Re)shaping Content in *Passing*; or, This Text Which Is Not One"; and Wall's *Women of the Harlem Renaissance*. Wall's essay "Passing for What?" is especially useful as it begins with a detailed discussion of one of Larsen's short stories, "The Wrong Man," tying it to Larsen's novels but also comparing aspects of it with other writings of the period. Instructors also recommend Pamela Caughie's *Passing and Pedagogy: The Dynamics of Responsibility* and John Young's chapter "Passing (on) Textual History: The Ends of Nella Larsen's *Passing*" in his *Black Writers, White Publishers: Marketplace Politics in Twentieth-Century African American Literature* for in-depth analyses of the ending of *Passing*.

Excellent resources for discussions of Larsen's transnational identity are Jeffrey Gray's "Essence and the Mulatto Traveler: Europe as Embodiment in Nella Larsen's *Quicksand*"; Hutchinson's "Nella Larsen and the Veil of Race" and "An End to the Family Romance: Nella Larsen, Black Transnationalism, and American Racial Ideology"; Lena Ahlin's *The "New Negro" in the Old World: Culture and Performance in James Weldon Johnson, Jessie Fauset, and Nella Larsen*; Arne Lunde and Anna Westerstahl Stenport's "Helga Crane's Copenhagen: Denmark, Colonialism, and Transnational Identity in Nella Larsen's *Quicksand*." Articles that address the plagiarism charge and speculate about its effects on Larsen and her career are Beverly Haviland's "Passing from Paranoia to Plagiarism: The Abject Authorship of Nella Larsen"; Hildegard Hoeller's "Race, Modernism, and Plagiarism: The Case of Nella Larsen's 'Sanctuary'"; and Kelli Larson's "Surviving the Taint of Plagiarism: Nella Larsen's 'Sanctuary' and Sheila Kaye-Smith's 'Mrs. Adis.'" For articles that raise issues of plagiarism in Larsen's novel *Quicksand*, see Erika Williams's "A Lie of Omission: Plagiarism in Nella Larsen's *Quicksand*" and Willie Tolliver's "The Wings of the Furies: Teaching Nella Larsen and the American Literature Tradition."

Allison Berg's *Mothering the Race: Women's Narratives of Reproduction, 1890–1930* (2002); Daylanne K. English's *Unnatural Selections: Eugenics in American Modernism and the Harlem Renaissance*; and Beth Widmaier Capo's *Textual Contraception: Birth Control and Modern American Fiction* discuss the politics of women's reproductive rights in literature, stressing the importance of fiction in helping shape public consciousness.

Selected Reference Works

For critical biographies and bio-bibliographical materials, instructors and students should consult Trudier Harris and Thadious Davis's *Dictionary of Literary Biography: Afro-American Writers from the Harlem Renaissance to 1940* (vol. 51); Cathy N. Davidson and Linda A. Wagner-Martin's *Oxford Companion to Women's Writing in the United States*; Pamela Kester-Shelton's *Feminist Writers*; Valerie Smith's *African American Writers*; Emmanuel S. Nelson's *African American Authors, 1745–1945*; Laurie Champion's *American Women Writers, 1900–1945*; Darlene Clark Hine's *Black Women in America*; and Yolanda Williams Page's *Encyclopedia of African American Women Writers*. Included in the Gale Literary Criticism series are *Black Literature Criticism*; *Contemporary*

Literary Criticism, vol. 37; *Twentieth-Century Literary Criticism*, vol. 200; *Contemporary Authors*, vol. 125; and *Contemporary Authors New Revision Series*.

For reference works that focus solely on the Harlem Renaissance, instructors and students should consult Bruce Kellner's *The Harlem Renaissance: A Historical Dictionary for the Era*; Cary D. Wintz and Paul Finkelman's *Encyclopedia of the Harlem Renaissance*; Aberjhani and Sandra L. West's *Encyclopedia of the Harlem Renaissance*; Jeffrey Brown Ferguson's *The Harlem Renaissance: A Brief History with Documents*; Henry Louis Gates, Jr., and Evelyn Brooks Higginbotham's *Harlem Renaissance Lives*; Hutchinson's *The Cambridge Companion to the Harlem Renaissance*; and *Harlem Renaissance: A Gale Critical Companion*.

Multimedia Resources

The documentary *The Life and Times of Sara Baartman* depicts the story of the woman also known as the "Hottentot Venus," who was taken from South Africa and then sexually exploited by being exhibited as a freak throughout Europe. It is an excellent film to use as historical background to help explain attitudes about black women's sexuality.

Several instructors suggested the films *Pinky* (1949), *Imitation of Life* (both the 1934 and 1959 versions), and *Scar of Shame* (1927) as older films that deal with interracial and intraracial class and skin color issues. Also recommended is Julie Dash's 1983 film *Illusions*, about an African American woman passing for white during the 1940s in Hollywood.

Audio resources include two NPR broadcasts (available online) featuring Heidi Durrow. In "Three Books to Rescue Nordic Lit from the Dark Side," she reads from and briefly discusses Larsen's novels; on NPR's *You Must Read This* series, she recommends Larsen's second novel, *Passing* (see 'Passing' across the Color Line). Finally, the LibriVox Free Audiobook Collection, an online source, has made unabridged versions of both novels available, and Griot Audio has put out unabridged audio cassettes of *Passing*.

NOTE

Unless otherwise indicated, most of the essays in the volume cite the 1986 Rutgers University Press edition of *Quicksand* and *Passing*, which features notes and an introduction by Deborah E. McDowell.

Part Two

APPROACHES

Introduction

Nella Larsen herself acknowledged the autobiographical nature of *Quicksand* in a letter to her friend Carl Van Vechten with the frank admission that "it's the awful truth."[1] Larsen's life was, indeed, similar to that of Helga Crane, the protagonist of her first novel. Like Helga, Larsen was born of mixed parentage—a Danish mother and a black father. According to Larsen, her early years were spent in predominantly white surroundings, her mother having married someone of her own race after the death of Larsen's biological father. That her mother was a white woman from Denmark is certain, but the truth of Larsen's statements about her black father has been debated in numerous literary venues, most particularly in the three biographies.

Two of Larsen's biographers, Thadious Davis, in *Nella Larsen: Novelist of the Harlem Renaissance: A Woman's Life Unveiled*, and George Hutchinson, in *In Search of Nella Larsen: A Biography of the Color Line*, differ in their accounts of Larsen's paternal parentage in significant ways. Davis states that Peter Walker, alleged to be Larsen's biological father, and Peter Larsen, her mother's alleged-to-be-white second husband, might have been one and the same (26–27), implying that Peter Walker passed for white as Peter Larsen (or "Larson"). Hutchinson argues that Davis's claim is improbable because it relies on what he deems the "faulty analyses of two census listings, a school record, a marriage license, and peripatetic spellings of "Larsen" as "Larson" (24). Hutchinson confirms Larsen's account that her biological father was black and her stepfather was white. Despite these differences, both biographers agree that racism complicated Larsen's childhood and family life. At an early narrative moment in *Quicksand*, the protagonist Helga Crane recalls her "unloved, unloving, and unhappy childhood" (29), feelings that resonate profoundly in Larsen's own life, accounting for her comment in an interview with Thelma Berlack of the *Amsterdam News* that "I don't see my family much now. It might make it awkward for them, particularly my half-sister" ("New Author"). In fact, after Larsen's death, her half-sister, Anna Larsen Gardner, commented that she didn't know she had a half-sister (C. Larson 119). That Larsen did not see her family demonstrates her firsthand knowledge of the alienation Helga feels; Larsen knew the loneliness and pain of racial dualism, which is why she focused her attention on these aspects of her protagonists' lives in her novels.

Larsen left or was sent from Chicago, where her family lived, at age sixteen. She then studied at Fisk University in their Normal Department, resided in Denmark two or three years (Hutchinson 64–78), entered the Lincoln Hospital and Home Training School for Nurses (in 1912), and worked as head nurse of the John Andrew Memorial Hospital and Nurse Training School at Tuskegee Institute (in 1915). Larsen remained at Tuskegee slightly less than a year, but the institute, its "system of rules and restraints," and one of her male colleagues all became models for other autobiographical elements of *Quicksand*, specifically the fictional southern school, Naxos, where Helga works at the novel's opening and the character James Vayle, to whom Helga is briefly engaged (T. Davis, *Nella Larsen* 101–10).

Two years after leaving Tuskegee and returning to New York, still working as a nurse, Larsen met Dr. Elmer Samuel Imes, apparently a brilliant physicist who eventually became chair of Fisk University's physics department among other notable accomplishments in his field. She married him on 3 May 1919. Her marriage to Imes most likely gave her the chance to meet some of the prominent African Americans in New York, which might account for her foray into the literary world. She published first in the *Brownies' Book* and then in *Young's Realistic Fiction*, where her short stories appeared. Both Davis's and Hutchinson's biographies provide great detail about the widening social circles that opened up opportunities for Larsen to pursue a literary career. One such opportunity was her employment at the 135th Street Branch of the New York Public Library and meeting Edward C. Williams, librarian and library administrator, writer, and son-in-law of Charles Chesnutt. When Larsen decided to attend library school, Williams provided her with a letter of recommendation (Hutchinson 142), and so began a career at the Seward Park Branch for the next several years.

Publication of the stories in *Young's* attests to the fact that Larsen had become serious about writing early on. In addition to "The Wrong Man" and "Freedom" in *Young's* and the 1930 controversial short story "Sanctuary" discussed below, according to information contained in the Harmon Foundation and Guggenheim Foundation files, Larsen wrote at least two other stories: "Tea," which may have been published pseudonymously, and "Charity," which was unpublished as of 1929, neither of which appears to have survived (T. Davis, *Nella Larsen* 184).

As previously mentioned, the short story that has received the most attention is "Sanctuary," probably because of the plagiarism charge. "Sanctuary" is a story about a black woman in the South who unwittingly hides her son's killer from a white sheriff and his men, thereby preventing a possible lynching. Larsen's publication of the story brought an accusation of plagiarism because a reader wrote to the editors of *Forum* that it bore striking similarities to the British writer Sheila Kaye-Smith's story "Mrs. Adis." *Forum*'s editors asked Larsen for an explanation and, satisfied with her account of how she came by the material, exonerated her. However, that did not prevent the gossip, some quite malicious among her contemporaries, that persisted in the accusation's wake.[2] Some critics have argued that the two stories are so similar as to make coincidence unlikely. Thadious Davis offers a detailed comparison of the two stories based on theme, story line, language, characterization, and plot, concluding that "Larsen may well have gambled on no one's recognizing the similarities" (*Nella Larsen* 351).

Others have either read into the incident autobiographically or speculated that it was in large part responsible for Larsen's disappearance from the literary scene. Beverly Haviland, for example, takes as a given not only that Larsen plagiarized the story but also that the act and accusation ended her career, calling it "literary suicide" (295). She fuses Larsen's life with the lives of her characters to such a degree that they are often indistinguishable, arguing that Larsen, like Irene Redfield in *Passing*, was paranoid. Haviland also argues that plagiarism was Larsen's way of taking "revenge against her own loved and hated white mother" for not protecting her as a child in the way that the black mother in "Sanctuary" "protects even the murderer of her own son" (302). Haviland states that Larsen's "brilliant and brief literary career came to a *sudden* end" as a result of the plagiarism charge, a statement that is, at the very least, misleading (emphasis mine). Although no known publications exist after "Sanctuary," Larsen continued to write and submitted at least one manuscript to Knopf ("Mirage"), which was rejected. No evidence exists to suggest that the plagiarism charge was a factor in Knopf's rejection, but there is evidence that Knopf readers did not think the submission was as well done as *Passing*.

Similar to Haviland's unfounded speculation about the effect on Larsen of the plagiarism controversy is Marcy Knopf's claim that "the scandal was so painful to Larsen" that she never published again" (xxxv). Yet the events that followed the plagiarism charge are too complex to make a judgment about any one major cause of Larsen's not publishing after "Sanctuary." It is important to note that the charge did not prevent Larsen's winning the highly competitive, prestigious Guggenheim fellowship, the first African American woman to do so, which enabled her to travel to Europe to continue her writing. However, the manuscripts on which she worked both alone and in collaboration with a white male friend, the aspiring writer Edward Donahoe, were never published, and neither were other writing projects mentioned in her correspondence.

Just as Larsen continued to write after the hurtful plagiarism charge, she also continued to write after the devastating discovery of her husband's infidelity. In a letter Elmer Imes wrote to Van Vechten dated 18 September 1930, he states that "early in the year and quite by accident Nella became possessed of information that I was at the time very much interested in another girl." The "girl" about whom Imes wrote was Ethel Gilbert, a white woman on the administrative staff at Fisk University. Within the space of a few years, Larsen was again the subject of, in her words, "a lot of gossip floating about."[3] When, in July 1933, Larsen sought a divorce in Nashville, Tennessee, she wrote to her friend Dorothy Peterson that it was because the divorce could be done there "discreetly."[4] However, that was not to be—the *Baltimore Afro-American* carried a front-page article about the divorce, complete with a photograph of Larsen.

Undoubtedly the divorce and the plagiarism accusation contributed to Larsen's abandoning her writing, but necessity might have contributed as much or more. She wrote to Van Vechten that she had requested a renewal of her fellowship but had been turned down because of a lack of funds.[5] Moreover, interest in black culture was rapidly going out of "vogue" as Langston Hughes would later write in his autobiography *The Big Sea.* Thadious Davis's point is well taken that the emergence of a "fresh generation of African-American writers" like Richard Wright "did not bode well for [Larsen's] chances of renewed success as a published author" (*Nella Larsen* 442). Despite numerous speculations, however, the precise reasons Larsen finally gave up a writing career and returned to nursing remain a mystery. Davis states that she had no "regular employment" until 1944, when she became a night-duty nurse at Gouverneur Hospital on Manhattan's Lower East Side (443).

After Larsen returned to nursing, she became increasingly reclusive. According to coworkers who were closest to her, she was lonely and unhappy (C. Larson 115–17). Larsen died on 30 March 1964, and she was buried on 6 April in Cypress Hills Cemetery in Brooklyn. Her grave went unmarked until 2006, when a young Black and Danish writer named Heidi Durrow, following the lead of Alice Walker, who erected a headstone on Zora Neale Hurston's unmarked grave, erected a headstone to honor Larsen.[6] It reads simply:

> Nella Larsen
> 1891–1964
> A Novelist Remembered

Critical Reception of the Novels

Over the years since the novels have come back into print, reviews and scholarly criticism, even when mostly favorable, have viewed Larsen's *Quicksand* and *Passing* almost exclusively as conventional "tragic mulatta" narratives whose mixed-race characters in most cases perpetuated the stereotype of the "divided self" in that they could not be white and would not be black. These stereotypes are characterized by racial self-loathing, the result of their "black" blood and the notion that "one drop" taints the rest. As I have written elsewhere, Larsen depicts racially mixed characters as more complex than "tragic mulattas" such as Zoe in Dion Boucicault's play *The Octoroon* (1859); Madame Delphine, the titular character in George Washington Cable's short story (1881); Rhoda Aldgate in William Dean Howells's *An Imperative Duty* (1891); and the "mulatto" character Peter Siner in T. S. Stribling's *Birthright* (1921), the specific novel whose characterizations Jessie Fauset, Larsen's contemporary, cited in an interview as unrealistic (McLendon, *Politics* 13–27).

Fauset named Larsen as a writer who, like herself, was "affected" by portrayals of blacks in general and mixed-race characters in particular in *Birthright* and other fiction. She stated in an interview for the *Southern Workman*, "Let us who are better qualified to present that truth than any white writer, try to do so" (Starkey 219). Some critics have argued that, like her contemporary Fauset, Larsen was preoccupied with the physical attributes among the lighter- or whiter-skinned segment of the "Negro" race. On the contrary, both writers in their novels satirize precursory, formulaic "mulatta" and "passing" tales. Larsen portrays the suffering of *Quicksand*'s protagonist, Helga Crane, as deriving from alienation, abandonment, and sexual and racial oppression.

Thus although many of Helga's problems stem from negative attitudes about miscegenation, Larsen challenges depictions that attribute such problems to the "blood" theory.

Yet Larsen's portrayal of miscegenation—an act that over time America has defined as felonious, bestial, adulterous, spurious, and, at the very least, unnatural—caused both praise and censure of the author and her novels from the very start. Although, to state the obvious, interracial sexual and marital relations do not occur only between black and white people, miscegenation is often perceived as such, a view that reflects the historically broader binary perception of race in this country. Many miscegenation laws were declared unconstitutional only as far back as 1967 with the ruling in *Loving v. Virginia*, and Alabama was the last state to overturn its law against interracial marriage in November of 2000, demonstrating how slowly attitudes toward interracial relationships have changed over the years.

Attitudes against "race intermingling" (*Quicksand* 39) resulted in *Quicksand* being labeled, among other things, a "black horror story" (see the back cover of the 1971 Collier Books reprint with Adelaide Cromwell Hill's introduction) and in *Passing* being compared with "a tradition of mulatto writers since William Wells Brown" by Hoyt Fuller, who sees in Larsen a preoccupation with the "white traits" of "society Negro characters" (19). Moreover, the critiques that accompanied the reprinting of Larsen's novels in the late sixties and early seventies often relied on inaccuracies about important aspects of her work.[7]

Serious attention to Larsen as an important literary figure seemed to take shape with Mary Helen Washington's landmark 1980 *Ms.* magazine article "Mystery Woman of the Harlem Renaissance" and to gain momentum with Deborah McDowell's insightful and provocative introduction to the single-volume reprint of both novels in 1986, after which scholarship not only increased but began to take on a different tone and configuration, evolving into scholarship that more often than not showed appreciation of Larsen's novels' subtleties and complexities.[8]

George Hutchinson's discovery that Larsen did, indeed, travel to Denmark at least twice in her life opened up the possibilities for scholars to pursue her transnationalism. Martyn Bone, in his essay "Teaching *Quicksand* in Denmark," in this volume, states that Hutchinson's work and other critical debates "transformed [his] teaching and classroom discussion of *Quicksand.*" Hutchinson's own scholarship on Larsen's transnationalism (esp. "End" and "Nella Larsen") has helped broaden an understanding of *Quicksand* and of Larsen's personal life.

In their essay "Helga Crane's Copenhagen: Denmark, Colonialism, and Transnational Identity in Nella Larsen's *Quicksand*," Arne Lunde and Anna Stenport argue that there is "much more to Helga Crane's relationship than previously noted" and that

> Larsen critiques a lingering silence with respect to Denmark's conflicted relationship to its own colonial past. At the same time, Larsen identifies as an artist with several of the major figures of the Scandinavian Modernist Breakthrough movement of the late nineteenth century—most notably Jens Peter Jacobsen and Henrik Ibsen. (228)

Lunde and Stenport suggest that Larsen's critique and dual heritage are important aspects that much Larsen scholarship has generally dismissed or glossed over, although they contend that Larsen's "own tendency toward self-mythologizing" to some extent explains this "critical oversight" (228–29).

Lunde and Stenport argue further that critics' "impulse to suppress Larsen's Danish family ties" is an attempt to "secure her status within a feminist, African-American literary canon" (229). Yet clearly the reasons many critics focus on Larsen's African American heritage and Harlem Renaissance identity are a great deal more complicated, having less to do with her cultural and racial identity and more to do with the genre in which she writes. Autobiographical or not, *Quicksand* (like *Passing*) is ultimately fiction. That *Quicksand* is about a woman, Helga Crane, who identifies as a "Negro" and, the Copenhagen section notwithstanding, that its settings are primarily in African American communities among people whose daily lives reflect a shared experience within the United States proper situates it in the tradition of African American literature. In other words, Larsen's "own identification with her 'Nordic' side and Danish roots" does not threaten the novel's status as belonging to a "feminist, African American literary canon," as Lunde and Stenport argue, because the novel functions in these traditions on its own merits: its plot, characterization, settings, and the many other ways suggested by the essays included in this volume (228–29).

That said, as Birgitt Flohr so aptly points out in "The Relationship between Fiction and Autobiography," "To avoid reading the autobiographical text as factual does not mean . . . to cut [the] text off from a reality outside of itself" (5). It follows, then, that situating *Quicksand* within an African American tradition does not negate its transnational identification and that adding the transnational dimension broadens an understanding not only of the Copenhagen section of the novel but also of the dilemmas in which the protagonist finds herself and the choices she makes to deal with those dilemmas.

With regard to Larsen's self-identification, although Larsen often acknowledged her Danish family background, she stated in an interview that because of her "economic status it's better to be a Negro" (Rennels). Besides this deliberate identification with "Negroes" for the reason stated in the interview, Larsen obviously felt keenly that social constructions of race also greatly influence the way one sees oneself. In other words, in the Du Boisian sense, people often see themselves as others do even if it is generally a distorted view, an issue that frequently materializes in Larsen's fiction.

Like society's attitudes toward interracial relations, though, social constructions of race have changed very little over the years. For example, the May

2011 issue of *Ebony* magazine carries a special report on various perspectives of biracialism. Adam Serwer, in his article "In the Mix: Being Biracial in America," quotes President Obama's answer to a *60 Minutes* host's question about "how he had decided he was Black": "Well, I'm not sure I decided it. I think if you look African-American in this society, you're treated as an African American" (86). And, as Serwer goes on to say, "Put another way, there's nothing contradictory about being biracial and being Black" (86). Similarly, because of such attitudes about race and class, along with Larsen's own attitude, most critics have found nothing contradictory about focusing almost exclusively on Larsen's African American heritage, nothing contradictory in placing her work within an African American literary canon.

Meeting the Challenges of Teaching the Novels

The interpretive and pedagogical challenges of teaching Larsen's novels, although diminished, have certainly not been eliminated. Scholars have not always given Larsen serious consideration as having fully participated in the transformation that marked the "New Negro" movement. Nor have they generally examined her work as, at the very least, marking a transition from the Victorian era to a new era concerned with power relations, ideas of freedom, opposition to religion, and questions of maternal destiny—although this is beginning to change as a book such as Susan Ware's *Modern American Women: A Documentary History* (2001) suggests, as well as the essays included in this volume. Perhaps more important, reading Larsen's novels as autobiography has also been problematic. Although Larsen's statement that *Quicksand* is "the awful truth" has influenced, perhaps overdetermined, analyses and interpretations of her work, several essays included in this volume provide ideas about ways to approach any similarities to Larsen's own life that appear in her novels or heavily influence the plots. Further, I have made the point elsewhere that Larsen's novels, especially *Quicksand*, recall texts of an African American literary tradition's foremothers such as *Incidents in the Life of a Slave Girl* and *Our Nig; or, Sketches from the Life of a Free Black* with regard to their hybridity (*Politics*). Keeping in mind that "literary forms and generic lines are fluid," one might say that *Quicksand* also is a "brilliant novel that makes autobiographical claims," as Gabrielle Foreman observes about *Our Nig* (xxxiii).[9]

Each of Larsen's novels, in its own way, resists the limitations of a single, definitive interpretation. The survey illuminated a need for further critical attention to Larsen's use of a range of metaphors as both political tool and artistic device to counter racist representations of blackness and black female sexuality. Instructors also indicated essays would be useful that identify and explore the many other issues the novels raise—those specifically germane to the period in which they are set and those that require at least minimal knowledge of prior historical periods and events. Providing a contextual framework of historical events helps students understand the complexity of Larsen's treatment of the intersections of race, gender, and class as they affect characterizations in the novels—especially of the female protagonists. The essays that follow were selected with these and other issues in mind.

Both of Larsen's novels take up the issue of motherhood, but *Quicksand* in particular shows the influence of eugenics debates as they occurred during the 1920s. Daylanne K. English argues in *Unnatural Selections: Eugenics in American Modernism and the Harlem Renaissance* that James Vayle, Helga Crane's fiancé when the novel opens, represents the "New Negro men [who] were trying to set an agenda for black reproduction and thus to establish control over modern black women's fertility" (132).[10] English's point is crucial to an understanding of black women's oppression. Furthermore, Vayle's views that "Negroes of the better class . . . must have the children if the race is to get anywhere" (103) echo the overall notion of racial uplift that many women themselves advocated. Larsen, however, criticizes such black upper-middle-class values, as Helga's response to Vayle's plea indicates: "Well I for one don't intend to contribute to the cause" (103). Helga's open expression of the pitfalls of marriage and children represents the views of those women who, English reminds us, Ann Douglas in *Terrible Honesty* calls "reluctant breeders."[11]

Helga's attitude and thereby Larsen's critique take on added significance when also read in the context of the birth control movement that took place between the 1910s and 1940s. Although Larsen did not write specifically for the special issue of the *Birth Control Review* devoted to the "Negro Project" as did other prominent blacks such as Angelina Weld Grimké and Mary Burrill, her portrayal of pregnancy and childbearing in her 1928 novel is in keeping with those of the other women's portrayals. These aspects of *Quicksand* and similar expressions in *Passing*—for example, Clare Kendry's lament that "being a mother is the cruelest thing in the world" (197)—lend themselves to discussions of more recent and ongoing debates over contraceptive equity and antifertility vaccines, TRAP (Targeted Regulation of Abortion Providers) and other state restrictions regarding the right to choose, and more recent anti-pro-choice activities that specifically target black women.[12]

Larsen and other women writers of the period such as Fauset, Grimké, and Hurston chose not to have children themselves and created characters that either had no children, felt trapped by the physical and emotional restrictions of marriage and children, or directly addressed issues of birth control. Despite the controversies surrounding the underlying motives of Margaret Sanger, the *Birth Control Review*'s founder, there is no reason to believe that these black women writers were anything but sincere advocates of reproductive rights.

Larsen's specific reference in her novel *Passing* to the highly publicized 1925 *Rhinelander* case in New York provides another means of contextualizing aspects of Larsen's views on 1920s attitudes about women—specifically black women. It opens up possibilities for discussing the ways in which Larsen challenges, instead of perpetuates, the cult of respectability regarding questions of black women's sexuality as well as the ways in which she challenges issues regarding interracial marriage or, again, "miscegenation." The case involved a white man, Leonard "Kip" Rhinelander, who sued for an annulment from Alice Jones Rhinelander on the basis that she had deceived him into marriage by lying about her race. According to Earl Lewis and Heidi Ardizzone, in *Love on Trial*, the very mention of the incident in Larsen's novel was a "fairly specific historical marker [that] conjured an event, a place, and a context. . . . In 1929 any American reader would have recognized the reference and understood its meaning" (253).

During the 1920s, "interracial marriages were outlawed in more than half of the United States" (Lewis and Ardizzone xii), which helps explain why in Larsen's novel the discovery of Clare's "passing" by the wrong people would be, as Irene's husband, Brian, states, "an unhealthy business" (185). Clare's marriage to the white Jack Bellew, like Alice Jones's marriage to the white Leonard Rhinelander, represents a threat to the status quo—indeed, symbolizes a threat to prevailing views about racial identity, as I have argued in "Double Nature."

Finally, the endings of the novels have continued to be the subject of debate—especially whether or not they are realistic, which earlier readings almost always questioned. *Passing*'s ending presents an even further challenge in that the final few lines of the novel in the original publication were omitted in Knopf's third printing and in some subsequent reprints. Currently, different editions have different endings, either with the original last few lines or without them. However, some scholars use this discrepancy to theorize about whether or not it is possible for instructors and students to feel confident about their analyses and interpretations of the ending, perhaps the entire novel, without knowledge of why the original was omitted or who was responsible for the omission. Thus, some of the more recent scholarship and several essays in this volume provide instructors and students with access to ways of dealing with textual issues such as this.[13]

The Essays and New Directions

The essays in the first section, "Historical and Cultural Contexts," provide practical ways to teach students about certain historical moments and how to read for multiple purposes. In addition to its artistic value and its usefulness in teaching students close reading, critical thinking, and interpretive skills, literature also has political, cultural, and social value, which "reveals to . . . students a kind of meaningful truth . . . that many [traditional history] textbooks might not," according to Lyde Sizer, who teaches Larsen's novels in her women's history courses. Beryl Satter ("'Anything Might Happen': Freedom and American Identity in Nella Larsen's *Passing*" organized under "Identity"), also a historian, teaches *Passing* as part of a United States history course that focuses on the "culture wars of the 1920s," including issues of Victorian sexual repression that she asserts were tied to economics and politics.

These essays reveal the complex social and cultural interchange between history and literature, showing that the two disciplines are not incompatible.

Indeed, Caresse John's essay on modernism in Larsen's novels, although taught in an American literature survey, introduces the novels of Larsen and other modernists (for example, Eliot, Pound, Stevens, and HD) as social and cultural history and also covers their more "literary" aspects: literal and figurative language, theme, and style. Likewise, Clark Barwick, in striving "to make the time period relevant" to his students, begins his teaching of *Quicksand* with what he deems the "cabaret" culture of the 1920s before embarking on reading and teaching *Quicksand* as fiction.

The second section, "Fiction and the Arts," contains two essays that focus on the relation between Larsen's novels and music and one essay on Larsen's novels and the visual arts. It is easy to find critical scholarship about African American literature's use of music, especially the blues and jazz. However, this kind of scholarship with regard to Larsen's work is noticeably scarce. Both Gayle Murchison's and Lori Harrison-Kahan's essays provide instructors and students, even those with little or no music background, the resources and strategies for examining the ways in which music figures thematically, symbolically, and structurally in Larsen's work, Murchison focusing on *Quicksand* and Harrison-Kahan on both novels.

In her essay for this volume, Cristina Giorcelli discusses how she uses performance and the "plastic" arts in teaching Larsen's *Quicksand* to challenge the assumption that verbal and visual art are too different to relate. Giorcelli provides background information about European primitivist and expressionist art to show how these forms work alongside literature to convey a better understanding of the social constructions of the black female body and sexuality. In addition to using the works of European artists in the classroom, Giorcelli recommends specific works of African American artists that she also shows in class through slides and photographs to demonstrate the ways in which primitivism and expressionism had an impact on African American art and Harlem Renaissance artists—for example, Aaron Douglas, Sargent Johnson, and Archibald Motley—and on the performance images of Josephine Baker.

For instructors interested in teaching about African American identity politics in Larsen's work, the next section, "Identity," offers a variety of approaches to the topic: racial and national identity, the subject of Beryl Satter's "'Anything Might Happen': Freedom and American Identity in Nella Larsen's *Passing*; sexual identity, as Suzanne Raitt discusses in "Teaching *Passing* as a Lesbian Text"; social constructions of gender, the focus of Beth Widmaier Capo's "Approaching Gender in *Quicksand*"; and masculinity and the "race man" concept, covered in Riché Richardson's "From 'My Old Man' to Race Men in *Quicksand*." These essays work together to show how to introduce students to Larsen's complex rendering of gender—both male and female—and sexuality. In placing attitudes about gender and sex in the context of the 1920s, the teaching strategies also work well in tandem with any of the essays in the volume but especially with those in the first section, "Historical and Cultural Contexts."

In her essay "Home at Last: Biographical Background to Pride and Prejudice," Ruth Perry raises the question that comes up time and again when teaching fiction: "how much should one make of the biographical contribution to a work of art?" (46). In the final section, "In the Classroom: Methods, Courses, Settings," three of the essays demonstrate strategies that place a special emphasis on the details of Larsen's life. (See Hutchinson's "The Uses of Biography," Bone's "Teaching *Quicksand* in Denmark," and Fabi and McLendon's "'In Some . . . Determined Way a Little Flaunting': Teaching with Nella Larsen's Letters"). Hutchinson argues that knowing biographical details "completely changes our notions of a text or of an author"; Bone states that the publication of the three Larsen biographies "has reshaped the ways in which teachers and students respond to the life and fiction of Nella Larsen"; and Fabi and McLendon suggest that Larsen's correspondence helps "introduce students to the complexity of Larsen's art." Yet, Fabi and McLendon's approach differs slightly from Hutchinson's and Bone's in that they strive to guide students "beyond the immediacy of biographical approaches to [Larsen's] fiction." Although the slight difference might create a minor tension with regard to using biographical details, introducing the various methods also provides ways to enrich classroom discussions. Whatever their differences, however, all the essays suggest that the described methods can lead to a greater appreciation of Larsen's work.

Zivah Perel Katz's essay, like Bone's, approaches teaching Larsen's work in a specific location, although Bone's approach hinges on Larsen's transnationalism, on the notion that Larsen's firsthand experience of having visited Denmark informs her novel *Quicksand*. Perel Katz's essay differs, too, in that her methods involve teaching excerpts of Larsen's *Passing* in an English composition course, which is part of the essay's value pedagogically. The two remaining essays in this section (Steven B. Shively's "The Matter of Beginnings: Teaching the Opening Paragraphs in *Quicksand* and *Passing*" and Young's "Versions of *Passing*") focus on teaching the novels by closely examining beginnings and endings, especially their relation to the whole texts and how they function to convey meaning. These essays, along with the others in the volume, and the syllabi and various other information shared by instructors as well as the responses by survey participants, indicate that close reading—ranging from a specific word or line to an entire passage—is still the most common method used to help students gain an understanding of literary texts, and, in these instances, instructors use this familiar pedagogical tool to illuminate the form and content of Larsen's novels. Indeed, although it is not a new method, close reading enables new or innovative analyses of texts and a wide range of perspectives.

The essays are divided into four sections, but each one fits into more than one category, underscoring the interdisciplinary nature and range of thematic, theoretical, and stylistic approaches to Larsen's work on display here. The essays assembled in this volume demonstrate how to teach the novels without either eliminating race or using racial identity as the only basis for analyses. In other words, as a number of survey participants asked, How does one teach the novels outside the categories of African American studies, generally, and African American literature, specifically?

Although the essays included in the volume represent a wide range of theoretical approaches to teaching Larsen's work, no volume on Larsen can be completely comprehensive. The pedagogical methods offered here are representative, and hopefully they will inspire more possibilities in future Larsen scholarship.

NOTES

[1] Larsen to Carl Van Vechten, 1 July 1926. The letters cited here are located in the Yale Collection of American Literature, the Beinecke Rare Book and Manuscript Library, Yale University.

[2] One of the chief offenders was Harold Jackman, an educator, known for his friendship with Countee Cullen. Jackman, under a pseudonym, wrote for the *Inter-state Tattler*, a short-lived, often described as "off-color" Harlem periodical.

[3] Larsen to Van Vechten, 14 May 1932.

[4] 29 July 1933.

[5] Imes to Van Vechten, 22 March 1931.

[6] In "Dear Ms. Larsen, There's a Mirror Looking Back," Heidi Durrow, author of the award-winning novel *The Girl Who Fell From the Sky*, writes that visiting Nella Larsen's grave was a "homecoming" that gave her the opportunity "to make peace with an artistic ancestor and literary role model" (101).

[7] A classic example, as I have argued in *The Politics of Color*, is Nathan Huggins's reductive analysis of the novels in *Harlem Renaissance*, which came out in the same year as the Collier reprints. One of the most significant inaccuracies is his statement that the Bellews—Clare, who is passing for white, and Jack, her racist white husband—have no children, suggesting a comparison of a physical sterility of her body to the spiritual sterility of her chosen "white life" (Huggins 159). He also states that Irene has only one child when, in fact, she and her husband have two. These are grave misreadings since the two women's views on the oppressiveness of marriage and motherhood are crucial to an understanding of the novel. See also Robert Bone's *The Negro Novel in America*. He places Larsen in a category he calls the "Rearguard" that excludes her from a "Harlem School" of male writers.

[8] Among other significant early critiques of Larsen's work are those of Singh; Youman; Arthur Davis; Christian, *Black Women Novelists* and *Black Feminist Criticism*.

[9] In her introduction to *Our Nig*, Foreman discusses "weaving together factual and fictional conventions" (xxxiii–iv).

[10] English also states that Vayle "had his real-life counterpart in male race leaders such as W. E. B. Du Bois" (133).

[11] Douglas states that "[w]hite and black women artists of the time were all reluctant breeders" and goes on to list them according to various sexual orientations, including Larsen among the heterosexual married women (98).

[12] Other resources for discussion might include the studies by the Guttmacher Institute that cite statistics on reproductive health and rights: one such report says that

several states in the first six months of 2011 enacted 162 new provisions, of which nearly half seek to restrict access to abortion services (http://www.guttmacher.org), and the September 2011 issues of *Spiritual Health*. Also, instructors might point students to *Spiritual Health* (10.9 [September 2011]) and various Web sites featuring information about the billboards in several cities that target black women and other women of color with regard to their reproductive rights (e.g., in New York City, one such billboard pictures an African American child with the caption: "The most dangerous place for an African American is in the womb").

[13] See Caughie's *Passing and Pedagogy* 124–43 and Young's *Black Writers* 38–64, as well as his essay in this volume.

Nella Larsen's *Passing* and the Literary and Legal Context of the Passing Narrative

Martha J. Cutter

Recent critical attention has turned to how Nella Larsen's novel *Passing* engages with the legal context of its time period. In her introduction to the Penguin edition of *Passing*, Thadious Davis mentions that *Plessy v. Ferguson* (1896), which allowed de facto Jim Crow segregation under the idea of a "separate but equal" status for African Americans, in effect gave light-skinned African Americans a license to pass for white (viii), while Miriam Thaggert, Mark Madigan, and others have examined how the unsuccessful marriage annulment trial *Rhinelander v. Rhinelander* (1925) may have influenced Larsen's depictions of racial identity. Larsen's novel refers to the Rhinelander case in relation to the possibility of Clare Kendry's divorcing her husband, Jack Bellew: "What if Bellew should divorce Clare? Could he? There was the Rhinelander case" (228). However, a number of provocative legal cases from the 1890s onward investigated the role, meaning, and legal status of the passing figure, and it is productive to ask students to think about how this broader legal landscape influenced Larsen's assessment of racial identity.

Considering the novel within such a broader legal context encourages students to move beyond a binary in which passing is read as either good or bad and toward an understanding of how external sociopolitical and legal debates influence this text's evaluation of the act and meaning of passing. Because case law from the 1890s forward concerning individuals who were accused of passing often attempted but failed to create a working definition of whiteness and blackness, students come to see that Larsen is in dialogue with legal debates about the meaning and coherence of racial difference. More specifically, Larsen uses passing figures in her text to challenge the law's ability to demarcate, legislate, or otherwise permanently stabilize racial difference. At the same time, through nonpassing figures such as Brian Redfield, she elucidates how the law also creates a temporary juridical imperative that does govern "black" or "brown" bodies, even while illuminating how arbitrary the imposition of this imperative may be.

The Meaning of Passing in Passing

I have argued elsewhere that within the galaxy of signifiers that is the novel *Passing*, Clare Kendry is a sliding signifier who disrupts other characters' fixed and stable identities ("Sliding Significations" 76). Because Clare floats from race to race, from class to class, and even from a seemingly firm heterosexual attraction to men into more ambiguous iterations of desire for women, she causes others to question the stability of their sexual, racial, or class status. In a textual sense, then, she functions positively to catalyze questions Larsen remains interested in throughout her career: What creates identity? How stable or unstable is race? How fixed are the categories into which we fit ourselves, be they categories of race, class, gender, or sexuality? Clare has no loyalty or fidelity to any one person, race, or group, as she tells Irene: "Can't you realize that . . . to get the things I want badly enough, I'd do anything, hurt anybody, throw anything away" (210).[1] Clare also comments that she passes not to abandon identity but to find or create one: "I was determined . . . to be a person and not a charity or a problem. . . . I knew I wasn't bad looking and that I could 'pass'" (159). Here passing seems to be a way to perform a new type of self-created individuality, and Clare's performance tests other characters' sense that the roles they inhabit are natural or innate.

Yet the ending of the novel appears to punish Clare for her inability to stay in one race, class, or sexual role. Her death is read by some critics as an invalidation of her attempt to have it all—to have her cake and eat it too, and even, as Irene says, to nibble on the cakes of others (182). After all, if she had stayed in her place as the white, upper-class, heterosexual wife of the millionaire John Bellew, she would not have fallen, jumped, or been pushed to her death. More specifically, in this interpretation, the decision to (first) pass for white and then (later) pass back and forth between the white world of husband and family and the black world of Harlem leads directly and inevitably to her death.

But the discourse of passing has a much more complicated social and legal history in the United States than this simplistic positioning of Clare's passing as either good or bad might suggest. Passing has been ongoing in the United States since at least 1747, and the term *passing* has also been used since this early time period to demarcate not only passing for white but also passing for free, for Indian, and for other nationalities (e.g., French) or statuses (married or employed as a tradesperson) (Cutler, "As White"). Of course, the valences and meaning of *passing* itself have changed greatly over time. One way to help students understand the complexity of passing within a specific sociohistorical context is to have them read some of the cases that influenced ideas of race in this time period.

Teaching Legal Trials and the Adjudication of Race, 1894–1925

While teaching *Passing* in upper-division (junior-level) classes on African American literature and in my senior capstone class for English and African American studies majors, Racial Passing, Performance, and Masquerade, I have incorporated four legal trials: *Van Houten v. Morse* (1894), *Plessy v. Ferguson* (1896), *Ferrall v. Ferrall* (1910), and *Rhinelander v. Rhinelander* (1925). Transcripts of these cases—with the exception of *Rhinelander*—can be accessed through the legal database *Lexis*, so students can go to this database and look them up, but I have generally posted links to these cases on *Husky CT*, our online course management system. The transcript of the Rhinelander annulment trial is not available, so I have students read selections from Elizabeth Smith-Pryor's book *Property Rites* (chapter 8, "Blind Love and the Visibility of Race," has been particularly well received by students) and Jamie Wacks's "Reading Race, Rhetoric, and the Female Body in the Rhinelander Case."

I generally ask students to read these materials before reading the novel. For each case, I request brief written responses to three questions: What markers are used to define race in this case? Does the definition of race appear to be stable? What role does race play in intimacy, marriage, or social relationships? I have also experimented with asking groups of students to present the cases in class in terms of these three questions, and this tends to work well in the junior-level class on African American literature.

I usually begin class discussion of the legal context with *Van Houten v. Morse*, a Supreme Judicial Court Case from Massachusetts, because the legal discourse is less complicated and detailed than *Plessy v. Ferguson* and *Rhinelander v. Rhinelander*. In this case, Anna Van Houten sued her (former) fiancé, Asa Morse, after he broke off their engagement, for breach of promise to marry. Morse's defense was that Van Houten had fraudulently concealed "the negro blood in her veins" and that he therefore had no legal obligation to marry her because this marriage would have been voidable under state law. The court ruled, however, that a potential spouse had no obligation to reveal racial identity before becoming engaged; moreover, it also ruled that "the fact, if it was a fact, that the plaintiff had some negro blood in her veins would not justify him as matter of law in breaking the contract." As Bella August Walker argues about this case, "Miss Van Houten only had to show that she did not provide misleading information. Mr. Morse was responsible for his own assumptions and his own ignorance" (14).

This judgment often surprises my students because they expect the court to follow a one-drop rule (in which "one drop" of "black" blood determines blackness) and side with the wronged white male. Instead, the court focuses on concealment: "So with regard to her parentage and family. She was under no obligation to tell the defendant about them in the absence of inquiry by him. But if she voluntarily undertook to make any statements concerning them, she was bound not only to state truly what she told, but also not to suppress or conceal facts which would materially qualify those which she stated." Interestingly, photographs of Van Houten's mother and sister were introduced into the courtroom by Van Houten, but the court refused to comment on whether they proved her whiteness. I encourage students to see that by focusing on the issue of fraud the court avoids the underlying question: what *is* racial identity, and in a mixed-race society, what would it mean to "conceal" the "facts" of race?

I next have students consider the more famous Supreme Court case of *Plessy v. Ferguson*, which appears to be more confident in its ability to juridically separate whiteness and blackness. In the majority opinion, written by Justice Henry Billings Brown, the court rules that Homer Plessy must ride in the Jim Crow cars on trains, even though he was "seven eighths Caucasian and one eighth African blood" and "the mixture of colored blood was not discernible in him." The court thereby seems to affirm a one-drop conception of racial identity. Yet I think it is important for students to see that a legal illogicality exists at the heart of *Plessy v. Ferguson*. First, the court specifically admits that blackness as such is not always visible:

> [W]e are not prepared to say that the conductor, in assigning passengers to the coaches according to their race, does not act at his peril. . . . The power to assign to a particular coach obviously implies the power to determine to which race the passenger belongs, as well as the power to determine who, under the laws of the particular State, is to be deemed a white, and who a colored person.

In acknowledging the "peril" of this action by the conductor, the court also acknowledges that the conductor might be wrong in his determination of who is a white, or a colored, person; racial difference is not, then, visible or apparent.

In class discussion, I also focus on a passage in which the court sidesteps the entire question by noting that although racial definitions vary by state, this case does not concern racial determination, despite appearances to the contrary:

> It is true that the question of the proportion of colored blood necessary to constitute a colored person, as distinguished from a white person, is one upon which there is a difference of opinion in the different States, some holding that any visible admixture of black blood stamps the person as belonging to the colored race, (State v. Chavers, 5 Jones, [N.C.] 1, p. 11); others that it depends upon the preponderance of blood, (Gray v. State, 4 Ohio, 353; Monroe v. Collins, 17 Ohio St. 665); and still others that the predominance of white blood must only be in the proportion of three fourths.

> (People v. Dean, 14 Michigan, 406; Jones v. Commonwealth, 80 Virginia, 538.) But these are questions to be determined under the laws of each State and *are not properly put in issue in this case*. (emphasis added)

Judge Brown relegates "black" bodies to their proper place within Jim Crow cars; yet, at the same time, he acknowledges the difficulty, even impossibility, of trying to define racial identity (and he leaves it up to each state to do so, creating a plethora of racial definitions). The decision therefore undermines the coherence of racial difference even as it adjudicates it. It also, as Mark Golub argues, illustrates the vivid discrepancy between lived experiences of race and the judicial necessity for clear rules defining racial identity (565). As we see when we discuss the novel, Larsen's text explores and exploits this same illogicality of racial identity as being determinative of social place yet also often undetectable and mutable.

Although in *Passing* Larsen specifically mentions *Rhinelander v. Rhinelander*, an earlier ruling by the Supreme Court of North Carolina may have influenced her thinking about marriage, the law, and race, so I turn next to this case. In *Ferrall v. Ferrall*, Frank Ferrall had sued his wife, Susie, for divorce three years earlier on the grounds that she "was and is of negro descent within the third generation" and that he did not know this "fact" at the time of the marriage. Susie Ferrall denied this allegation:

> While plaintiff [Frank Ferrall] was courting defendant [Susie] he was repeatedly informed that there was a strain of Indian or Portuguese blood in [her] veins, and he was also informed that some people insisted that there was a strain of negro blood in [her] veins, and defendant said he proposed to marry her in spite of such rumors.

A lower court had ruled against Susie Ferrall because "the evidence tended to fix a strain of negro blood in Julius Coley, a great-grandfather of defendant"; because "said Julius Coley was a real negro," the lower court held in favor of the plaintiff and granted his decree for divorce.

Susie Ferrall appealed this decision to the Supreme Court of North Carolina. Ultimately the Supreme Court reversed the lower court ruling due to tenuous assertions about what constituted "a real negro," noting instead that

> [i]f indeed, the plaintiff had discovered any minute strain of colored origin after the youth of his wife has been worn away for his pleasure and in his service, justice and generosity dictated that he keep to himself that of which the public was unaware. . . . Certainly of all men he should have welcomed the verdict that decided his wife and children are white.

If students do not notice this passage, I draw their attention to it because here the court opines that the "facts" of racial ancestry—if they are indeed facts—are much less important than the reality of a white-looking wife whose husband is attempting to abandon her. Again, I hope that students will see that the court avoids the question of how to determine racial identity.

Rhinelander v. Rhinelander would seem to have a different outcome than *Ferrall v. Ferrall* in that racial identity is affixed to a body in what seems to be a clear and stable way: Alice Jones Rhinelander was determined to be unambiguously black. Yet when examined closely in class, students can come to see that this case, like *Plessy v. Ferguson*, operates in a contradictory manner through a faulty and unstable circular logic: a body is black because it looks black, yet it looks black *only* because the viewer *is told* that the body *is* black. Leonard "Kip" Rhinelander sued his wife, Alice Rhinelander, for an annulment of his marriage on the grounds that he did not know she was black when he married her; Alice's defense lawyers contended that Kip knew her race because he had seen her naked before marriage and that her race was visible on her body. In an infamous court scene, a weeping Alice appeared partially disrobed in front of an all-male jury so that they might judge whether her race was visible. The jury concurred with Alice's defense lawyers that her race was apparent from her body (although how her race was manifested is not made clear), and the case was resolved in her favor: no annulment was granted.

The case thus appeared to affirm that race was—that it had to be—visible on the body, as attorneys for Alice would make clear: "I let you gentlemen look at a portion of what he saw. You saw Alice's back above the bust. You saw her breast. You saw a portion of her upper leg. He saw all of her body. And you are going to tell me that he never suspected that she had colored blood! . . . You saw that with your own eyes . . . that colored blood was coursing through her veins" (Wacks 174). Yet Kip's own testimony was more ambiguous. He had bathed Alice, been intimate with her, and examined every nook and cranny of her body, yet he could not tell her race and he married her, believing her to be white, as the following exchange with his attorney, Isaac Mills, shows:

MILLS: If you had known what is now conceded to be true before you married Alice, that she is of colored blood, would you have married her?
LEONARD: Absolutely not, no.
MILLS: When you married her did you believe her statement that she was white?
LEONARD: I did. I always believed her. (Smith-Pryor 110)

Smith-Pryor has argued that the *Rhinelander* case symbolized "the chaotic future that awaited Americans if racial lines could not be clearly drawn" (5). But at the heart of the case are several unresolved ambiguities that students can profitably ponder as they begin reading *Passing*: Did Kip know of Alice's race and marry her anyway? Or did she "fool" him into thinking she was white? And, if Alice did adequately perform her whiteness in such a way that it went unquestioned by Kip, what does this say about whiteness itself? Moreover, the facts of this case should reveal to students that race was read onto Alice's body by the jury, but only *after* it had learned of her mixed-race background by hearing about her mixed-race relatives and her "black" father. Without knowing this background, race was not, it seems, visible on Alice's body, as Kip's own testimony shows; he claims he would not have married her if he had known she was black. So what creates a black body may be knowledge that this body is black—a circular logic that Larsen's novel will unravel through Clare Kendry.

The Visibility and Invisibility of Race in Nella Larsen's Passing

In class time spent discussing these four trials, I encourage my students to see how the courts attempted, with varying degrees of success, to script racial identity onto bodies and to stabilize racial difference. Yet these cases also raise questions about the logic of this process and whether race (or more specifically blackness) can be known. When we begin discussing the novel, I focus on several key scenes that also imply that blackness is read onto white-looking bodies only after the "facts" of black racial ancestry are known. For example, when Clare Kendry and Irene Redfield meet after a period of many years, Irene cannot discern Clare's race and instead believes that she herself might have been detected while passing: "Did that woman, could that woman, somehow know that here before her very eyes on the roof of the Drayton sat a Negro? Absurd! Impossible! White people were so stupid about such things for all that they usually asserted that they were able to tell" (150). Presumably knowledge of race could only come if someone observing Irene was aware that she normally classifies herself as "black"; race is created by a person's placement of him or herself within racial groups, instead of by a reading of physical attributes.

It perhaps makes sense, then, that Irene does not know what Clare's race is until she remembers Clare's background: "Ah! Surely! They were Negro eyes! Mysterious and concealing. . . . Yes, Clare Kendry's loveliness was absolute, beyond challenge, thanks to those eyes which her grandmother and later her mother and father had given her" (161). Eyes here become a symbol of Clare's race—they are "Negro eyes"—but this race is only discernable through references to her family background (to her "black" grandmother and mixed-race father and mother). I urge students to see that, like Alice Rhinelander, Clare is placed within a racial hierarchy only *after* the "facts" of her racial lineage are known. Attention can also be drawn to how Irene replicates the mystification of race present in case law—to how Irene constantly attempts and fails to stabilize race. In a conversation with her husband, for example, she asks Brian why passers come back to their true race, to which Brian responds: "If I knew that, I'd know what race is" (185). Race is an illogical set of discourses that get sutured onto bodies. But the seams of the suturing show, and instead of being stabilized by this discourse, race remains unknowable through a visual logic.

Nowhere is the unknowability of race made clearer than in the case of Clare's husband, John Bellew, and I invite students to think carefully about his claims concerning race in the context of the cases they have read. Bellew claims that he knows that Clare is "no nigger" and that there are "no niggers in my family. Never have been and never will be" (171), only to learn eventually that Clare is "a nigger, a damned dirty nigger!" (238). Bellew believes that he can "draw the line" (171) between blacks and whites, but he cannot. Thus his cry at the end of the novel is one of both "rage" and "pain" (238) as he is forced into categorical crisis by the abrupt revelation of Clare's blackness. Like the court in *Plessy v. Ferguson* and *Rhinelander v. Rhinelander*, Bellew fails to stabilize race. Indeed, his knowledge of Clare's race comes not from her body but from her association with others: he sees Irene with the darker-skinned Felise Freeland and then comes to believe (or at least suspect) that Clare is passing. Something beyond or before the body—association, kinship, or even proximity—creates a raced black body, not the body itself.

In the marital trials described above (*Van Houten v. Morse*, *Ferrall v. Ferrall*, and *Rhinelander v. Rhinelander*) students can see that passing does not automatically lead to a rationale for divorce or annulment, because race itself is so hard to determine. Instead, fraud becomes an avenue for divorce or annulment: Was the husband deluded? Did the wife conceal knowledge she should have revealed? Larsen may mention *Rhinelander* because it emblematizes a series of cases in which the court failed to create a coherent bodily or visual logic of race. Even in the *Rhinelander* case, where the body seemed to reveal race, race changed once information about its "blackness" became known on an intellectual level. Initial newspaper accounts of the case described Alice as possessing a "light complexion," but as knowledge of the "facts" of her racial background were brought forward, the newspaper reporters increasingly depicted her with "dark skin" (Smith-Pryor 27). Moreover, the courts engaged in the same project as many characters within the novel: like John Bellew and Irene Redfield, the courts tried to define blackness in terms of a visual logic, or in terms of coherent markers of racial difference. Yet race remains unknowable and unfathomable within the trials and within the text—a position best represented by the characters of Clare Kendry and Brian Redfield.

This does not mean that certain bodies—bodies that "couldn't exactly 'pass'" (168), such as Brian Redfield's—are not governed by discriminatory discourses of racial visuality. But it does mean that other bodies—such as those of Anna Van Houten, Susie Ferrall, and Clare Kendry—enter a realm where racial difference is not knowable through a visual logic of the body. In the end, I hope students understand that Larsen interpolates the *Rhinelander* case to gesture toward a whole series of trials that attempted to script race onto the bodies of individuals in ways that defy logical or coherent categorization. For my students, I hope that these trials illuminate Larsen's larger project in the novel: contemplating how the passer might momentarily slip free from a binary black/white logic of racial difference and visuality, thereby forcing the reader into a categorical crisis wherein he or she can no longer "know" race.

NOTE

[1] This and all quotations throughout the essay are taken from the 1989 Rutgers edition.

Nella Larsen's Modernism

Caresse John

> It is impossible to say just what I mean!
> —T. S. Eliot, "The Love Song of J. Alfred Prufrock"

> Here is a place of disaffection
> —T. S. Eliot, *Four Quartets*

Though modernism and the Harlem Renaissance are by no means disparate movements, they are often treated as such. The separation is partly due to the critical emphasis on the innovative styles of modernism, styles inspired by Ezra Pound's call to "make it new!" contrasted with the critical interest in the thematic and social concerns that figure prominently in the work of Harlem Renaissance writers. The demands of teaching are a further incentive to the division. In the college-level classroom, the implicit intertextuality of these movements sometimes gets sacrificed in favor of an organized calendar of readings or syllabi and class discussions that lend themselves to categorization. Yet, instead of simply adhering to the convenient boundaries of literary movements, perhaps we should be asking our students to engage with and critically examine the amorphous nature of these boundaries.

Even a cursory glance at most American literature anthologies and critical articles on modernist and Harlem Renaissance authors highlights the continued marginalization of the Harlem Renaissance. Readers and critics often understand modernism to be the larger and more influential of the two movements; there is, perhaps, nothing wrong with this understanding. Yet the Harlem Renaissance was more than just a submovement of modernism, more than just something happening on the outskirts. Indeed, because the Harlem Renaissance encompasses much of what we see as characteristic of modernism *and* embodies the voices and experiences of a particular group of people in a particular time period, we might say that the Harlem Renaissance stands both within and outside modernism. Nella Larsen's work is an excellent place to explore the complex relation between modernism and the Harlem Renaissance. Her oeuvre provides students with an inimitable understanding of the uncertainties of life in 1920s America: epistemic, social, racial, sexual, and class uncertainties. Yet, although her works exhibit the thematic and stylistic traits of modernism in complex and highly skilled ways, critics and teachers almost never categorize her as such; thus, her texts provide a valuable opportunity not only to introduce our students to the traits of both modernism and the Harlem Renaissance but also to have them think about the boundaries of literary movements and the categorization of texts.[1]

Not surprisingly, students are often overwhelmed by modernist literature. In my American literature survey course, I introduce students to T. S. Eliot,

Pound, Wallace Stevens, HD, and their contemporaries about midway into the semester, after we have read texts from realism, naturalism, regionalism, and Reconstruction. Students find authors like William Dean Howells, Edith Wharton, Jack London, and Sarah Orne Jewett accessible and enjoyable. As we turn to modernism, they become a bit shell-shocked, and understandably so. Eliot famously wrote in 1919 that "[t]he poet must become more and more comprehensive, more allusive, more indirect, in order to force, to dislocate if necessary, language into his meaning" ("Metaphysical Poets" 248). Students certainly feel this dislocation. Relinquishing narrative continuity in order to represent the lives of characters as fragmented and filtering scenes through multiple subjective perspectives instead of mimetically reflecting the world through an objective narrator, the modernist text presents multiple truths and seems to revel in gaps. The deliberate fragmentation presents intellectual challenges for students. They are forced to bridge the gaps and merge truths, partaking in the construction and interpretation of meaning in a way very different from their textual engagement in the earlier part of the semester.

Within this framework of stylistic and thematic estrangement, Larsen's works are particularly rewarding to teach.[2] Thematically and stylistically, Larsen communicates feelings of dislocation, desperation, and alienation and also conveys an ambiguity of meaning that results from the subjectivity inherent in both interpretation and experience. In order to give fellow teachers of Larsen specific ways of approaching her novels as modernist texts, I focus on two thematic concerns (the fear of "something" and Larsen's practice of ambiguous endings) and one stylistic technique (Larsen's use of focalization).[3] Taken together, these marks of Larsen's art earn her the well-deserved yet still overlooked position as a modernist author.

Both Helga in *Quicksand* and Irene in *Passing* consistently come up against the fear of "something." There are a number of scenes in which the women cannot name, describe, or sometimes even comprehend this "something." *Quicksand*, for example, opens with Helga deciding, in a characteristically self-assured way, to leave Naxos, the school at which she has been teaching, because she cannot adhere to its policy of racial uplift or its "suppression of individuality and beauty" (20).[4]

Yet, the very day after she has made this decision, the reader finds her, just as characteristically, questioning her former assurance:

> The uneasy sense of being engaged with some formidable antagonist, nameless and ununderstood, startled her. It wasn't, she was suddenly aware, merely the school and its ways and its decorous stupid people that oppressed her. There was something else, some other more ruthless force, a quality within herself, which was frustrating her. . . .
>
> But just what did she want? . . . Helga Crane didn't know, couldn't tell. But there was, she knew, something else. Happiness she supposed. Whatever that might be . . . She couldn't define it, isolate it, and contemplate it. (10–11)

It doesn't take long for students to see this vacillation as characteristic of Helga (the same is true, as well, for Irene in *Passing*). One way, then, to begin discussion of these novels is to ask students what this "nameless and ununderstood something" might be. The rest of the narrative consists, on many levels, of Helga's fight with this force inside herself and her search for this indefinable happiness. As we read about Helga moving from place to place in this search, never staying anywhere long enough to confront and endure the difficult moments she encounters, my students and I think about what, if anything, might allow for Helga's happiness.

One of the possibilities we discuss is a racial identity. Helga comes to an important realization after her trip to Copenhagen, when she asks herself, "why couldn't she have two lives, or why couldn't she be satisfied in one place?" (93). Directing students to another passage, I walk them through close reading, showing them that the questions raised by the text can be answered by the text:

> *These* were her people. Nothing, she had come to understand now, could ever change that. Strange that she had never truly valued this kinship until distance had shown her its worth. . . . Ties not only superficially entangled with mere outline or features or color of skin. Deeper. Much deeper than either of these. (95)

Helga may not always know what she's searching for or be able to articulate or commit to what she finds, but given our broader outside perspective as readers, my students and I can draw important conclusions about Helga's inability to self-define. In the literature survey, before looking at the Harlem Renaissance and modernism, I have of course covered at least W. E. B. Du Bois and Booker T. Washington. Given that we have discussed at length Du Bois's "double consciousness," students and I can think more broadly than Larsen allows Helga to do so about her questions of duality.

Compared with the earlier constantly vacillating Helga, students see her decision to return to America as, perhaps, the most cognizant and healthy decision she makes in the narrative. Finally, she realizes that racial barriers exist no matter where she goes; she can resist them, but she cannot escape them. Yet Larsen does not sustain this moment of hope. I lead my students through this duality, this vacillation, by directing them to the contexts provided by *both* modernism and the Harlem Renaissance. This social and historical framework lets them develop multiple interpretations of the text, interpretations that take into account the complex realities Larsen reflects in her work.

Once she returns to America and marries the Reverend Green, Helga convinces herself for a time that she is happy, that being married and having a home is the "something" she has been searching for: "Here, she had found, she was sure, the intangible thing for which, indefinitely, always she had craved. It had received embodiment" (120). Yet this happiness soon turns into Helga's characteristic discontentment, and her body is literally overtaken by motherhood.

After her fourth, particularly dangerous childbirth, she lies in bed for weeks, oblivious to all around her, even the death of her child. Eventually, as her strength returns, so does the old Helga, the self-assured, strong-willed Helga. She begins to imagine a way out:

> For in some way she was determined to get herself out of this bog into which she had strayed. Or—she would have to die. She couldn't endure it. Her suffocation and shrinking loathing were too great. Not to be borne. Again. For she had to admit that it wasn't new, this feeling of dissatisfaction, of asphyxiation. Something like it she had experienced before. In Naxos. In New York. In Copenhagen. This differed only in degree. (134)

Something like this she has experienced before, but the difference this time is more than just degree; this time, she is tied to this "bog" not by abstractions, like love and race, but by the reality of her children. As her thoughts turn to them, she talks herself out of the decision to escape, and the narrative closes with her next pregnancy.

When I teach *Quicksand*, I spend an entire class period on these final pages. Students are dismayed by the ending. Helga has been sucked into the quicksand of domesticity, and Larsen does not provide any sense that she will be able to escape this time. As we move into Harlem Renaissance works, students are drawn to and delighted by the hopefulness they find in authors like Langston Hughes and Zora Neale Hurston; they love the racial pride they find in "The Negro Artist and the Racial Mountain" and "How It Feels to Be Colored Me." Nellie McKay and Henry Louis Gates, Jr., identify an "unrivalled optimism" within the works of the Harlem Renaissance, an optimism that is markedly different from Washington's quiet pride and Du Bois's politically charged rhetoric (932). Yet the Harlem Renaissance is not just optimism—there is an equal amount of sadness, bitterness, and contemplation of destruction. In other words, the Harlem Renaissance intersects with modernism in striking ways, ways that often get lost in a classroom setting.[5] Particularly in a survey course, it becomes too easy to compartmentalize works and draw boundary lines that are both limiting and misleading. Because it represents elements of modernism and the Harlem Renaissance, *Quicksand*'s ambiguous ending, this unfulfilled search for something, allows us (and, frankly, forces us) to engage our students in a conversation about the boundaries, or lack thereof, between the two movements.

Passing affords a similar opportunity. Like Helga, Irene avoids and represses that which she cannot name. On the surface, Irene's life seems perfect: she has a loving and successful husband and two beautiful children, and Irene herself is an upstanding society woman. Because we read *Passing* over the course of three to four days, students at first are sympathetic to Irene, seeing her in the same way she sees herself: a true race woman, a loving wife and mother. But as they move into the text, students begin to see that below the surface Irene is deeply troubled. Irene holds firm to her false reality because it provides her with security, because she convinces herself it isn't false. When Clare Kendry comes back into her life, the security threatens to deteriorate. Irene fears something about Clare, something about Brian, and something about Brian and Clare together, none of which she can define or articulate. In class, we focus on the following passages, attempting to uncover Irene's true fears.

When Clare and Irene run into each other, as they are both passing on the rooftop of the Drayton, Irene doesn't recognize Clare at first, but she feels as if she should: "about the woman there was some quality, an intangible something, too vague to define, too remote to seize, but which was, to Irene Redfield, very familiar" (151). Later, after Irene has learned all about Clare's marriage to a white man, she describes Clare's eyes: "Arresting eyes, slow and mesmeric, and with, for all their warmth, something withdrawn and secret about them. Ah! Surely! They were Negro eyes! mysterious and concealing!" (161). This nameless, vague something about Clare that Irene sees over and over is Clare's blackness. Irene fears that aspect of Clare because it ties her to Clare and, more troubling to Irene, because it identifies her own blackness. Irene hates Clare, but she does not sever their relationship since, as she convinces herself, they are racially connected: "She was caught between two allegiances, different, yet the same. Herself. Her race. Race! The thing that bound and suffocated her" (225). We discuss this passage at length, and I often compare it with the passage in which Irene thinks about how important security is and asserts that she is an American (235).

I ask students to think about and discuss what race really is for Irene: is it a duty? Is it something of which she is proud? Is it something to hide behind? Is it a burden? Early in the narrative, students are reluctant to judge Irene for her passing, but they are quick to condemn Clare for hers. But by this section, as Irene wishes "for the first time in her life, that she had not been born a Negro," students are beginning to see how disconcerting race is to Irene (225). We talk at length about how other pieces of Irene's life, such as familial and financial security or a national identity, hold more power over her than race does, despite her protestations.[6]

Like her relationship with Clare, Irene's relationship with her husband is strained, at best. And while this discontentment seems, in Irene's mind, to hinge on Brian's desire to go to Brazil and Irene's refusal, I focus my students' attention on two extended scenes between Brian and Irene to explore how race and sex are obstacles in their marriage. In the first scene, Brian and Irene discuss passing and have wholly different notions of it. Brian sees it as slightly "humorous," something that has "conveniences" (185). While Irene's actions suggest that she agrees, she would never admit it, instead seeing it as "abhorrent" (161). Their conversation ends after a tense discussion over what Brian calls the "necessary education" about sex that their boys are receiving from older boys at school; Irene again abhors the idea, while Brian believes that, for the boys, learning about sex when they're young will "keep [them] from lots of disappointments later on" (189).

The second scene finds Brian and Irene's son asking about lynching. His parents again have opposite reactions: Brian believes that the children need to know about it now because "the earlier they learn it, the better prepared they'll be"; Irene, on the other hand, wants "their childhood to be happy and as free from the knowledge of such things as it possibly can be" (231). Like Clare, then, Brian threatens Irene's notions of race and sex by refusing to reside within the same barriers she does. His refusal thus threatens her need for security and propriety. These scenes are telling for students; while a few students sympathize with Irene's desires to protect her children, most students (if not all) see that the "protection" is not in the interest of the boys. In other words, when we look at these scenes, students come to see that Irene's true concern is her own security.

By the final scene in *Passing*, students have already moved very far away from their early impressions of Irene. As with *Quicksand*, I spend a good deal of class time looking at the end of *Passing*. As Clare, Brian, and Irene walk to the party at the Freelands', Irene feels "a something in the air, something that had been between those two and would be again. It was like a live thing pressing against her" (237). Although Irene has no conclusive evidence that Brian and Clare are having an affair, she has long ago convinced herself of this "fact" (234). The threats that Brian and Clare pose to Irene separately come together in this final scene and give Irene the motive that readers need to convict her.

Clare's death at the end of the narrative can certainly be seen as murder—and, in fact, often is. Although Larsen resolutely does not provide irrefutable evidence that Irene kills Clare, critics and students alike are often convinced that she does. Because of this conviction, I first ask students why they are so sure that Irene murdered Clare. They have pretty compelling evidence, compelling enough to convince other students who had been unsure of Irene's complicity. Then I ask them what I see as the more important question: "if it is so clear to us that Irene murdered Clare, why would Larsen leave the ending ambiguous?" We spend a good amount of time discussing this; the one thing we do agree on is the fact that Irene's life does not get significantly better, murderer or not. Larsen closes this narrative off in darkness as well. As with *Quicksand*, Larsen's ambiguity on both the stylistic and thematic level leads to discussion of the similarities between works of the Harlem Renaissance and modernism.

Near the end of *Quicksand*, as Helga escapes from the rain into a revival meeting led by the Reverend Mr. Pleasant Green, she undergoes what she temporarily sees as a religious conversion. The narrative describes this moment ambiguously: "in that moment she was lost—or saved" (113). In her book *Freedom's Empire: Race and the Rise of the Novel in Atlantic Modernity, 1640–1940*, Laura Doyle suggests that, in this unresolved description, "Larsen holds us in a hovering position" (406). I take this notion one step further; Larsen holds us in this hovering position throughout the entire work, in fact throughout both novels. And when I teach these texts, I highlight this position during every discussion. In other words, students and I think very carefully as we move through these novels about the ambiguity in content and in style. The fact that Larsen does not save these women even at the end of the narratives highlights not bad writing, as has sometimes been suggested, but modern writing. The inconclusiveness, the ambiguity, the "something" we (and the protagonists) are met with throughout the novels, particularly in their conclusions, highlights the very lack of options and opportunities available to these women in 1920s America that could have led to the recognition and achievement of a fulfilling identity.

In comparison to the hopeful tone of some of her Harlem Renaissance contemporaries, Larsen takes a different approach, exposing a different experience, an experience we often designate as modern. Her stories represent the kind of fragmented fear of being alienated in one's own world. Defining the "something" that Helga and Irene both fear perhaps doesn't even matter. What ultimately modernizes these texts is the fear and ambiguity that is all around the protagonists, ruling their thoughts and driving their actions, leading to what can only be a dismal and destructive future. My students and I also, inevitably, discuss Larsen's role in all of this; certainly, her decision *not* to save these women suggests something about her own position in the world. But what does it say? Is she critical of Irene and Helga? Is she sorry for them? We arrive at potential answers to these questions by looking at one more element of the texts: the focalization.

Larsen underscores the thematic ambiguity through, among other techniques such as free indirect thought and free indirect discourse, her use of focalization, something that students often overlook, making it all the more important to the teaching of Larsen. There are a variety of types of focalization, but Larsen exclusively uses internal focalization, which is "a type of focalization whereby information is conveyed in terms of a character's (conceptual or perceptual) point of view or perspective" (Prince 45). In other words, Irene and Helga do not narrate these texts; instead, there is a third-person narrator who provides occasional commentary. But the focalization is so intense and profuse (indeed, each novel is almost entirely focalized through the protagonists) that it is easy to forget they are not the narrators. Having students pay attention to and think seriously about the fact that the texts are focalized through rather than narrated by the main characters is essential to their careful, critical reading.

As I noted, focalization requires the presence of another voice, another point of view besides that of Helga or Irene. Although there are very few passages that are not focalized through the two women, the passages that aren't help shed light, perhaps, on Larsen's position. I have students look, for example, at the following two passages from *Quicksand* and *Passing*, respectively. The first passage reads:

> As always, at first the novelty of the thing, the change, fascinated her. There was a recurrence of the feeling that now, at least, she had found a place for herself, that she was really living. And she had her religion, which in her new status as preacher's wife had of necessity become real to her. She believed in it. Because in its coming it had brought this other

> thing, this anesthetic satisfaction for her senses. Hers was, she declared to herself, a truly spiritual union. This one time in her life, she was convinced, she had not clutched a shadow and missed the actuality. (118)

The second passage reads:

> No, there had been, in all the years that they had lived together since then, no other talk of [Brazil], no more than there had been any other quarrelling or any other threats. But because, so she insisted, the bond of flesh and spirit between them was so strong, she knew, had always known, that his dissatisfaction had continued. . . .
>
> A feeling of uneasiness stole upon her at the inconceivable suspicion that she might have been wrong in her estimate of her husband's character. But she squirmed away from it. Impossible! She couldn't have been wrong. Everything proved that she had been right. More than right, if such a thing could be. And all, she assured herself, because she understood him so well, because she had, actually, a special talent for understanding him. It was, as she saw it, the one thing that had been the basis of the success which she had made of a marriage that had threatened to fail. (187)

Enacting a close reading of these passages with my students allows them to see how easily the narrative moves between the consciousness, even the exact wording, of the characters and the voice of the narrator. I call attention to the use of qualifiers, phrases like "as always," "she declared to herself," "so she insisted," "she assured herself," which are phrases from the narrator and, notably, phrases students often gloss over. Helga and Irene would not say these phrases to themselves. These qualifiers call attention to what Helga and Irene *want* to believe, *want* to think, while at the same time suggesting that what they are telling themselves is not true. More important, they disclose the fact that the narrative authority wants us to see the inherent subjectivity of their perspective.

This extra voice, provided by the narrator, is easy to miss because we hear it very rarely. But if one pays attention to it, this voice adds another perspective and, in doing so, provides students with the opportunity to engage with multiple perspectives instead of having their conclusions inextricably tied to the subjective experience of one person (as would happen, for example, in a first-person narrative such as *The Great Gatsby*). This other voice also draws attention to a controlling figure behind the text. My students can't help wondering, when we look at these qualifiers, what Larsen thought about Helga and Irene. We generally arrive at three options for Larsen's position: (1) she is critical of Helga and Irene; (2) she purposefully remains ambiguous about them, withholding her own judgment to avoid influencing readers' judgment; (3) she literally can't save them, for two possible reasons—she doesn't have the rhetorical means to do so or she herself doesn't know how to save them.

No matter which option we discuss, we always come back to the fact that Helga and Irene are very similar to Larsen. In other words, the world in which they live, a world in which they are ultimately unable to thrive, is a world much like Larsen's.

As we examine Larsen's position as a mixed-race woman writing in 1920s Harlem, a position as a voice of the Harlem Renaissance, my students also begin to see her as modern, even more modern, perhaps, than other canonical modernist authors like Eliot and Pound. Larsen's situation, one could argue, was to a greater extent ruled by dislocation than that of many others; she was always between worlds: black and white, male and female, art and experience. Having ties to all of them, she ultimately did not fully belong in any of them. Laura Doyle comments on this position:

> While Larsen keeps us just outside her community's and heroine's interiors through her use of limited point of view, her novels establish her own stance as critical onlooker, positioned at least partially outside her community. . . . It seems that, as for Hawthorne and Eliot, her authorial acts of defiance proved her embrace of freedom—her transcendence of race, for the race. (408)

Although I agree that Larsen is a critical onlooker, and critical not of her protagonists but of the systematic social oppressions affecting her protagonists, I cannot agree that Larsen was able to, or even trying to, transcend race through her writing. Instead, Larsen's works are grounded in the lack of freedom to embrace anything solid and real. Indeed, her works embody the modern condition, skillfully illustrating Eliot's "place of disaffection," and they do so through a racial and gendered lens that is often missing from canonical modernist works.

As I have noted, Larsen's novels are often designated as texts of the Harlem Renaissance. But having students think about them as modernist texts focuses attention on the complex, multilayered ambiguity they contain. There is worth in letting the ambiguity be instead of trying to solve it. Recognition and analysis of the ambiguity lead students to important questions about Larsen's characters, Larsen herself, and the political, social, sexual, and racial realities in modern America. In her deeply unsettling content, in her depiction of what Daylanne English calls "racially specific wastelands," Larsen illustrates that no sense of fulfilling identity existed for these women to grasp ("Selecting" 815). In her deeply unnerving style, a style that refuses to be conclusive, Larsen illustrates the unavailability of rhetorical positions that would allow her to openly criticize the interlocking oppressions of sex, race, and class. Indeed, Larsen heeded Eliot's call to dislocate language into meaning. Larsen did not shore up the fragments of these women's lives to try to make sense of them, to embrace freedom. Instead, she leaves the fragments as is, leaving it up to her readers to create meaning. For many potential reasons, it was impossible for Larsen to say just what she meant, which was, after all, a very modern predicament.

NOTES

[1] To my knowledge, there have been few critics who designate Larsen as a modernist. A recent exception would be Charles Scruggs in his article "Sexual Desire, Modernity, and Modernism in the Fiction of Nella Larsen and Rudolph Fisher." Even Scruggs, however, ends his article with this pronouncement: "Once considered minor writers, both Larsen and Fisher have emerged as two great literary figures of the Harlem Renaissance" (168).

[2] I regularly teach *Passing*, and I have done so in a variety of classes: American Literature Survey, Introduction to Fiction, Gender Studies, and African American Literature. Approaching *Passing* as a modernist text has worked best in my American literature survey courses and African American literature course because I include in those courses discussion of historical and cultural contexts. In my survey courses, we begin with works from realism, naturalism, regionalism, and Reconstruction. Then, we turn to modernist and Harlem Renaissance poetry, ending the time period with *Passing* and *The Great Gatsby*. In my African American Literature course, we begin with slave narratives, turn to Reconstruction texts, and then read Harlem Renaissance works, ending with *Passing*.

[3] Prince defines *focalization* as "the perspective in terms of which the narrated situations and events are presented; the perceptual or conceptual position in terms of which they are rendered" (31). Prince's definition nicely summarizes the rhetorical distinction between "who sees" and "who speaks" that Genette discusses in his *Narrative Discourse: An Essay in Method*. In Prince's words, "point of view ("who sees") should be distinguished from voice ("who speaks"): it is not equivalent to expression but institutes the perspective governing expression. Yet, especially since the work of Lubbock on narrative technique, point of view has often been taken to involve not only a perceptual or conceptual apparatus but also factors like the narrator's overtness, the types of treatment favored (drama or panorama), and the types of discourse adopted" (74). Thus, I employ the term *focalization* for its specificity. See Genette's *Narrative Discourse Revisited*, especially chapters 11 and 12, for further clarification.

[4] This and all quotations throughout the essay are taken from the 1986 Rutgers edition of Quicksand *and* Passing, edited by Deborah E. McDowell.

[5] As I note above, while the Harlem Renaissance and modernism are certainly not mutually exclusive, they are often seen as such. In her article "Selecting the Harlem Renaissance," English discusses McKay and Gates's view, arguing that seeing the Harlem Renaissance through this lens causes us to overlook important works, works such as Larsen's, because they do not fit into this assessment of optimism. English further argues that there are vital connections to be made between modernist and Harlem Renaissance works. Additionally, and often with upper-level majors or graduate students, I also read Baker's influential "Modernism and the Harlem Renaissance," in which he argues that the Harlem Renaissance and modernism were vastly different literary movements. Both articles present connected yet opposing arguments, and they provide a valuable way to engage in this discussion.

[6] In her article "Clare Kendry's 'True' Colors: Race and Class Conflict in Nella Larsen's *Passing*," Brody convincingly argues that it is Irene, not Clare, who desires to be white. This article is an important resource for teachers of *Passing* and, if time allows, for students as well.

Helga Crane in West Egg: Reading *Quicksand* and *The Great Gatsby* as a Case Study in Canonicity

Shealeen Meaney

"How can any self-respecting English major not have read Nella Larsen's *Quicksand*?"

This is the question with which I half-jokingly berate my Canon, Canonicity, and Coverage students every spring at the Sage Colleges in Troy, New York. They look mystified every time, which is really my point. My question follows an ice-breaking exercise inspired by an episode from David Lodge's novel *Changing Places*, in which literary academics try to outdo one another in a game of "Humiliation" by admitting to canonical texts that they have never read. As I point out to my students, in the novel the game has high stakes: one scholar is refused tenure not long after admitting never to have read *Hamlet.* Since my students are soon-to-be high school teachers who hope to earn tenure themselves someday, they laugh and look wary at the same time.

In our version of Lodge's game, I ask students to identify one book that they are *humiliated* to admit that they haven't read as a college English major. *The Great Gatsby* is invariably someone's response. Tellingly, every year this same title comes up as one of the few that new English majors in my American literature survey course can name when asked to list some titles of works of American literature (they are often much more familiar with British literature). In neither course is Nella Larsen a familiar name when she turns up on the syllabus, and my Canon, Canonicity, and Coverage students have no idea how to respond when asked if they are embarrassed not to have read her novel *Quicksand.* Perhaps they should be, after all, but they aren't sure. They *are* sure, on the other hand, about *Gatsby. Everyone* should have read that.

The divergent receptions these texts receive on day 1 of my class reflect their divergent histories in American literary culture. As Deborah McDowell points out in her introduction to Rutgers's *American Women Writers* 1986 edition of *Quicksand* (bound with *Passing*), upon its initial publication the novel received praise from critics like W. E. B. Du Bois and was awarded a second-place prize in literature from the Harmon Foundation in 1928 (ix). Du Bois called it the "best piece of fiction that Negro America has produced since the heyday of Chesnutt" (qtd. in McDowell ix). Fitzgerald's novel received praise as well, but early reviews were mixed, and some potential serial publishers were wary of its overtly sexual content (Green 39). Review headlines called forth "New Fitzgerald Book Proves He's Really a Writer," but also "F. Scott Fitzgerald's Latest a Dud" (Bruccoli 188). As Robert Beuka summarizes, "[M]ost critical appraisals of *The Great Gatsby* that appeared in 1925 praised Fitzgerald's 'facility' with language, while grappling with the question of the novel's literariness" (4). Amy Green notes that "luminaries within Fitzgerald's immediate circle, including Gertrude Stein, Ernest Hemingway, and T. S. Eliot, immediately showered his new novel with praise" (39). Indeed, Eliot called it "the first step that American fiction has taken since Henry James" in a letter to Fitzgerald. In a similarly enthusiastic letter, the high-profile critic H. L. Mencken wrote, "I think it is incomparably the best piece of work you have done" (qtd. in Bruccoli 178); however, his published review of the book was more layered. Noting its "fine texture" and "careful and brilliant finish," he nevertheless famously opened his review with the statement that "*The Great Gatsby* is in form no more than a glorified anecdote, and not too probable at that," noting that most of the characters are "not quite alive" (Mencken, "As H.L.M." 156–57). The simple fact that multiple academic volumes have been dedicated solely to chronicling and assessing the critical reception of this novel speaks to the complexity of its rise to canonicity.

Nevertheless, *The Great Gatsby* went on to be translated into many languages from Arabic to Turkish and to inspire diverse adaptations from the 1926 silent film directed by Herbert Brenan to the Elevator Repair Service's 2005 six-hour performance reading entitled *Gatz*. Meanwhile, *Quicksand* virtually disappeared from the literary landscape for nearly half a century before being rediscovered by scholars of African American women's writing in the 1970s. Fitzgerald became and remained a household name while Larsen became an obscure figure of interest largely to specialists. In part, these different trajectories make these novels useful when read together, but this is only the beginning. Published a mere two years apart, they are both engagements with the urban cultures of the Jazz Age, both are integrally caught up in questions about the modern woman, and both—in their ways—offer fascinating opportunities to think about the ethnic landscapes of the United States during the era of the Great Migration. These are foremost among the many reasons that I often teach them together, and when taught this way, the novels produce an excellent case study for talking about canonicity.

In Canon, Canonicity, and Coverage, I ask students to read both *Quicksand* and *The Great Gatsby*, and we do not discuss either novel until we have read them both. For upper-level undergraduate and graduate students, these novels are accessible enough and brief enough that this unusual approach works, as long as the students understand ahead of time that they are meant to be reading them independently alongside the critical materials of the course. In lower-level courses, I have taught the novels sequentially—starting with Larsen—and kept critical readings to a minimum, relying on the novels themselves as material for pointing out issues of canonicity, modernity, and the politics of representation and interpretation. There are really two kinds of work that this textual pairing undertakes. The first, as this article's title suggests, is to encourage students to think about canonicity and the various processes and factors that shape cultural reading practices. The second is to demonstrate a form of contextual reading that challenges simple notions of fiction as a "window to the past" while maintaining that a critical engagement with a range of cultural texts can deepen our thinking about not only an individual literary text but also the culture that produced it. One of the critical texts I often assign alongside the novels is Lillian S. Robinson's "Treason Our Text: Feminist Challenges to the Literary Canon," which suggests that feminist challenges to the canon can be carried out in multiple possible ways: we might read (canonical) texts differently or we might read different texts (and argue for their canonicity). This "case study" method is a great way for students to see the possibilities held out by both approaches.

As Canon and Canonicity caters to English education students, readings and assignments tend to emphasize the relation between canon and curriculum, and because our course is focused on these subjects, the students are well steeped in critical discussions about canonicity by the time we discuss these well-steeped novels at the midterm point. In a broader course, a relatively small group of excerpted texts can provide students with a general understanding of the key concepts, terms, and stakes of canon debates. An instructor might select critical texts or have students purchase an edited collection that lays the groundwork for the assignment. Many effective selections can be found in David H. Richter's collection *Falling into Theory: Conflicting Views on Reading Literature* (the framework of which I use to organize the course into basic questions: what, why, and how do we read?) or Lee Morrissey's *Debating the Canon: A Reader from Addison to Nafisi.*

Whichever selections one chooses, the critical texts function to open up questions about the ways that the novels become canonized and commodified in United States culture (and in educational contexts in particular). They also foreground the ways that cultural location shapes reading practices, urging students to problematize their initial readings of the characters and cultures they encounter in texts. Finally, they can serve as a basic introduction to theoretical approaches, should this be an objective of a given course. In the remainder of this essay, I briefly discuss how a few of these critical excerpts feature in students' discussions of *Gatbsy*, *Quicksand*, and canonical culture, sticking with examples of critical theories that can be found in one or the other of the aforementioned collections. In doing so, I foreground some of the questions and issues that have emerged in class discussions.

"Why haven't we ever heard of this book?" students often ask when they read *Quicksand* for the first time. Well, that's the big question of the class, I remind them. What would Toni Morrison say? What about Barbara Herrnstein Smith? We brainstorm together, thinking about how we *know* that *Gatsby* is canonical literature. One thing we consider is the pervasiveness of Gatsby in mainstream culture: students can usually come up with references to the novel in popular culture that I've never heard of (most recently, for instance, an episode of Comedy Central's *South Park*, in which the novel features prominently). We flip through E. D. Hirsch's *Dictionary of Cultural Literacy*, which ostensibly tells us "what every American needs to know," noting that not only does Fitzgerald have his own entry but so does *Gatsby*. Larsen, unsurprisingly, is conspicuously absent from each of these contexts, and students are quick to recognize that Fitzgerald's novel is canonical by the exact measures that Larsen's is not.

In preparation for our discussion, students read McDowell's aforementioned introduction to *Quicksand*, from which they garner a basic knowledge of its publication and reception history. Their edition of *The Great Gatsby* also comes complete with an introduction, but *Gatsby*, they assume, they know all about. They are, in fact, surprised to hear that the now blockbuster *Gatsby* itself fell out of print for a while in the 1930s before coming into literary vogue (Sealts). Matthew Bruccoli notes that Scribner's printed only 23,870 copies of *The Great Gatsby* during Fitzgerald's lifetime and that not all of these sold (175): "Though Fitzgerald would ask his publishing house, Scribner's, repeatedly over the years to issue an inexpensive paperback edition of the novel, with the hope of improving sales and generating a revival of sorts of the book, Scribner's refused" (Beuka 2). This is not what we might imagine of a novel that has come to epitomize canonicity in our own era.

Considering this historical transition in the light of other events and issues of the period provides students with a concrete illustration of why some critics argue that "greatness" is a culturally and historically specific construct. Some basic questions about the economics of literary production and publishing can also be raised. Starting the "case study" questions with the historical fluctuations of Gatsby's "greatness" provides useful background before we turn directly to the reception and disappearance of, as well as the renewed interest in, Larsen's work. It can be tempting for some students to dismiss Larsen's recovery by feminist and black studies scholars as *just* politically motivated multicultural grasping for representation. In fact, some of the assigned readings by Harold Bloom, E. D. Hirsch, and William Bennett can encourage them to read this way. After all, they remember Bloom's "Elegiac Conclusion" (from *The Western Canon*) and his railing against a modern university in which "the teaching of poems, plays, stories, and novels is now supplanted by cheerleading for various social and political crusades" (227). By considering the historical fluctuations of *Gatsby*'s popularity, students have a more complex context for making sense of Larsen's disappearance and recovery. Furthermore, they are encouraged to see both texts, rather than just the latter, as susceptible to cultural whims and open to critical reevaluation. This significantly complicates their assumptions about literary greatness and about the kinds of critical work they themselves feel entitled to do.

One of our critical mantras in the course becomes "good for what?" The question emerges from our reading of Jane Tompkins's "But Is It Any Good?" Among other things, she inquires into the concept of universal aesthetic greatness and articulates alternative criteria for reading *Uncle Tom's Cabin*—as contrasted, for instance, with *Moby-Dick*. What if we replace the oft taken for granted association of complexity with quality in fiction and replace it with a reevaluation of its efficacy as socially transformative? By what criteria, we ask, might Larsen's text be considered "great?" Are these the same criteria by which we evaluate *Gatsby*?

Do they change over time? For instance, in thinking about Gatsby's rise to greatness, it is interesting to consider that while Beuka notes that early reviews were impressed by the author's "'facility' with language" (4), Jackson R. Bryer's 1980 assessment of scholarship on Fitzgerald is only able to identify one article on style and language in *Gatsby* before the 1970s (264). Style may have been part of what made *Gatsby* great, but apparently it also had other merits compelling to scholars. So, is *Quicksand* great in terms of language and style? Or is it great by other scholarly or popular measures? This is an idea that we also consider when we read Herrnstein Smith's "Contingencies of Value," and the novels offer an opportunity to ground Herrnstein Smith's discussion in specific texts. It is helpful that so many students have already read *Gatsby* once, since they can reflect back on how their high school or introductory college classes read the text. I ask them to try and remember what their teachers focused on when they studied the novel the first time and how classroom readings of the text might relate to Herrnstein Smith's explanations for how a text's value is reproduced.

Herrnstein Smith offers several possibilities for explaining any given text's "endurance," and many of these are easily explored in relation to these two novels. For instance, is a text "the best of its kind," "exemplary" in some particular way that makes it a good teaching tool? Well, yes, students sometimes say. Those who encountered the text in high school frequently remember an emphasis on the novel's formal qualities and lessons on literary terminology; in particular, it appears that *Gatsby* is often taught to them as a way of understanding "symbolism." Inevitably, this leads students to discuss the ways that other texts—the obvious example being Larsen's—might be used to meet the same objectives. Anne Hostetler's article on the racial aesthetics of the novel can be a valuable resource for this discussion; the novel, she argues, "is richly encrusted with symbols chosen from the object world of haute-bourgeois culture" (45). This then raises the question of why Larsen's novel *isn't* a common choice for studying this particular literary quality. They also note that *Gatsby* is often taught as a sort of window on the 1920s (what I see as a potential substitute for complex historical analysis of an era). *Quicksand*, of course, offers a fascinating vision of New York in the 1920s, and it offers one that imagines that city and its immediate surroundings in relation to its national and global contexts in a way that Fitzgerald's novel arguably does not. The "new woman" of the era, the emergent youth culture of the postwar period, the economic boom and its disparities—all of these can be explored in depth through a careful study of Larsen's characters and the diverse social and geographic spaces that she locates them within.

However, the canonical *Gatsby* appears to be most frequently taught as an exploration of that ever-popular classroom theme "the American dream." This makes sense: as Arnold Weinstein notes, "There is doubtless no more perfect piece of Americana in all of literature. Horatio Alger, rags-to-riches, the American Dream, upward mobility: it is all there. Fitzgerald has grasped the enormity of the American cliché" (30). But what about Helga's American dream? Her struggle to be independent, self-sufficient, and upwardly mobile? It is not hard for students to make the jump to Larsen's text themselves, and the ensuing discussions can be very fruitful.

Students can also draw from their own experiences with the text, and they are often quite interested in thinking about *why* a particular text has been taught to them (something they have not always thought much about before). Why would *Gatsby* speak to critics and readers of the 1950s differently from the way it spoke to those of the 1930s? Beuka, for one, argues that Fitzgerald's work was unpopular in the 1930s because critics were interested in works that dealt with the struggles of the "suffering masses," and he notes that by 1945 Lionel Trilling was praising *Gatsby*, "seeing *Gatsby*'s timeliness as part and parcel of its potential timelessness" (4). Richard Anderson suggests that "the general wave of nostalgia for the Jazz Age that swept the United States in the 1950s" fueled popular awareness of Fitzgerald (17). However, Green notes that in the 1950s, when the American dream "found itself subject to scrutiny," critical attention to the novel often focused on the failings and corruption of Gatsby's world (42). Perhaps readers were ready for the social critiques implicit in the novel in a way they had not been before. Bruccoli asserts that, although Fitzgerald's literary friends "*singled out* Gatsby *for recognition*" after his death, "the Fitzgerald Revival was essentially a reader-driven revival, not critic-driven or professor-driven" and that *Gatsby* was popular with book buyers themselves in the mid-1940s and 1950s (217). In 1957 a student's edition of the novel was issued, and it was on its way to becoming the classroom classic it is now (R. Anderson).

Whether we focus on teachers or critics or general readers, this evolution surely prompts us to ask, What about our ideas of greatness changed? How can we understand the process that Herrnstein Smith calls the "cultural reproduction of value" in relation to *Gatsby*? What about *Quicksand*? Herrnstein Smith argues that "what may be spoken of as the 'properties' of the work—its 'structure,' 'features,' 'qualities,' and, of course, its 'meanings'—are not fixed, given, or inherent in the work 'itself,' but are at every point the variable products of some subject's interaction with it" (148). So how, then, can what we know about different periods of the twentieth century help us understand the shifting value of these texts in United States culture?

This topic opens up some provocative conversations about Gatsby's "incorruptible dream" and how it relates to Helga's moments of satisfaction, which "didn't last long," as Larsen regularly reminds us. If Fitzgerald's treatment of the American dream is often offered as a reason for his novel's centrality in the American canon and curriculum, Helga's dream complicates such easy thematic understandings of canonicity. Furthermore, the failure of Jay Gatsby's elaborate schemes for buying happiness casts Helga's own consumerist fantasies and failed escapes in a new light. It can be frustrating, indeed, to watch Helga take off time and again, just when it seems like she might *finally* be happy somewhere, and trying to find her a home in Gatsby's world reframes our readerly frustrations in interesting ways. What are the options for Larsen's character? If we have difficulty understanding Helga's choices, would her contemporaries have shared our difficulties, or would some historical context help us make sense of her? How might readers' discomfort with the choices the novel offers and those that the character makes affect the reception and status of the text? This brings us back to Herrnstein Smith's point about the ways that the qualities of a text "are at every point the variable products of some subject's interaction with it" (148).

This is a fairly extensive unit, and I also have some contextual materials that I use to sketch out the historical circumstances and cultural climates from and to which these texts speak. I find that such material helps us complicate some basic questions students invoke about "reality" and "accuracy." An added benefit of these materials is that students are fascinated by images of Jim Crow railway signs, flapper fashions, and Harlem nightclubs, and articles about miscegenation and "petting," and this interest helps draw them further into the contradictory visions and ideological issues presented by the texts and their respective canonical locations.

Herrnstein Smith argues that once a text has attained canonical status, there are mechanisms by which it retains that status, ways in which the culture nearly renders the text sacrosanct. Elements of a work that "conflict intolerably with the interests and ideologies of subsequent subjects . . . for example, incidents or sentiments of brutality, bigotry, and racial, sexual, or national chauvinism—will be repressed or rationalized" (149). I am not the first person to ask students why African Americans are so curiously absent from the jazz and youthful landscapes of Fitzgerald's *The Great Gatsby*. Nevertheless, students don't immediately see race as an issue in *Gatbsy*, and even reading the novel alongside *Quicksand* doesn't always make the issue stand out for them. Once race is zoomed into focus for them, however, students are almost immediately troubled—largely because they realize that they have read and discussed Fitzgerald's novel extensively without ever having noticed its racial representations (never mind its engagements with anti-Semitism and domestic violence). I reassure them that they are not alone. As Jeffrey Decker argues,

> At first glance, nothing seems more remote from *The Great Gatsby* than the issue of racial segregation or black empowerment. Despite the novel's being set in metropolitan New York, African Americans almost never appear in Gatbsy's world. Yet, from Garveyism to the fledgling Harlem Renaissance, New York was becoming the mecca of black American politics and culture. The near complete absence of blacks from the novel can be comprehended only if we factor in the ubiquitous power of racial segregation. The absence of African Americans alongside the novel's conspicuous appropriation of black culture is what makes it a definitive text of the so-called Jazz Age. (56)

I can think of no better way of introducing this context than by reading the novel alongside Larsen's work. Along with raising questions about the relations between race, politics, and readership, the comparison offers an interesting opportunity for students to think about a national context in the United States for Edward Said's concept of "contrapuntal reading" in postcolonial studies. In "Connecting Empire to Secular Interpretation" (from *Culture and Imperialism*), Said writes, "As we look back at the cultural archive we begin to reread it not univocally but *contrapuntally*, with a simultaneous awareness both of the metropolitan history that is narrated and of those other histories against which (and together with which) the dominating discourse acts" (227). We thus attempt to read Larsen's black New York into Fitzgerald's novel and vice versa. What would Helga Crane's place in West Egg be? Could she be one of those "beautiful people" at Gatsby's parties? Invariably the answer is no. And that no is a helpful one for prompting us to think again about the Harlem of Helga Crane and Anne Grey and the anxieties over "mulatta" identities, "jungle beasts," and the exoticized Africanist fantasies of Axel Olsen in Copenhagen. How are the Dahls' social events in Copenhagen related to Gatsby's parties? Both are racially homogenous zones of social interaction in which a figure like Helga would be visibly marked as an outsider.

Helga's journeys make clear not only that when the raced and gendered body travels, it takes on diverse meanings but also that in the modern world most spaces are already global spaces and that wherever cultural productions travel, ideology does as well. Helga's frustration at the "certainty of the division of her life into parts in two lands, into physical freedom in Europe and spiritual freedom in America" simply has no parallel in the lives of Fitzgerald's characters (96). The Jim Crow trains that define Helga's experience of mobility in the United States are a sharp contrast with the restless and reckless inhabitants of West Egg. Why is it that the "three modish negroes, two bucks and a girl," that pass Nick and Gatsby on the Queensboro Bridge make Nick so uneasy? What would it take for Nick, we might ask, to be one of those white jazz voyeurs that Audrey Denney "goes about with" (60)?

Toni Morrison's "Black Matter(s)" (an excerpt from *Playing in the Dark*) can also be useful in asking students to think about how black characters are used to construct ideas about whiteness in the novels and vice versa. Morrison's analysis focuses on the "potent and ego-reinforcing presence of an Africanistic Population" in American literature that she argues is essential to the construction of free, independent ideal of Anglo-American selfhood (317). It becomes very easy for students to engage Morrison's ideas through the few black characters in *Gatsby*, particularly the infamous scene on the bridge into the city, the racist stereotypes of which are hard to ignore, though generations of classrooms have done just that. How, students wonder, is it possible that so many different high school classes have managed to "*gloze over*" such scenes, to use Herrnstein Smith's terminology? The conversation becomes even more difficult when we draw out the connections to Larsen's novel. "Autonomy, newness, difference, authority, absolute power," Morrison writes, "these are the major themes and concerns of American literature, and each one is made possible, shaped, and activated by a complex awareness and use of a constituted Africanism that, deployed as rawness and savagery, provided the staging ground and arena for the elaboration of the quintessential American identity" (317). "Autonomy," "newness," "difference," and "authority" are very much at the heart of Helga Crane's struggles, and these "themes" demand that we complicate questions of race and gender by reading them together.

In both novels, each female character embodies a wealth of contradictions and contained crises that illustrate the range of raced and classed ideologies of femininity at work in American society of the 1920s. The famously freewheeling characters in *Gatsby* offer a valuable contrast to the constraints, conventions, and consequences of which Larsen's desperate seeker struggles to make sense. How can it be that Jordan seems relatively unscathed by her sexual encounters but that the mere presence of Helga's green negligee is scandalous at Naxos? This textual juxtaposition allows for some interesting conversations about how we read the sometimes troubling "choices" made by Larsen's Helga in the light of the consumer femininities offered up by Fitzgerald's characters like Daisy and Jordan. For some students (particularly those in lower-level classes), the emotional exhaustion they experience vicariously through Helga takes a toll, and this can lead them to condemn her fairly quickly. When they attempt to read Jordan or Daisy into Helga's place, they sometimes begin to suspect that Helga has held together rather well under the historical circumstances of her life. While such conversations may be less tightly related to our questions of canonicity, I find that they are valuable in keeping students engaged with Larsen's characters despite the challenges they present.

Interestingly, many students ultimately argue that they find *Quicksand* to be the more interesting of the two texts, and the one that they would choose to teach themselves if asked to choose a text to represent American literature of the 1920s. Two major course assignments bring students back to this case study. One asks students to select a single text that they believe is important for other students to read and then to develop a teaching unit to present in class. The second asks them to create a "canon" for American high school students and to articulate a logic and justification for the choices therein. Students regularly go back to the example of *Quicksand* when they talk about their own canons, frequently explaining that the experience of reading the novel in the context of canon debates has, indeed, made them rethink what, why, and how they read. While I have emphasized students' engagements with supplemental readings in this essay, I would like to suggest that the juxtaposition of these novels can be quite effective even without such theoretical texts. In lower-level courses in which theoretical materials are not easily integrated, a brief critical introduction of the above issues by the instructor can help students set up *Quicksand* and *Gatsby* to illuminate one another—and questions of canonicity—in quite interesting ways.

In a recent essay arguing for a rereading of *Gatsby* as an ethnic novel that can decenter the canon, Joe Kraus argues that

> *Gatsby* is very much concerned with questions of ethnicity . . . and that fact matters for two reasons. First, putting the novel in such a light brings into relief its representations of immigrant crime and jingoism and puts it into conversation with a range of other literature, much of it ethnic. Second, proposing *Gatsby* as ethnic reemphasizes the idea that much of canonical American literature—however we define the canon—is centrally concerned with categories of social difference. (127)

How canonical literature has engaged these categories, however, deserves further attention, as does the question of which categories of difference tend to be elided in canonical contexts. When read in conjunction with a canonical counterpart like *The Great Gatsby*, Larsen's finely wrought depictions of lived social difference in *Quicksand* can help students enter into conversations about these and other questions of canonicity and culture.

"A Whole World of Experience and Struggle": Teaching Literature as Cultural and Intellectual Women's History

Lyde Sizer

> *Quicksand* and *Passing* are novels I will never forget. They open up a whole world of experience and struggle that seemed to me, when I first read them years ago, absolutely absorbing, fascinating, and indispensible.
>
> —Alice Walker

A dozen years ago now, in the line collecting lunch in the faculty dining room, a colleague turned to speak to me about my syllabi. He'd been analyzing them as a senior member of my division; I was up for tenure. Leaning over, not unkindly, he noted that I used a *lot* of literature when teaching cultural and intellectual history, implying that this was a mistake. Remember, he told me, to make sure the students know that this isn't the *truth*. He was right: among other primary sources, like autobiographies, memoirs, and collections of shorter pieces like letters, editorials, and speeches, I *do* use literature to teach history, sometimes a number of times in a semester. But to my mind he was wrong, too. Then, as now, I do believe that literature reveals to my students a kind of meaningful truth, an accessibility and complexity that many textbooks might not; if they are literary texts, they are also political, cultural, and social documents of a particular moment. In short, they are history.

Teaching at a small liberal arts college, I have come to wear a number of hats. Trained in United States cultural and intellectual history and women's history, in particular the Civil War era, I have had to stretch as a scholar in teaching courses spanning from the late eighteenth to the late twentieth century. (This has been, I've found, very intellectually productive.) Most courses taught at my college are seminars, very often yearlong, and there are few requirements. This has given me a great deal of latitude in the ways I have been able to design courses, even as I am very conscious that my students may only take one history class in their career. I am therefore eager that they have a sense of the sweep across time, the crucial overlapping shifts in ideas and culture that still inform their world. Nella Larsen has been a regular choice in my classes, from courses that focused broadly on cultural and intellectual history to those in women's history or culture and politics. She was included in an early course I taught on the history of sexuality, along with one that focused on US and European intellectual history at the turn of the twentieth century.

I have taught both of Larsen's novels, sometimes in the same class: each is remarkably useful in its way. *Quicksand* explores ideas and politics of African American leaders and the effects of the early years of the Great Migration;

Passing traces ideas about race and essentialism as well as sexual mores in the urban 1920s (although there are many other clues to the 1920s in both novels). What has been notable over the years is the delight that my students take in both novels. They marvel at the graceful and clipped language and are intrigued by the modernist ambiguity, especially when they have spent a semester with the often didactic certainty of late-eighteenth- and nineteenth-century writers. The truth they read here is not about fixity but about movement, about the ways a writer chooses to depict a world, about what she chooses to include (and how she chooses to include it), and what she chooses to omit.

My students come to Larsen with some grounding in larger social, political, or intellectual shifts. I most often move between more traditional history textbooks and primary documents so that students are primed: this allows them new ways to read and appreciate the work as more than a piece of literature, as also historical evidence of a particular and valuable kind. My colleagues in literature have at times suggested that the way I use novels is "instrumental," and perhaps they are right. Texts like the novels of Larsen can and should be read in multiple ways and for multiple purposes. If my students leave their reading of Larsen with a deeper sense of the conflicts at the center of the Harlem Renaissance, with a realization of the complexity and nuance of sexual desire among and between women in the 1920s, with a grave sense of the narrowness of the choices bright, intellectual African American women faced in the early twentieth century, among other revelations, then her work would have continued to make meaning in the world. If that's "instrumental," so be it. For the most part, I leave purely aesthetic considerations to others, though I'm certainly not opposed to their emerging in the course of discussion.

Perhaps most profoundly, *Quicksand* and *Passing* are novels both about and of the Harlem Renaissance. Larsen opens *Quicksand* with a stanza of a poem by Langston Hughes and *Passing* with a dedication to Carl Van Vechten and a stanza written by Countee Cullen. Part of my work in the classroom is to introduce Harlem—the physical and urban space, the way it became inhabited by African Americans, and the culture, movement, music, and politics they brought to it in its heyday in the 1920s—along with the Renaissance in literary culture. Larsen is not so much representative of the Renaissance as a window on it: clearly influenced by an older generation of intellectuals represented by the sociologist W. E. B. Du Bois (my students typically also read *The Souls of Black Folk*), she is also a bit of a sexual radical, inspired by the playfulness, resistance, and vigor of a new generation of writers, represented by Langston Hughes, among others.[1] And while very much committed to African American culture, she was unwilling to be exclusive, to deny the part of herself that was European and white.

In their reading, I ask my students to think hard about the context, the way the historical environment surrounding the novel reveals and obscures the lives of both protagonists and minor characters. In both novels, for example, the economic limits faced by African American women in the North shape the stories themselves. Helga, once she has cast herself outside the suffocating shelter of Naxos, can do little with her education and skills. Library work, when an African American woman could get it, required further education, and "the shops didn't employ colored clerks or sales-people, not even the smaller ones" (*Quicksand* 32). What African American women could do was housework or, it was hinted, sex work. Pervasive in Larsen's work is a sense of the predatory and entitled white man, those who jostle and entreat Helga both on the street and in her pretentious elite life in Copenhagen, where the painter Axel Olsen offers marriage only after it is clear she will not accept a "more informal arrangement" (88).

Even the happy accidents in both novels evoke a sense of danger, a bullet dodged in pursuit of a comfortable life. When Helga is hired, it is for an unusual short-term job as an assistant to Mrs. Hayes-Rore, a prominent "race" woman. This is unusually fortuitous, for without references or family connections, Helga could not have found a job even with a newly established Negro insurance company, and would never have found herself amidst the black elite in Harlem. Clare Kendry knows well what her status will be, and remain, if she stays with her white aunts as their servant, or even if she returns to the South Side to live off the families of her sympathetic friends. The fact that her aunts never revealed her racial origins allowed her to pass. The American dream for an intelligent African American woman with aspirations to an elegant life came only with considerable help from mentors or with marriage.

Both novels also suggest the significance of the enormous social change precipitated by the Great Migration. World War I not only opened previously closed factory doors to African American workers (often as a strike-breaking tool) but offered soldiers a glimpse at another way of living. In *Quicksand*, the Great War took the life of Ann's first husband; in *Passing*, it fostered a deep sense of grievance and restlessness in Brian, Irene's husband. James Vayle, Helga's ex-fiancé, tells her that as much as he wanted to get back to his people from his stint in the army, being in Europe helped him see "the country and the difference in treatment" (101). Terrible economic and political conditions in the South, an upswing in numbers of lynchings, a renewed KKK, along with the draw of opportunity triggered a massive migration north and westward. Aware of the importance of these shifts, my students ferret out the ways in which Larsen reveals the consequences for those who came and stayed, as well as those already established in the North.

The twentieth century ushered in a new social role for women of the leisure classes, and Larsen makes clear the relevance of this role for African American women in both Harlem and Chicago. The protagonists of both novels are notable for the quality and intensity of their consumption. Helga is introduced while surrounded by beautiful and carefully selected things—a blue Chinese carpet, numerous books, a shining brass bowl, an oriental silk covering a stool—and these things matter a great deal to her, so much that the first activity she indulges in, to comfort her after her bruising interaction with her uncle's new wife, is buying a book and a tapestry bag she "could not afford" (32). Larsen acknowledges and does not condemn Helga's yearning for beautiful and colorful things.

For my women's history students in particular, these novels are a revelation. After the novels of the nineteenth century, the students are dazzled by a new sense of sexuality and its possibilities. Larsen, described in "Modern Sexuality and the Myth of Victorian Repression" by the historian Christina Simmons as a sex radical, opens up a world by challenging the truisms of the Victorian past, defying the sexual straightjacket more careful women and writers wear as a kind of protection against the stereotype of the promiscuous African American woman. In *Quicksand*, Helga awakens to her own desire with a passionate kiss, and if it leads her to a prison of sorts, it also offers the moments of the text where she is freest from ambivalence. *Passing*, with more than a hint of same-sex desire, represents a decisive move away from the buttoned-down silence of even the Boston marriages of the late nineteenth century. As we parse the language of desire in *Passing*, we stop to consider the sexual revolution, with its new language, culture, and associations.

At the center of both of Larsen's novels is the question of race. Her position on race is complicated, deliberately ambiguous: much like her character Brian Redfield, she calls into question just what race *is*. Irene Redfield, *Passing*'s unreliable narrator, has a revealing conversation with a prominent white philanthropist, Hugh Wentworth, at a Negro Welfare League dance as they contemplate the dancers and wonder about the phenomenon of racial passing. How, asked Hugh, could one tell if a light-skinned woman was a Negro? Not by looking, Irene tells him, nothing "definite or tangible," but she asserts there is something nonetheless real, "a thing that [can't] be registered" (206). While we are not to trust Irene, the yearning of both Clare Kendry and Helga Crane to return to the African American community is palpable in both novels, offering them a sense of profound meaning and belonging even for these marginalized, racially mixed characters. Both are aware of the limits of living "even in Harlem," a world "too cramped, too uncertain, too cruel" (96), but also a kind of magnet because, as Helga muses in *Quicksand*, "Ties were of the spirit. Ties not only superficially entangled with the mere outline of features of color of skin. Deeper. Much deeper than either of these" (95).

What my students bring to as well as get from this text, I hope, is a complicated sense of the ways race is—and continues to be—constructed historically. The mid-to-late-twentieth-century binary of "white people" and "people of color" was under construction in the 1920s: in that historical moment, a complex hierarchy of races predominated, each with accompanying stereotypes and meanings. As the historian Matthew Frye Jacobson argues in *Whiteness of a Different Color*, "White privilege in various forms has been a constant in American political culture since colonial times, but whiteness itself has been subject to all kinds of contests and has gone through a series of historical vicissitudes" (4). Given the rather abrupt drop in immigration with the Johnson-Reed

Act of 1924, the alchemy of race in America was shifting, and white European immigrants were beginning the struggle to be accepted as white, a struggle that heightened the stakes of race considerably.

Interracial unions were the focus of considerable interest and conflict in the 1920s. An Alabama court case over racial intermarriage was overturned because the wife of a black man, Edith Labue, was a Sicilian immigrant, and this could "in no sense be taken as conclusive that she was therefore a white woman, or that she was not a negro or a descendant of a negro" (Jacobsen 4). Larsen alludes to the fraught implications of this angle of the color line at one point in *Quicksand*, when Helga has the flippant thought that "it would serve Anne right if she married a white man" (97). In *Passing*, there is a brief mention of the *Rhinelander* case, in which an African American wife, Alice Jones, won her case against her wealthy New Yorker husband, Leonard Kip Rhinelander, who sued for an annulment, claiming he did not know of her Negro background, if at a considerable cost to her dignity (Kaplan xvii–xviii).[2] Helga is well aware of the costs of "mixed marriages," even if her aunt Katrina is not, especially "to the children" (78).

Larsen's work usefully complicates ideas of racial stereotypes for my students. They come to the texts thoughtfully uncomfortable with the idea that African Americans are more musical, more spiritually passionate, more colorful, warmer, and more sexually voracious than Anglo-Saxons. These are ideas that writers in the Harlem Renaissance both resist and play with: Larsen in particular is suggestive rather than dramatic in the ways that she both reinforces and rejects stereotype. By reading Deborah McDowell's introduction to the text, students learn that overt celebrations or even explorations of sexuality were condemned by the powerful social critic Du Bois, who loathed the "nastiness" he felt Larsen's friend Carl Van Vechten encouraged (xv).

What *Quicksand* and *Passing* also allow my students to see with clarity and specificity are conflicts and struggles in the African American elite. They are almost startled at the profundity of Helga's critique of the world of Naxos—representing a mix between Tuskegee Institute in Alabama and Fisk University in Tennessee—and its attempt at erasure of all that does not project respectability and acceptance of white bourgeois norms. Her flight from Naxos—an anagram for Saxon—is precipitated by the respectful hearing given a "patronizing" but "renowned white preacher" when he advises them that "it was their duty to be satisfied in the estate to which they had been called, hewers of wood and drawers of water" (2, 3). What had begun as an idea—and maybe, she hints, at first a good one—had become a "machine," a "show place" that "tolerated no individualisms" (4). She could not befriend the smiling but submissive children there, nor could she connect to her smug and self-satisfied colleagues, who claimed to be uplifting the race while simply working to shape them into cogs for a white-controlled world.

If the politics of Naxos seemed to represent the ideas of Booker T. Washington, those of Harlem were more allied to those of Du Bois and his celebration of the political work of the talented tenth. Yet Larsen ironically comments on the similarity of their worldviews, which in history textbooks can seem so starkly opposed. Here too one finds a program of uplift, and Larsen suggests that here too is smug self-satisfaction masquerading as sacrifice and commitment, even in the work of generous Mrs. Hayes-Rore, whose lectures were "bodily lifted" from the work of "Wendell Phillips, Frederick Douglass, Booker T. Washington, and other doctors of the race's ills." Hayes-Rore cared little, it seemed, for consistency, throwing in "a peppery dash of Du Bois and a few vinegary statements of her own" (38). Anne Grey in *Quicksand* and Irene Redfield in *Passing* are also "race women," but in both cases they are drawn as more interested in the hierarchies and internecine battles within Negro society than the work itself. Larsen's critique can be startling to my more earnest students, and it encourages them to think harder about the motivations and complexity of benevolence.

Buried but suggested here are the ideas and work of other African American leaders, notably the socialist A. Philip Randolph and Marcus Garvey, whose Universal Negro Improvement Association (UNIA) rose and fell in the 1920s. Randolph in particular was critical of Du Bois and the NAACP, and he sought to draw working-class blacks into unions. Garvey's was a more popular cause, almost a spiritual movement, celebrating black pride and accomplishment and encouraging self-help and loyalty to the black community. At Mrs. Tavenor's party, which Helga attends after returning from Copenhagen, the political struggle among opposing factions is clear: "Helen, Mrs. Tavenor, had given vent to a malicious glee, and had invited representatives of several opposing Harlem political and social factions, including the West Indian, and abandoned them helplessly to each other" (99). Anne Grey, otherwise a careful proponent of uplift, is particularly incensed by any hint of sexual or romantic intermingling across the color line, echoing the critique that Garveyites had for their community: "That's what's the matter with the Negro race. They won't stick together" (61). Yet for all Anne's rage, she "turned up her finely carved nose" at the culture of working-class Southern blacks, with their "lusty churches, their picturesque parades, their naive clowning on the streets" (48).

Criticized bitterly too is the African American church. If Helga is bemused—and dismayed—by Anne Grey's hypocrisy and elitism, she carefully held herself aloof from the embrace of the church until the end, when it becomes the leading edge of the quicksand of the title. Caught in a drenching rainstorm, distraught by the intensity of her desire for Dr. Anderson, Helga stumbles into a storefront church. Here she is surrounded by the sounds and emotion of the Southern African American evangelical church, and she is stunned by the "writhings and weepings of the feminine portion, which seemed to predominate" (113). Moved by a profound desire for "simple happiness," she gives in to a world "unburdened by the complexities of the lives she had known" (114). She yields both to sexual desire and to the embrace of the church: "her religion was to her a kind of protective coloring, shielding her from the cruel light of an unbearable reality" (126). In the aftermath of a devastating pregnancy—her fourth—Helga's postpartum depression allows her enough rest to reconsider what she comes to see as a "fatuous belief in the white man's God" (133). But Helga is now well and truly caught: she cannot desert her children, and so cannot desert her husband, the preacher, or the church community.

Like many other readers, my students are dismayed by the dark endings of both novels. What we work toward understanding, however, is how this darkness is true to the America that Larsen presents. Both Helga and Clare yearn to be individuals, to express a sensual freedom, to be free, and yet neither is allowed to live that yearning. Much as both of them tried to escape the "race problem"—one by fleeing to Copenhagen, the other by passing—neither could, or even entirely wanted to, given their loyalties and desires. After thinking about returning to America—"To America, where Negroes were allowed to be beggars only, of life, of happiness, of security" (82)—Helga chooses to stay in Copenhagen, only to reconsider, yet again, and return. This America, this Harlem, is a dangerous, desirable place, with a hint of sexual and intellectual freedom framed by economic and physical constraint.

NOTES

[1] One of the best books on women and sexual radicalism in this period is Simmons, *Making Marriage Modern*. For an excellent history of the culture of the 1920s, see Dumenil. When I teach Larsen in a women's history course, paired with a textbook, I use Buhle, Murphy, and Gerhard.

[2] See Larsen, *Passing* [2007], and Madigan, excerpted in Kaplan's Norton Critical Edition, 387–93. Both sources provide an enormously useful collection of documents for a historian (among others), and it is often what I teach if I do not include *Quicksand* on the syllabus.

Nightlife and Racial Learning in *Quicksand*

Clark Barwick

One of the primary challenges of teaching the Harlem Renaissance, and Nella Larsen's *Quicksand* in particular, is attempting to make the time period relevant. For students today, much of what made the 1920s feel thrillingly modern now seems prehistoric. Silent films, phonographs, even books—technologies that brought exciting forms of culture to Americans in new ways—appear incredibly dated, if not altogether foreign, to young people. *Jazz* is a term that undergraduates are probably familiar with, but most students would be hard-pressed to name more than a handful of important jazz artists, either from the 1920s or otherwise. Flapper fashion, as styled by three women on the cover of the edition of *Quicksand* that I teach from, now seems almost costume-like, if still striking. Smoking cigarettes, once a sign of glamour and hipness, has lost its luster. Yet, nightlife itself—connected to all the aforementioned modes of culture and crucial to our understanding of the Jazz Age—remains incredibly relevant to college-aged men and women. Although their dress, speech, and music may differ, today's students understand very clearly the complexity of "going out" as staged in the literature of the 1920s. Undergrads can comprehend, often from firsthand experience, how a nightlife space such as the Harlem cabaret in *Quicksand* can be a venue for testing social codes. They know the sexual energy, anxiety, and exhilaration inherent in such landscapes. They can articulate how house parties, local bars, dance clubs—not unlike the places that Helga frequents—are stages for identity making and performance. In sum, students recognize nightlife as a place of the unexpected, where unusual contact invites experimentation and creates possibility.

Nightlife, then, is an important point of entry for me as I teach *Quicksand*. Helga Crane's most profound moments of disorientation, self-reflection, and learning occur in the context of nightlife spaces. The cabaret, dinner parties, vaudeville theater—these social environments, with their capacity for cross-racial and cross-class contact, force Helga (and Larsen's audience) to navigate, in a very practical way, the flawed logics of both Jim Crow segregation and the intraracial elitism of African American uplift. What happens, for instance, when sexual desire crosses the color line? As we see in *Quicksand*, anything can happen at night, and Helga's shifting responses in these environments demonstrate the pressures that color-line politics place on everyone involved and most acutely on those who cannot easily identify with just one (or any) group.

When I teach *Quicksand*, I begin by situating Larsen's first novel in its proper "cabaret" context. *Quicksand* was published by Knopf in March 1928, at the height of the so-called "Negro vogue." A few years before, the "Harlem" special issue of *Survey Graphic* helped inaugurate mass interest in modern black culture. This new attention brought various consequences. Thousands of white tourists, for instance, ventured to Harlem's nightclubs, in what Chad Heap has called "the most popular slumming vogue of the early twentieth-century" (189). Nightclubs such as the Cotton Club and Connie's Inn presented world-class African American performers like Fletcher Henderson, Louis Armstrong, Duke Ellington, and Ethel Waters to almost exclusively upper-class white crowds. The interiors of these venues propagated racist stereotypes of black culture. Stages were built to recall southern plantations. Palm trees carried "jungle" connotations. Light-skinned African American women danced in "exotic" costumes with feathers or leaves. While recent scholarship on this period demonstrates how African American musicians and dancers performed this "primitivism" to their advantage, the potent image of white voyeurs slumming in Harlem (and other American cities) troubled African Americans during this era and has had a lasting effect on the way that the Jazz Age is remembered.[1]

In reality, Harlem was also home to a vibrant black nightlife scene that neither began with the "Negro vogue" nor was solely designed for white consumption. For every cabaret like the Cotton Club, there were many more bars, dance halls, speakeasies, and even less formal nightlife spaces where African Americans spent their free time. The Savoy Ballroom (home to the Lindy Hop) and the Renaissance Casino were major dance halls in Harlem. The Lafayette Theatre was one of the first theaters in New York to allow African Americans to sit anywhere in the audience (as opposed to just the balcony). Blacks patronized integrated establishments ("black and tan" clubs) like Small's Paradise, Bamville, and the Nest, where it was not uncommon for whites and blacks to break social codes and dance together. "Negro" cabarets such as the Sugar Cane Club, which Wallace Thurman described in his essay "Negro Life in New York's Harlem" (1927), were usually more intimate places where couples would "push back their chairs, squeeze out from behind the tables and from against the wall, then finding one another's bodies, sweat gloriously together" (48). In this same vein, rent parties, thrown ostensibly to help Harlemites pay their landlords, were primarily African American affairs. For the admission price of about a quarter, men and women were invited into someone's apartment, where they could eat homemade food, drink bootleg liquor, and dance to the music of a single piano player or a small band.

At the moment that *Quicksand* appeared, nightlife was front and center within debates about how African Americans should be represented. Cultural and political leaders such as W. E. B. Du Bois staged their uplift efforts directly against the backdrop of the supposed criminal and sexual degeneracy of nightlife. "In general," the editors of the NAACP's *Crisis* magazine wrote, "the individual [nightlife] portrait may be true and artistic, [but] the net result to American literature to date is to picture twelve million Americans as prostitutes, thieves and fools and that such 'freedom' in art is miserably unfair" ("Negro" [Feb. 1926] 165). Nightlife, characterized in terms of deviance and pathology by social scientists, gave definition to the black middle class by showing what it was *not*. In literature, one response was to avoid nightlife altogether. Another approach was to depict scenes where a protagonist "goes bad" for a moment—a youthful excursion later corrected or a moral lapse in a time of turmoil. Jessie Fauset's *There is Confusion* (1924) and Du Bois's *Dark Princess* (1928) feature passages where a prominent male character momentarily compromises himself in a cabaret before resuming an otherwise upwardly mobile path.

Yet for other (often younger) black artists, the cabaret emerged as a productive landscape for challenging normative uplift ideology. As Shane Vogel demonstrates in *The Scene of Harlem Cabaret*, "Cabaret School" writers and performers "used the cabaret to imagine and enact alternative possibilities for racial, sexual, and socioeconomic subjectivities" (36) that ran counter to the narrow representational fields sanctioned by elitist uplifters. Speakeasies, rent parties, dive bars, and juke joints, with their endless potential for creation and exchange, became stages of resistance and empowerment. Langston Hughes, perhaps the most visible of this group, famously urged black writers to "let the blare of Negro jazz bands and the bellowing voice of Bessie Smith singing blues penetrate the closed ears of the colored near-intellectuals until they listen and perhaps understand" (694). Indeed, by the late-1920s, there was a proliferation of writers heeding this call. Rudolph Fisher's "The City of Refuge" (1925) and *The Walls of Jericho* (1928), Hughes's *The Weary Blues* (1926) and *Fine Clothes to the Jew* (1927), Carl Van Vechten's *Nigger Heaven* (1926), Wallace Thurman's edited journal *Fire!!* (1926) and novel *The Blacker the Berry* (1929), Zora Neale Hurston's "Muttsy" (1926), James Weldon Johnson's *The Autobiography of an Ex-Coloured Man* (published anonymously in 1912 and reprinted in 1927), Claude McKay's *Home to Harlem* (1928)—each of these texts, as well as numerous others to come, foregrounded nightlife as a space for racial, gender, and class possibilities that resided outside uplift circumscription.[2]

Nella Larsen's *Quicksand* was an important participant in this critique. What is interesting, though, as George Hutchinson notes, is that many reviewers hailed Larsen's novel precisely for *not* being of the cabaret school (Allison Davis). No matter, it seemed, that *Quicksand* featured many of the elements that the uplift anthropologist Allison Davis considered the "distinctive sordidness" of nightlife culture (268)—drinking, jazz, cross-racial and homoerotic desire, minstrel performance, even violence (when Helga slaps Robert Anderson). No matter that a cabaret scene appears literally at the center of the novel. Or that Larsen enjoyed a very close friendship with Carl Van Vechten (Davis referred to cabaret writers as "Van Vechtenites," charging the white author with bringing the nightlife "movement" to its "complete fruition" [268]). Or that Larsen was a fairly regular presence in New York's nightlife scene.[3] George Schuyler lauded *Quicksand* as "no story of bull-dikers, faggots, slums, cabarets, prostitution, gin parties, and whiskey socials" ("Views"). Gwendolyn Bennett, in echoing Schuyler, wrote that "many folks will be interested to hear that this book does not set as its tempo that of the Harlem cabaret. . . . Negroes who are squeamish about writers exposing our worst side will be relieved that Harlem night-life is more or less submerged by this author." Du Bois, in his oft-referenced assessment, praised *Quicksand* as "the best piece of fiction" that Negro America had produced in decades, in direct contrast to the "drunkenness, fighting, lascivious sexual promiscuity and utter absence of restraint" ("Browsing Reader" 202) of McKay's *Home to Harlem*. Such tendencies to downplay nightlife in *Quicksand* may be partially explained by the way that the novel was advertised and packaged. (Unlike most of Knopf's other publications by African American authors, *Quicksand* did not feature a cover illustration that immediately connected it to jazz or even black culture). Further, the personal agendas of the reviewers—namely Du Bois—figured prominently into how commentators chose to situate *Quicksand* (Hutchinson, *In Search* 284–85). Yet these selective readings contributed to the fact that for many decades Larsen's novel would be reduced to a "simple" plot working within a "genteel tradition" (Lewis, *When Harlem* 231–32).

With this context in mind, I turn my students' attention to how nightlife functions in *Quicksand*. I often open class discussion of the novel with the following question: How do we learn race? The board quickly fills with responses. Some students explain that they were introduced to race through institutions or social mediums: school, church, sports, television. Others immediately refer to personal experience. Undergraduates may recall a defining moment of cultural pride or familial practice. They may describe traveling to another part of the United States or to a new country. Or, sometimes students will recount an initial encounter with racism. Once we have compiled a diverse list, I then invite students to reflect on what we have generated. Are there any broader conclusions that we can draw about the ways in which we learn race? Two observations, among many other unexpected and often provocative connections, usually emerge. First, most of us believe that we learn race in childhood. Almost everything on the board will usually relate to an experience that occurred either before or around the time of elementary school. Second, we tend to speak about racial learning in the past tense. Even though my original question is not close-ended, students normally respond as if their impressions of race were formulated and fixed long ago. "I learn*ed* about race when . . ."

Nightlife in *Quicksand* challenges students to see racial learning as something that is constantly happening. For Helga, as for the protagonists of "The Wrong Man" and *Passing*, nightlife becomes a space for *figuring out*. Here, strange contact among nightlife participants produces a testing ground for the "absolutes" of Jim Crow and uplift ideology. Yet one of the defining aspects of *Quicksand*—what makes the novel tangibly different from much of the rest of Harlem Renaissance literature—is that there are never definite answers. Even when something becomes "quite clear" (83) for Helga, the racial landscape shifts.[4] Therefore, to read the novel's various nightlife scenes together—the Harlem cabaret, the minstrel show at the Circus, the Tavenor's cocktail party, for example—is to begin to see race in terms of performance and perpetual revision. Helga's questions become our own. What does it mean, at a given moment in the narrative, to be "Negro"? What does it mean to be "white"? Or neither? What is the relationship between race and sex? race and money? race and family? race and nation? Who is the spectator? Who (or what) is the spectacle?

Helga's visit to a Harlem cabaret, which occurs almost at the middle of the novel, is one of the best passages for discussing racial learning with students. The chapter opens with Helga encountering race in radically new terms. Before descending through the "furtive" entryway of the cabaret, Helga has little expectation for the evening. She has just endured an unwelcomed dinner party, and she "half unwillingly" submits to a cabaret outing on this "atrocious" evening. Yet, immediately after entering the club, Helga becomes overwhelmed. Jazz music "split[s]" (58) her ears. Everything begins to spin around. While dancing, Helga feels "drugged, lifted, sustained, by the extraordinary music, blown out, ripped out, beaten out, by the joyous, wild, murky orchestra." When the music stops, this euphoria—the likes of which we have never seen before in Helga—suddenly disappears. In a revelatory moment, Helga comes to the "shameful certainty that not only had she been in the jungle, but she had enjoyed it." This feeling taunts her: "She wasn't, she told herself, a jungle creature" (59).

There is a lot to unpack here. First, students may notice that this is the initial instance in the novel where Helga completely identifies (albeit briefly) with African American culture. We see Helga transition, in a matter of moments, from being "singularly apart" (58) to totally immersed in her surroundings. Other students may raise questions about the "primitivist" aspects of this scene. Why does the narrator code this space in terms of "jungle" imagery: "tomtoms," a "wild" orchestra, "savage" music (59)? Is this not racism? Still, others, like many critics, may seize on Helga's shame. What is wrong with her enjoying this feeling? Whichever line of inquiry our discussion follows—and we see these issues being rewritten in each of the subsequent nightlife scenes—the cabaret chapter presents the opportunity to discuss race as performance. Indeed, Helga's impulse to extract herself from the dancing is problematic. Yet the fact that Helga sees such distancing as *even an option* underscores how the "jungle" is an act. Throughout *Quicksand*, Larsen foregrounds the ways in which dress, gesture, hairstyle, and speech figure into racial identity (for example, "race" proponents like Mrs. Hayes-Rore consistently wear drab or outmoded clothing). Now, as Helga retreats from the dance floor, she "marvels" at the staging of her "oppressed race" (59). Her detailed observation, which emerges as a list of the possibilities of blackness ("sooty black" to "pasty white," "straightened hair" to "woolly hair," "semi-barbaric" [59] to "sophisticated" [60]), gives the lie to any prevailing legal or neo-scientific "evidence" that would reduce African American culture to a single set of characteristics or traits.

In the latter half of this chapter, the cabaret becomes a space for Helga to interrogate the sexual rules of the color line. When Helga's gaze shifts from the "moving mosaic" (60) to the individual tables, her eyes meet those of Robert Anderson. Yet it is Anderson's partner, Audrey Denney, who captures Helga's attention. What unfolds is a scene of discovery. First, Helga stands alone and "studie[s]" Audrey's "lovely" appearance: her "pale" skin, her "shivering apricot frock," her "red, softly curving" mouth, her "pitch-black" eyes, her "drooping" lashes, and her "black smears" for eyebrows (60). Then, when Anne Grey joins Helga and begins to articulate her hatred for Audrey, Helga systematically questions Anne's logic. Why does Audrey deserve to be ostracized? Simply for attending interracial parties? At each turn, Helga exposes Anne's hypocrisy. Eventually, the truth emerges: for Anne, Audrey represents the potential for interracial sex (and procreation). Finally, the chapter concludes with Helga shifting her focus back to Audrey and Robert Anderson, who are now "closely clinging" on the dance floor. During this act of watching, Helga is seized by another moment of intense disorientation. As the room begins to recede and her heart throbs, Helga escapes from the cabaret, "panting" and "confused" (62).

What exactly causes Helga to flee? When I present this question to our class, some students will argue that Helga's impulse to withdraw comes as a direct response to witnessing Robert Anderson, her object of desire, share a moment of intimacy with another woman. As evidence, students may point to the fact that Anderson continues to "obtrude" (64) into Helga's thoughts as she travels to Denmark in the next chapter. Helga's subsequent insistence that "she wasn't, she couldn't be, in love" with Anderson seems to indicate that there is indeed some level of attraction (64). So it is plausible that Helga's escape is a reaction to Robert. Yet what happens if we read the final paragraph of the cabaret chapter in terms of Helga's "envious admiration" (62) for Audrey Denney? Throughout this scene, Helga identifies with Audrey. Both women live their lives crisscrossing the color line, and both are "misunderstood" (62). Helga is the child of an interracial relationship, of the sort that Anne despises Audrey for pursuing. Therefore, Helga's unsettlement in the cabaret may arise from the fact that she experiences Anne Grey's attack on Audrey as an attack on herself.

At this point, I direct my students to the following lines that appear just before Helga departs from the cabaret: "Helga turned her glance to Dr. Anderson. Her disinterested curiosity passed. While she still felt for the girl envious admiration, that feeling was now augmented by another, a more primitive emotion" (62). What exactly does this mean? As a class, we enumerate the possibilities. Since Helga's perspective shifts to Anderson, do we read this as Robert displacing Audrey in Helga's mind? In other words: "Helga *was* curious about Audrey, but now her primary focus returns to Anderson." The "primitive emotion," then, could be understood as sexual desire ("sex" is always conveyed through euphemism in *Quicksand*), anger, or something else.

Or, what if Anderson is the "curiosity" that passes? What if Helga's "envious admiration" is supplemented with an even deeper emotion for this same woman? In the preceding sentences, Helga is highly attentive to the sensuousness of Audrey's body ("Her long, slender body swayed with an eager pulsing motion. She danced with grace and abandon, gravely, yet with obvious pleasure, her legs, hips, her back, all swaying gently" [62]). Helga explicitly connects Audrey's "courage [to] . . . ignore racial barriers" with her "beautiful, calm, cool" appearance (62). For Helga, Audrey's transgressiveness is erotic. What if Helga's urgency to flee emerges, then, from a recognition (or frustration) that her same-sex desire is not sanctioned within the dominant social paradigm (which would have Helga marry a financially successful, "alluring brown or yellow" man [45])? Or that Audrey's current closeness with Robert forecloses her own access to Audrey? Or that this scene of "pleasure," which causes Helga to forget everything around her, seems disturbingly unattainable?

The Harlem cabaret, like the dinner party at the end of *Passing*, fosters indeterminacy. Any of this—and all of this—is possible. Yet as we see here, the knowledge of the cabaret, based as it is in firsthand experience, can be overwhelming. As *Quicksand* develops, nightlife continues to be the stage for Larsen to engage the novel's most difficult issues. Each scene revises the previous, and as the settings shift, we find Helga constantly relearning the rules of race.

NOTES

[1] Two films are useful for introducing students to this popular (and problematic) version of Harlem's Prohibition-era cabaret culture. Francis Ford Coppola's *The Cotton Club* (1984), in focusing on white organized crime in Harlem, presents race and performance in complicated ways. Eddie Murphy's *Harlem Nights* (1989), packaged as a comedy, approaches similar subject matter from the perspective of African American underworld participants.

[2] To help students understand the terms of the debate between the uplift and cabaret schools, I often assign shorter essays or articles from the 1920s to read before we encounter *Quicksand*. Of particular value is "The Negro in Art: How Shall He Be Portrayed," a symposium published in the NAACP's *Crisis* magazine between February and November 1926. This discussion includes a diverse range of opinions, including those of Carl Van Vechten, Langston Hughes, Walter White, Jessie Fauset, and Countee Cullen. I also recommend the following essays that deal with nightlife: Chandler; Rogers; Hughes, "Negro Artist"; Harrison, "Cabaret"; Fisher, "Caucasian Storms Harlem"; Allison Davis, "Our Negro 'Intellectuals'"; and Hurston, "Characteristics."

[3] Many of the nightlife scenes in *Quicksand* connect to Larsen's own experiences. According to Hutchinson, Larsen and her husband, Elmer Imes, traveled in "one of the roaringest party circuits of the Twenties" (*In Search* 243). From Greenwich Village to Harlem, Larsen spent evenings at interracial dinner parties, cabarets (including the Cotton Club), charity balls, theaters—often in the presence of Carl Van Vechten and his wife, Fania Marinoff. Larsen counted among her friends and acquaintances many prominent African American performers, including Nora Holt, Ethel Waters, Paul Robeson, Bill "Bojangles" Robinson, and Roland Hayes. For more on Larsen and New York City nightlife, see Hutchinson, *In Search of Nella Larsen*, esp. 240–93.

[4] Citations to *Quicksand* are from McDowell's Quicksand *and* Passing (1986).

Sounding and Being: A Resource for Teaching Musical References and Symbolism in Nella Larsen's *Quicksand*

Gayle Murchison

Teaching about the *use* of music in a novel presents a challenge different from teaching students either music or literary history or from leading them through a close reading of a poem or novel. Here, one does not necessarily focus on the music itself or the aesthetics of a composer, musician, or some other musical artist. Rather, one approaches the music through a filter, that of how an author *uses* the music in his or her text rhetorically and symbolically. The reader must always keep in mind how the author wants us to *hear* the music as we read certain passages. Doing this is often a balancing act, for one has to know more than simply what music was contemporary during the time the author wrote his or her work. One has to wear many hats: that of a music researcher who can find appropriate bibliography and reference sources; a music critic who can listen critically to the music and formulate a thesis about what one hears; and a literature critic, able to perform a close reading of the text. Finally, one must synthesize these, linking the music to the text.

Throughout her 1928 novel *Quicksand*, Nella Larsen makes frequent and extensive references to music. These vary, from mention of ethnic and national musical traditions, genres, and styles to quotation of specific song lyrics to invocation of classical works. This variety of music can seem daunting to those outside the field of music. Understandably, one teaching the novel to high school and undergraduate students would be tempted to forgo discussions of the music in favor of concentrating on other aspects of the novel. Discussing music in the novel, however, leaves students with a more nuanced portrait of the protagonist, Helga Crane, and a better understanding of Larsen as a literary artist. This essay outlines how to read and interpret the musical references and music symbolism in Nella Larsen's *Quicksand*, with a threefold goal: to provide resources, to provide strategies, and to provide an interpretation that would prove useful in the classroom.

Framing Questions

The central questions in approaching Larsen's use of music revolve around the how and why: First, how does Larsen use music? Does she refer to musical traditions and genres only generally or does she mention specific songs and musical works? Second, why does Larsen use music? What is the rhetorical purpose of doing so? To advance the narrative? To provide insight into the protagonist's emotional and psychological state? Does her use of music convey the social and cultural context of the Harlem Renaissance era, the societal mores and values of the time period?

To answer the "how" questions Larsen's use of music falls into four broad categories: oblique, descriptive, direct reference, and direct quotation. Oblique references are those in which Larsen does not mention music specifically. Rather, she provides a context in which music would be heard. Larsen is carefully descriptive of music in several instances. In chapter 11, she vividly describes the music of a Harlem cabaret and its effect on Helga. Later, Larsen similarly describes two religious services of two working-class congregations. The first occurs when Helga seeks refuge in a Harlem storefront church; the second, when Helga recuperates after the difficult delivery of her son, who dies shortly after birth.

Larsen makes direct references to musical traditions, genres, and works, as well as to musicians and composers. The first occurs in chapter 2, when she mentions "The Star-Spangled Banner." In later chapters, Larsen refers to specific musical traditions, such as African American music and dance (chs. 9 and 14), American popular song (ch. 9), and European classical music (chs. 9, 14, and 16). She also quotes lyrics, here using music as a highly effective artistic device. She quotes directly from four genres: a popular song, a gospel song, a hymn, and a spiritual. To answer the "why" framing questions, in all cases, the reader has to use his or her imagination to hear the music internally (in other words, audiate), to understand the music's cultural meaning and social function at the time Larsen wrote and published the novel, and to link the sound with the novel's text in order to perceive its symbolism. This is discussed in more detail below.

Resources

When studying the use of music in Larsen's (or any) novel, it is useful to devote some attention to the music itself. Students benefit from gaining familiarity with the following: how the music sounds, a brief history of relevant composers and musicians, and how the music and these musical figures were understood during the time Larsen wrote her novel. High school and university libraries have varying holdings of commercially available and archival sound recordings, although, predictably, they will not have recordings (or sheet music or song folios) of all the music Larsen mentions.[1] Fortunately, online databases of sound recordings provide access to the music.

Larsen quotes directly from two gospel songs, "There Will Be Showers of Blessings" and "None of Self and More of Thee"; therefore, I suggest some attention be given to the genre of African American religious music. Recordings of concert spirituals by African American university choirs (such as Howard, Fisk, and Hampton Universities) are typically commercially available and are among those most often found in university library collections. Also available are concert recordings by notable singers (Roland Hayes, Paul Robeson, Marian Anderson, for example)—all are suggested listening, since these singers established the tradition of recital singing of spirituals. Assigning at least one such recording (Robeson is suggested) would be illuminating for students.

Throughout *Quicksand*, Larsen also alludes to jazz, ragtime, and Tin Pan Alley songs—all music to which Americans and Europeans danced in the late 1920s. To gain a general understanding of this music, as well as of the types of social dancing popular during this time, instructors might consult any of several good introductions: Burton W. Peretti's *Jazz in American Culture* and Gary Giddins and Scott DeVeaux's *Jazz* both provide a good overview of 1920s jazz. Charles Hamm's *Yesterdays: Popular Song in America* is a classic study of the history of American popular song. Eileen Southern's *The Music of Black Americans* remains the standard history of African American music in the United States. Paul Allen Anderson's *Deep River: Music and Memory in Harlem Renaissance Thought* and Samuel A. Floyd, Jr.'s *Black Music in the Harlem Renaissance: A Collection of Essays* relate specifically to music of the Harlem Renaissance. Two African American intellectual histories that are useful are Alain Locke's *The New Negro: An Anthology* and W. E. B. Du Bois's *The Souls of Black Folk*. In her frequent references to classical music, Larsen refers to two works by name: Antonin Dvořák's *Symphony no. 9 in E minor, From the New World*, popularly referred to as the *New World Symphony*. She also refers to "Nielsen's 'Helios,'" which, more specifically, is the *"Helios" Overture*, op. 17, by the Danish composer Carl Nielsen. The two composers whose names the character Fru Fischer mentions are Peter Heise and Niels Gade, both Danish composers. All—Dvořák, Nielsen, Gade, and Heise—are considered nationalist composers. That is, though they composed in the German classical tradition, all drew on the folk music and culture of their respective nations, sometimes quoting actual folk songs in their concert and stage works. Dvořák's work is well-known, and recordings are plentiful. Recordings by the other composers are less common but can be found at online music databases such as *Classical Music Online* and *Naxos Music Library*. If instructors want to assign students the task of finding more information about these composers, two useful standard reference works are *Baker's Biographical Dictionary of Musicians*, edited by Nicolas Slonimsky, and *The New Grove Dictionary of Music and Musicians*, edited by Stanley Sadie, also available online. Again, the instructor need not assign all these. A movement from Dvořák's symphony (either the first or second) would be useful.

Typically, instructors tend to reserve one class session for music, often inviting in a guest lecturer with expertise. Though pragmatic (since the music is covered at once), this relegates music, which is contrary to what Larsen attempts to do in the novel. Indeed, as I discuss below, music precipitates Helga's epiphany moments. To fully incorporate music into the class, students might listen to music regularly throughout the Larsen unit of a course with small, relevant listening assignments. For example, as students read the first chapter (set at Naxos), students can be assigned at least one spiritual sung by Paul Robeson and one sung by a concert choir. To accompany the passage where Helga is in Denmark, an instructor might ask students to listen to *Helios*. For the passage in the Harlem cabaret, a selection from Ellington's 1920s recordings would suffice (*Black and Tan Fantasy* is suggested as a starting point, since this work has two contrasting sections, one that is representative of Ellington's "jungle style," which he developed while performing at the Cotton Club, the other representative of so-called sweet jazz as played by a jazz orchestra such as Fletcher Henderson's). The Ellington recordings would be usefully accompanied by a 1920s selection from either James P. Johnson or Willie "the Lion" Smith (these represent the kind of piano jazz typically heard at Harlem rent parties). Once the music sources have been located (especially the music itself *and* the secondary sources), the challenge is to integrate them as instructors and students read the text. The music as heard in the sound recordings can be "read" or studied critically as texts, even if the selections are abstract music, that is, if they lack lyrics or a song text. (See the appendixes for several assignments and a list of questions that instructors might ask students during the various assignments.)

Interpretation

The third purpose of this essay is to provide an example of one interpretation useful for the classroom. It is not the only interpretation of Larsen's use of music. Rather, it is intended to provide a model that can be adapted for practical use by those who face challenges in incorporating music into discussion of the novel. With this goal in mind, a segment of Deborah E. McDowell's introductory essay in the Rutgers edition, in which she addresses the issue of how to represent black women's sexuality, provides a useful starting point:

> To be writing about black female sexuality within this conflicted context, then, posed peculiar problems for Larsen. The questions confronting her might be formulated: How to write about black female sexuality in a literary era that often sensationalized it and pandered to the stereotype of the primitive exotic? How to give a black female character the right to

> healthy sexual expression and pleasure without offending the proprieties established by the spokespersons of the black middle class? The answers to these questions for Larsen lay in attempting to hold these two virtually contradictory impulses in the same novel. We might say that Larsen wanted to tell the story of the black woman with sexual desires, but was constrained by a competing desire to establish black women as respectable in black middle-class terms. The latter desire committed her to exploring black female sexuality obliquely and, inevitably, to permitting it only within the context of marriage, despite the strangling effects of that choice both on her characters and on her narratives. (xvi)

As McDowell argues, although Larsen and her peer writers lived and worked in an age in which women's sexuality found liberation, they were constrained both by African American middle-class values that prescribed and proscribed certain behaviors, as well as the aesthetic ideology of Harlem Renaissance intellectuals. McDowell notes this dialectic, "between pleasure and danger," and argues that the combat of racial stereotypes of hypersexualized black women trumped, in a sense, artistic exploration of sexual desire and sexuality for those working "high culture," or the cultivated areas of literature (I also include the fine and performing arts, such as art music). Thus, as McDowell writes, "Even in Larsen's day, the Freudian 1920s, the Jazz Age of sexual abandon and 'free love'—when female sexuality, in general, was acknowledged and commercialized in the advertising, beauty, and fashion industries—black women's novels preserve their reticence about sexuality" (xiii).

For Larsen and her peers, the "familiar narrative" safe zone was "within the genre of the romance in which sex for women is enacted and legitimated within the boundaries of marriage and generally harnessed to its biological consequence, motherhood" (xxii). McDowell also quickly points out that not all African American women were constrained by aesthetic politics and adopted the Victorian narrative of romance and motherhood. On the contrary, one group of African American women freely celebrated an unfettered sexuality. McDowell cites blues women Ma Rainey and the unrelated Smiths—Bessie, Clara, and Mamie—all of whom had the freedom to sing openly and boldly about sex and relationships. Indeed, it is this very openness that Angela Y. Davis writes about in her study *Blues Legacies and Black Feminism: Gertrude "Ma" Rainey, Bessie Smith, and Billie Holiday*. To illustrate her point, McDowell quotes lyrics from Ma Rainey's "Tight Like That," which is filled with double entendre and 1920s African American sexual references (xiii).

Although constrained by convention, Larsen does have one device with which she can explore the protagonist's sexuality: music. McDowell notes how Larsen uses clothing to express Helga's desire. Music functions similarly. Moreover, in *Quicksand* Larsen presses music into service for other topoi as she explores several binaries surrounding racial identity and class, in addition to the usual bifurcation of black/white racial identity of our biracial protagonist, Helga Crane.

In her ever-shifting circumstances, Helga must navigate a constantly changing kaleidoscope of geographic, class, and national worlds: northern/southern, American/European, urban/rural, privileged/middle-class/poor. Helga Crane is always defined in contrast to those around her, as she wanders from a southern educational institution to the urban northern cities of Chicago and New York to Denmark, before descending into despair at the end of the novel, negotiating these external worlds and her own psyche. Externally, music locates our protagonist in a specific cultural and social milieu: through music, Larsen comments on the cultural and social contexts in which Helga Crane finds herself. Internally, music reveals Helga's innermost psyche; through music, Larsen can probe Helga's vacillating psychological state. In more vernacular terms, music creates a geographic and psychological soundscape.

Race

Although in her introduction McDowell concentrates on sexuality, issues of race are at the heart of *Quicksand*. Larsen does not always explicitly foreground race, but it is always present. Music marks race and race is marked by music, meaning that since it is common knowledge that certain musical traditions and styles originate with or are popular among specific socioeconomic, racial, and ethnic groups, reference to their music can be used to identify a character as a member of a certain social group. In *Quicksand*, one theme is that Helga feels that she is never quite at home among any social group and never belongs anywhere she goes, whether at an African American educational institution, African American communities in Chicago or Harlem, or in Denmark. Larsen establishes this at the outset and uses music to amplify her point. The novel opens with Helga reading in the solitude of her room at a southern African American educational institution. After Larsen establishes Helga Crane's solitude, she describes her physical features (2). In chapter 3, Larsen refers to Helga as a "mulatto" (18). Here at the beginning of the novel is the point where we begin our study of Larsen's use of music, not with its presence, but its absence: the quiet in which Helga sits in her room.

This opening is marked by the care with which Larsen describes the *lack* of sound, or in other words, the lack of music. The novel begins with a careful, detailed description of silence. Ironically, for a novel in which the presence of music figures as a key literary device, the novel begins with Larsen notably underscoring the *absence* of literal sound through an oblique use of it. Silence is followed by Larsen's play with assonance, and here assonance is not just literary, but musical. The school is identified as "Naxos," and the reader might pause at this Greek name. In her introduction, McDowell notes that this is an anagram of "'Saxon,' suggesting the school's worship of everything Anglo-Saxon" (xvii).[2] I offer an alternative reading. The use of this two-syllable word actually functions as the first use of music—albeit oblique—in the novel. Two basic definitions of *music* often cited by music scholars and critics are that music is simply organized sound, or, at its most basic, heightened speech. One of the most basic sounds human beings make is ordinary speech. There is a continuum from speech to music. For example, speaking rhythmically and with melodic inflection results in chant. Intensifying this results in melodic singing. Here, one offers an example of conceptualizing music in this fashion by simply saying the word "Naxos"—heightening the "melody" and "rhythm" of the inflections of Standard American English (see List). Rendered thusly, "Naxos" sounds remarkably like "noxious" and "nauseous." In her play of Naxos/Saxon/noxious, Larsen subtly injects a critique of Helga and race.

McDowell makes the point that in choosing the anagram of Saxon, Larsen subtly critiques African American educational institutions and their mission of uplift (which, later, Helga Crane somewhat vainly sees as her role of a preacher's wife among her husband's parishioners in their rural, southern community). Uplift was one of the goals of some Harlem Renaissance intellectuals and certainly the mission of Black Women's Clubs, of which Mrs. Hayes-Rore is a member. One avenue toward uplift was through assimilation of the values—and self-prejudice—of the hegemonic Anglo-American culture. But Larsen paints with a broader stroke and strikes at the heart of perceived, understood, and unchallenged assumptions of "Western" and "other" with this three-way play of phonemes. *Naxos/noxious* suggests something toxic. Helga finds Naxos toxic on many levels: first, the Eurocentric culture and values the school, its faculty, and students embrace are toxic. The education promulgated there (and the one Helga herself receives) is toxic for Helga, students, and African American culture. Second, the environment is toxic for Helga—its stifling propriety, its Victorian strictures on female sexuality, and the stifling environment that prizes elitism and pedigree. This relative privilege we see underscored both in Helga's engagement to James Vayle, the scion of one of Atlanta's "best families," and in Dr. Anderson's discussion of family. Third, as a biracial woman, Helga is neither Saxon nor fully comfortable in this stilted African American environment with its embrace of middle-class and Victorian Anglo-Saxon values.

Music illustrates Helga's lack of belonging in Harlem, as the description of the Harlem cabaret in chapter 11 demonstrates. Larsen vividly describes the urban soundscape. We learn that despite the gaiety, Helga feels apart from it. As she enters the cabaret, she is greeted by the sound of blaring jazz. Larsen alludes to primitivism and invokes Africa as she describes "a thumping of unseen tomtoms" (59). Our protagonist is seduced by and gives herself over to the music, only later to reject the sensuousness. Seeing herself apart from the others—"[s]he wasn't, she told herself, a jungle creature"—she expresses disgust at the entertainers' dance.

In this Harlem cabaret scene the most descriptive and sensual writing of the novel occurs. Larsen takes us from the silence of the beginning to the blare of jazz. Throughout the novel, she makes indirect references to jazz, especially at parties where dancing occurs:

> They danced, ambling lazily to a crooning melody, or violently twisting their bodies, like whirling leaves, to a sudden streaming rhythm, or shaking themselves ecstatically to a thumping of unseen tomtoms. . . . She was drugged, lifted, sustained, by the extraordinary music, blown out, ripped out, beaten out, by the joyous, wild, murky orchestra. The essence of life seemed bodily motion. . . . (59)

Here, Larsen literally puts the music in motion as she couples description of the music to description of the physical body and its allure. As Helga looks about the club, she does not feel solidarity with or a connection to the other African Americans; similarly, at Naxos Helga feels alienated from her own race (59–60). Yet to consort with whites would be a transgression, as her friend Anne makes clear when denouncing a mutual acquaintance, Audrey Denney, who frequently attends interracial parties (61).

Music also figures prominently in Helga's Copenhagen sojourn and her foray into consorting with white Europeans. Larsen uses music as a metaphor to juxtapose the black and white races. European classical music is set against African American music. Just as music reveals Helga's alienation from her own race, here Larsen uses music to represent Helga as a racial other. During her first year, Helga encounters Fru Fischer in a café, the Vivili (the café's name recalls the Italian composer Vivaldi). Fru Fischer expresses her open racism: she dislikes the Russian and Japanese patrons, who, she says, make the place "common" (80). Fru Fischer also strongly dislikes American jazz, preferring Danish nationalist composers—that is, those who draw on Danish folk songs and subjects in their compositions. Larsen's portrait of the Dane, however, is rather shrewd, as vividly outlined by the music references as by the derogatory names Fru Fischer uses to refer to those patrons she so intensely dislikes. Here, American jazz serves as a metonym for African Americans, and, similarly, the Danish composers serve as metonyms for Europeans. Helga encounters racism just as she had encountered racism on the Jim Crow car and from her uncle's new wife. Here, however, it is made more vivid by music that both alludes to racial and national groups and evokes soundscapes recognizable to those familiar with American culture and classical music (compare the jazz recordings with the Dvořák symphony).

Music leads Helga to an epiphany. Larsen's first direct quotation of music awakens in Helga *Heimweh*, or homesickness. Now pursued "romantically" by the Danish painter Axel Olsen, she attends a vaudeville show at the Circus. The closing act features two African American performers who sing and dance. Here, Larsen quotes from a coon song, "Everybody Gives Me Good Advice." Since their inception, coon songs proved both wildly popular and controversial. While they obtained a vogue among white Americans, many African Americans objected to their derogatory and offensive nature. If, following McDowell, clothing has served as a metaphor for Helga's sexuality, Larsen's quotations from this song further highlight Helga's racial otherness. As the rest of the Danish audience applauds wildly, Helga remains silent. For the Danes, the song is new and unfamiliar, but for Helga the song is old:

> [S]he was filled with a fierce hatred for the cavorting Negroes on the stage. She felt shamed, betrayed, as if these pale pink and white people among whom she lived had suddenly been invited to look upon something in her which she had hidden away and wanted to forget. And she was shocked at the avidity at which Olsen beside her drank it in. (83)

This performance leads Helga to understand that her Danish relatives, Olsen, and Fru Fischer view her as an other.

Helga is "profoundly disquieted." She returns to the vaudeville house to see the two men again and again, much the same way that a cloying melody sticks in a listener's mind or a child insists on listening repeatedly to a favorite song. This is a turning point, brought about not by something explicitly stated but by a song and dance (83). When Olsen later proposes and Helga refuses him, race is the major reason she gives for refusing: she flatly states that one day he would come to be ashamed of her and hate her (86–88), much the same way she is ashamed of the racial display of the vaudevillians.

Racial identity and the epiphany that her Danish family and friends consider her an exotic is precipitated by the affront of seeing the vaudeville performance and hearing what Helga alone recognizes as a coon song, "Everybody Gives Me Good Advice." Larsen, furthermore, injects irony. Here the instructor should ask the students to consider the lines of the song's lyrics:

> Ev'rybody gives me good advice,
> But then nobody offers me the price,
> Well, a glad handshake and a
> "You're my guest today . . ."

Larsen does not specify the lyric that Helga remembers, but the lyric and hook resonate with the situations in which she finds herself. Repeatedly, her friends and acquaintances *have* offered their advice—Dr. Anderson, Uncle Peter, Aunt Katrina, and Uncle Poul. One also considers the song's lyrics: more than good advice, our singer laments being abandoned by fair-weather friends as much as he bemoans the lack of financial resources. Similarly, once she rejects acceptable avenues to middle-class respectability—whether in the form of employment or acceptable marriage to either desirable suitor (Olsen or Vayle)—Helga finds herself abandoned by her African American friends (Anne is about to marry Dr. Anderson, no less) and, at this moment in the novel, alienated from her Danish would-be suitor and friends. She also finds herself repeatedly in financial straits and, later, in poverty.

Larsen uses music as a device that precipitates Helga's decision to return to the United States, which comes during her second year in Denmark, following a concert at which she hears Dvořák's *New World Symphony*. She is affected not by the composition's orchestral magnitude but by its echoing of African American spirituals, the "sorrow songs" as Du Bois had called them. And, indeed, Helga feels sorrow in her homesickness. Hearing this work in Denmark, at a distance from her native land, leads Helga to another racial epiphany. Here, the instructor could refer to the lyrics of the spiritual Larsen mentions: "Swing low, sweet chariot / coming for to carry me home." Not only does memory of this spiritual lead to her awareness of what had been missing in her life, but it also gives insight into her parents' failed marriage. As she acknowledges that she is "homesick, not for America, but for Negroes" (92), her hard emotion toward her father has now softened. Formerly, she had blamed him for deserting her mother when she was a child. Now, she understands and feels sympathy for her father because she experiences the same longing to be amid African Americans and her own culture. In being able finally to forgive her father, she seems to have reached a degree of psychological transcendence.

Sexuality

Helga is at odds with her own sexuality and society's mores. Throughout most of the novel, three men pursue her: James Vayle, Dr. Anderson, and Axel Olsen. Only during the transatlantic crossing on the ocean liner does Helga begin to acknowledge that she may be in love with Dr. Anderson. Although an earlier chance meeting at a Harlem church (with its attendant music) had stirred Helga's desire for Anderson and although that desire increased when she later sees him *dancing* in the Harlem cabaret with Audrey Denney (60–62), precipitating her flight to Copenhagen, it is not until she finds herself in his arms at a party in New York after her return that she fully acknowledges the depth of her feelings (104). Weeks following the confrontation with Anderson at a Sunday afternoon tea, Helga, still in emotional turmoil, happens upon a storefront church on 138th Street during a service one rainy evening. Here, music serves as a vehicle through which Larsen articulates Helga's repressed sexual desire and what appears to be its hoped-for resolution.

This climactic moment in the novel—the scene in the storefront church—is precipitated by music and parallels the epiphany about race Helga experienced at the vaudeville house. Rather than secular, this music is sacred, and both types of music symbolize Helga's struggle with her own sexuality. Throughout the novel, Larsen presents two choices for Helga—premarital sex or matrimony—each of which corresponds to the type of music that proves dramatically pivotal. The risqué music of the Harlem cabaret and vaudeville house is secular, worldly, and low-culture. The music Helga hears in the storefront church is sacred, a presage of the institution of "holy matrimony" and her eventual marriage to the Reverend Mr. Pleasant Green.

In this chance encounter of the Harlem church, Larsen unleashes her most emphatic and effective use of music. As Helga enters, seeking refuge from the storm, a metaphor for Helga's desire for refuge from her emotional turmoil, her love for Anderson, and her repressed sexuality, she is, ironically, mistaken for the opposite of the model of black, middle-class, and Victorian propriety: the congregants think she is a common streetwalker, a prostitute. Again, Larsen relies on the quotation of song lyrics to intensify the drama. As Helga opens the door to the church and enters, she hears music from her past, just as she heard a song from her past at the Circus in Copenhagen. Larsen quotes two lines from the chorus of a nineteenth-century revival gospel hymn; I have included the first verse and whole chorus below from the sheet music:

> Verse 1:
> "There shall be showers of blessing:"
> This is the promise of love:
> There shall be seasons refreshing,
> Sent from the Saviour above.
>
> Chorus:
> Showers, showers of blessing,
> Showers of blessing we need;
> Mercy drops round us are falling,
> But for the showers we plead.
> ("There Shall Be Showers")

In this scene, music gradually transitions from formal, written revivalist hymnody to the African American spiritual. Larsen turns the revival service on its head and proves herself a keen satirist of religion (just as she satirizes African American educational institutions with her play on the word *Naxos*). Love and a healthy relationship have eluded Helga. She sees the irony between the scene before her and her life, sits on the floor, and breaks into laughter, thereby disrupting the service. The congregants come to her assistance and begin "a low wailing thing" (at this point, instructors might review the examples of the traditional African American religious music referred to above, especially the example that is preceded by a sermon). The congregation then sings another revival hymn, "None of Self and All of Thee," of which Larsen quotes two verses. This hymn addresses conversion, as our seeker transforms from worldly "all of self / none of Thee" to spiritual and transcendent "none of self / all of Thee" (111–12).[3]

Larsen builds tension throughout the novel, as Helga's sexual frustration increases until she reaches the breaking point. This storefront church promises Helga salvation, brought about by the singing and weeping women. Deliverance comes not just from the words that are sung, but from the *manner* in which they are sung. The *sound* of the music is powerful, as Larsen's choice of words conveys: "low wailing thing . . . moaning" (111–12). The actual hymn is in triple meter, or (more simply) "waltz-time." Larsen again injects irony, for the text of the hymn is uplifting: the melody literally soars as advice is given for submission to Jesus, from whom deliverance and salvation will come. Ostensibly, through this lilting melody, Helga will be saved from her overwhelming desires. Larsen, however, turns this on its head: instead of rendering a joyous revival hymn, the congregation performs this as what in African American church parlance is called a "moan" (suggested listening: "Been in the Storm So Long").

In African American worship tradition, the moan—or "raising up a hymn"—occurs at an emotional high point, as a sinner confesses. The song can serve many functions; most typically, it brings about emotional release. Those familiar with traditional African American Pentecostal and sanctified worship would recognize what is happening and what is about to happen: the altar call, when those on the mourners' bench (figuratively or literally) come forward seeking redemption. As the congregation sings the spiritual, they shout. Here, "shout" does not mean to raise one's voice; rather, it means the body movement, or dance ("Holy Dance"), that accompanies musical performance in traditional African American worship. The emotion heightens, as the point in the services is reached where the seeker confesses transgressions and opens to receive Jesus Christ. When Helga, weak from hunger and alcohol, falls against the altar, the congregation mistakes this physical collapse for repentance: "At that moment, she was lost—or saved" (113). Helga begins to plead for God's mercy, and the ecstatic worship service reaches its climax.

The sacred music ushers in the turning point in the narrative and the beginning of Helga's descent. In the midst of the religious fervor, Helga meets the Reverend Mr. Pleasant Green, a meeting that promises to bring her what she so desires. In addition to spiritual and religious calm, Helga's conversion brings her a husband, a reverend who, in turn, will bring the social respectability of being a preacher's wife. Relocating to his small Alabama town, where she lives in poverty, she imagines that she will engage in the mission of uplift so instilled in her by institutions like Naxos and the Cult of Black Womanhood (represented by her former employer, Mrs. Hayes-Rore). As a preacher's wife, Helga will indeed live a life that is "none of self, and more of Thee" (112).

The storefront church and its spirituals also presage Helga's sorrowful fate. Larsen quotes the spiritual "Jesus Knows All about My Troubles." Helga's troubles have just begun. The children come, and the pregnancies and responsibilities of motherhood begin to wear Helga down and ruin her health. As Helga goes into labor for the third time during Sunday service, Larsen introduces music. This time, it is "Ah am freed of my sorrow." This is the last direct reference Larsen makes to music—suggesting another moan, sung as part of a prayer and healing service. Helga is lying in bed when her husband, Rev. Green, tells her of an upcoming prayer service for her recovery and asks if there is something she would like sung. Here, music is once again silent—Helga makes no request. Instead, her thoughts turn to "freedom and cities" and social gatherings with their "tuneless music." The reader is left to wonder what *will* be sung for Helga. How will her song end?

The suggestions for research, resources, and interpretations given above lead students to a deeper and more nuanced understanding of Helga Crane's psyche and dilemmas and to Larsen as a writer. From an interpretive standpoint, the intertextuality between Larsen's prose and the music illuminates Helga's racial, gendered, and class complexities as a biracial woman navigating race in the United States and Denmark. The music especially marks class, as Larsen locates Helga in both northern urban and southern rural communities by contrasting the music of urban African sophisticates against that of rural and transplanted southerners. Each music tradition (African American and European, jazz and popular versus gospel and spirituals) accompanies Helga's awakening sense of herself and reveals her as an always racial, gendered, and classed other.

Instructors and students are encouraged to expand beyond the suggestions and examples given here. By doing some research into music current during the 1920s, instructors and students will uncover other facts about music and other musical selections that will stir their critical imaginations as they probe more deeply the passages in which Larsen is oblique or merely describes the effect music has on Helga Crane. The recommended readings, assignments, and the discography in the notes will guide the reader to more primary sources that will provide not only more insight and tools into interpreting how music functions in *Quicksand* but also a guide for approaching her second novel, *Passing*. Moreover, the instructor and students will become more comfortable and skilled in discussing the way Larsen and other literary artists—both her contemporaries and later writers—use music in their works as artistic device.

NOTES

[1] Larsen quotes from or mentions two spirituals, a popular song, and two gospels. For the spirituals, see "Swing Low, Sweet Chariot," of which numerous recordings are available, and entries in the list of works cited for "Jesus Knows All about My Troubles." For the popular song, see "Everybody Gives Me Good Advice," available on the *Levy Sheet Music Collection* Web site. The gospel hymns "There Will Be Showers of Blessings" and "None of Self and More of Thee" can be found in *Gospel Hymns No. 1 to 6,* compiled by Ira D. Sankey, James McGranaham, and George C. Stebbins.

[2] See also xxxivn23 and page 243.

[3] The text and tune of "None of Self and All of Thee" can also be found on *Hymnary* (www.hymnary.org/text/to_the_bitter_shame_and_sorrow).

APPENDIX: LISTENING ASSIGNMENTS

The assignments below are considered integral, not supplemental, to helping students gain a full understanding of Larsen's novel. To this end, they are most useful when assigned in tandem with the passages where Larsen refers to music. With each assignment, always ask students, "What do you hear?" Having an idea of what the music sounds like and knowledge of a specific genre proves essential to illuminating the subtlety and power of Larsen's use of music. Aim to keep music selections less than ten minutes long, but encourage students to listen to a selection several times, since they will hear and understand more each time they hear a musical work.

Questions for Listening Assignments

(Note that some questions may not apply to a given selection.)

1. Tradition: European classical? American popular? African American?
2. Genre?
3. Ensemble: Is it a symphonic work? solo vocal? small ensemble? What instruments are used?
4. When was it composed (classical work) or recorded (jazz/popular music)? Is it relatively contemporary with Larsen?
5. Tempo: Is it fast? slow? Is the tempo suitable for dancing?
6. Is there an element of drama?
7. What emotions does this selection evoke?
8. Can you tell if the harmony is simple or complex?
9. What is the melody like? Can it be sung (lyrical)? Is it highly rhythmic? syncopated?
10. Does the work have a complex form made of several different sections? Is the form relatively simple and straightforward? Does the melody repeat? Do you hear only one melody or are there several? Are they played one after the other, or are two or more melodies played simultaneously?

Listening Assignment 1

Ask students to listen to "Jesus Knows All about My Troubles," performed by the Congregation of the Wesley Methodist Church or by the Moving Star Hall Singers, and to pay close attention to the preacher and the vocal interjections and call and response between the preacher and the congregation heard before the choirs begin to sing. This is an example of a tradition of African American preaching and worship service, similar to the one Helga happens upon in Harlem and the kind found at the rural southern church of her husband, the Reverend Mr. Pleasant Green. The Congregation of the

Wesley Methodist Church and the Moving Star Hall Singers are examples of the folk tradition.

Listening Assignment 2

To familiarize students with jazz popular during the time Larsen wrote *Quicksand,* have students listen to recordings from the 1920s by Duke Ellington, which provide examples of ensemble jazz found in Harlem's nightclubs and ballrooms such as the Cotton Club. Rather than bands, parties in private homes (e.g., the Harlem rent party) featured pianists who played a style of piano jazz called Harlem stride. James P. Johnson and Willie "the Lion" Smith serve as excellent examples. Introduce students to the blues sung by classic (city) blues singers such as Ma Rainey and Bessie Smith and ask them to pay close attention to the lyrics (here, Angela Davis's book on blues women might be consulted) and to consider their frank and sometimes explicit nature. One example of each should suffice.

Listening Assignment 3

If instructors want to include classical recordings as a listening assignment, I recommend Nielsen's work. The *Helios* example serves to illuminate late-nineteenth-century European classical music and its similarities to African American religious and jazz music.

Listening Assignment 4

Larsen refers to the genre of popular song, especially the "coon song," which is one subgenre of Tin Pan Alley. Before listening, students might be asked to consider the following questions: What are "coon" songs? When did they originate? When were they popular? Did white Americans, African Americans, or did both compose them and perform them? Hamm's *Yesterdays,* Floyd's *Black Music in the Harlem Renaissance,* and a reference source such as Stanley Sadie's *The New Grove Dictionary of Music and Musicians* (also available as part of the *Grove Online* subscription database) are useful resources. Students can then listen to "Everybody Gives Me Good Advice," streamed from either the *National Jukebox* Web site or the *Cylinder Preservation and Digitization Project* Web site. They can also find the sheet music on the *Levy Sheet Music Collection* Web site and follow along with the words. For comparison, they can be directed to a performance by the African American blackface comedian Bert Williams—"All Going Out and Nothing Coming In" will serve as a good example—and discuss the similarities (the *National Jukebox* Web site streams a recording of this selection that Williams recorded for Victor in 1901). Both are examples of coon songs. Students might be asked if these coon songs resemble African American jazz of the 1920s (Ellington, Henderson, Johnson, among others) in any respect and how they compare to "Jesus Knows All about My Troubles." During the late nineteenth and early twentieth centuries, white Americans who lacked knowledge of African American music, as well as understanding of their stereotypical and offensive nature, considered coon songs such as Williams's "All Going Out and Nothing Coming In" representative examples of African American music.

Nella Larsen and the Racial Mountain: Teaching Black Musical Aesthetics in *Passing* and *Quicksand*

Lori Harrison-Kahan

In his 1926 manifesto "The Negro Artist and the Racial Mountain," Langston Hughes famously advocated an African American literary aesthetic that would take its inspiration from the vernacular, especially black music. Hughes's essay opens by criticizing an unnamed African American poet for relying on traditional forms. Hughes describes such reliance on Western high culture as "the mountain standing in the way of any true Negro art in America—the urge within the race towards whiteness, the desire to pour racial individuality into the mold of American standardization, and to be as little Negro and as much American as possible." Hughes's own writing, in contrast, found its source in "the meanings and rhythms" of blues and jazz music. According to Hughes, only when black artists adapted "the blare of Negro jazz bands and the bellowing voice of Bessie Smith singing the Blues" would they "stand on top of the mountain, free within" themselves.

Passing and *Quicksand*—the two texts that form the basis of Nella Larsen's small but undeniably influential literary corpus—offer rich opportunities to discuss how black writers (and especially black women writers) adhere to and enact Hughes's injunction to overcome "the racial mountain." In this essay, I demonstrate how providing students with tools to interpret *Quicksand* and *Passing* in the context of black music opens a space for them to engage in close readings of Larsen's form. This practice teaches students that structure can often equal, and produce, meaning, guiding them toward placing Larsen's novels in a musical and oral rather than solely literary and written tradition. Through this exercise, students also develop a better understanding of what was at stake in establishing criteria for African American art during the Harlem Renaissance.

I should say at the outset that this approach to teaching Larsen's novels does not require prior knowledge of black music on the part of students. *Introducing* students to blues and jazz is one of the lesson's objectives. However, I have also found that many students who are musicians, or simply music lovers, embrace the opportunity to draw on their outside knowledge and passions. Encouraging students to bring this expertise into the literature classroom relieves the burden on instructors, who may not themselves possess any special musical knowledge; in the process of teaching Larsen's work, I have learned much from students who have formal musical training. The approach I describe here thus models an interdisciplinary pedagogy in which student engagement with other forms of art is brought to bear on literary texts. At the same time, this practice requires them to adapt techniques of literary analysis to nonliterary cultural forms by closely "reading" lyrics, as well as aural aspects of music, to decipher the cultural-historical significance of blues and jazz.

To introduce students to the genre of the classic blues and to the scholarly conversation that places Larsen at the forefront of debates surrounding the relation between black women's writing and music, I assign Hazel Carby's essay "It Jus Be's Dat Way Sometime: The Sexual Politics of Women's Blues." In this important study of the empowered agency of black female blues singers, Carby uses Larsen as her counterpoint, critiquing the tendency among black feminist theorists to privilege "literate forms of black women's intellectual activity" above popular forms. In contrast to Larsen's novels, which reproduce "the denial of desire and the repression of sexuality," Carby argues that black female singers, working in the genre of the classic blues, compose "an alternative form of representation, an oral and musical women's culture that explicitly addresses the contradictions of feminism, sexuality, and power" ([1998] 472).[1]

Once students have read Carby's essay, we listen to a number of blues recordings as a class. Bessie Smith's "I Need a Little Sugar in My Bowl" and Ethel Waters's "My Handy Man" have been favorites with students for their thinly disguised sexual innuendos, lending support to Carby's description of the blues as a genre in which black women figure as agents, rather than objects, of erotic desire. In an effort to encourage students to think critically about form as well as content, we also examine the formal properties of the classic blues. For example, we discuss the aural qualities of the music as it is played aloud and perform close readings of songs such as Clara Smith's "Freight Train Blues" and Bessie Smith's "In House Blues," whose lyrics are conveniently cited in Carby's essay.[2]

To facilitate discussion of the ways that African American writers translate musical principles into literary forms, Larsen's novels can also be paired effectively with the work of African American writers whose work owes more apparent debts to black oral traditions. In courses that I teach on ethnic American literature and jazz age culture, for example, Hughes often precedes Larsen on syllabi. Familiarizing students with the polemic of "The Negro Artist and the Racial Mountain" allows them to develop a deeper appreciation of Hughes's formal innovations as well as those of other African American writers from the Harlem Renaissance and beyond. My students have found it especially helpful to hear Hughes reading and discussing his work on *The Voice of the Poet* series. In his introduction to the blues poem "Wide River" on that recording, Hughes explains how his style emulates "the strict poetic pattern" of the "real blues" with "one long line repeated, and the third line . . . rhym[ing] with the first two." His description of the classic blues verse—its two repeated (or minimally varied) lines followed by a third that, though different, has an end rhyme with the preceding ones in an *aab* scheme—leads students to uncover how modern black writers, from Sterling Brown to Zora Neale Hurston, adapt similar patterns of repetition and variation, thus implementing Hughes's guidelines for "true Negro art."

While my students readily identify the oral qualities of Hurston's prose through her use of dialect in particular, they typically approach Larsen's novels on the level of plot and require some prompting to engage fully with her formal strategies. The opening of *Passing* provides an ideal segue to a consideration of the novel's structure. In the first few paragraphs of *Passing, the* protagonist, Irene Redfield, scrutinizes the details of a mysterious envelope recently received in the mail, as she delays opening the letter and reading its contents. To Irene, "the long envelope of thin Italian paper with its almost illegible scrawl" was "a thin sly thing which bore no return address to betray the sender" (143). Yet, despite her claim of "illegibility," Irene has correctly deduced that the letter is a plea from her childhood acquaintance, Clare Kendry, who desires the renewal of their friendship. The opening image of the envelope, I suggest to my students, directs us toward an observation of how form informs content. After all, Irene has more than an inkling of what the letter will reveal based on its "outward appearance" (143). What exactly does the envelope containing the contents of *Passing* look like, I ask them, and what does this "outward appearance" tell us about its content?

Outlining the structure of *Passing* together on the board, we note that it is divided into three parts titled "Encounter," "Re-encounter," and "Finale" and that each part is then subdivided into four short chapters, numbered one through four. Having studied blues music in conjunction with Hughes and other black writers of the period, they recognize that *Passing* mimics the form of the classic blues: twelve bars, spread across three lines with four measures to a line. *Passing* is thus structured so that each part represents a classic blues line, the four chapters in each part representing the four measures. With the first two lines labeled "Encounter" and "Re-encounter," the titles of the parts speak to the novel's pattern of repetition with slight variation. From there, we discuss how the contents of the parts can reinforce a "blues" reading.

Parts 1 and 2, for example, narrate encounters between Irene and Clare marked by a number of telling similarities. Part 1 of the novel dwells on the reunion that occurs between the two women when they coincidentally find themselves taking refreshment on the roof of the Drayton Hotel in Chicago, where they are both passing for white. In contrast to Clare, who has married a white man and disappeared into the white world, Irene, ostensibly loyal to her race and to her dark-skinned husband and sons, passes only occasionally out of convenience. Silently condemning Clare for permanently crossing the color line, Irene fruitlessly tries to resist accepting the other woman's invitation for tea. Students note that the novel establishes a central pattern of repetition involving Irene's repulsion from and attraction to Clare; Irene continually tries to maintain distance from or break ties with the other woman, only to find herself pulled further in by her. When she does take tea with Clare, the episode provokes Irene to declare once again that she is "through with Clare Kendry" (163), going so far as to vow to "turn away her eyes, to refuse her recognition" (178) if fate should bring them together. In part 2, Irene, despite the extremity of her vow, finds herself powerless against Clare's magnetism; the two revive their acquaintance as Clare—regretting her decision to pass—infiltrates Irene's Harlem social set, becoming a regular fixture in her home and at society events.

In blues terminology, Irene's reiterated statements of ambivalence might be understood as "worrying the line," the repetition of a similar phrase or idea, often expressed with minimal differences, in order to underscore and play with meaning. *Passing* also applies strategies of repetition that resemble riffs, the short musical phrases that are sounded over and over to create faint echoes of one another. For example, my students adeptly identify patterns of vertical movement in the novel. Scenes of characters ascending and descending various heights, and several symbolic episodes of falling objects, such as cigarette ash and teacups, allude to the limits on upward mobility sought by the characters and foreshadow Clare's plunge in the third part of the novel. In part 3, Irene wishes her newfound friend out of the way again, but the finale introduces an additional dimension of intrigue, since Irene's fear of the other woman is now based on her unconfirmed suspicions of an affair between Clare and Irene's own husband, Brian. In the novel's startling conclusion, Clare's white husband, John Bellew, tracks his wayward wife to a party at a Harlem penthouse, where his sudden appearance causes her fall from an open window, an "accident" that allows for the possibility that she was pushed to her fate by Irene. Though differing significantly from parts 1 and 2 in content, part 3 effectively "rhymes" with them, especially in its use of the rooftop apartment from which Clare falls—an image that echoes the roof of the Drayton Hotel on which the two women initially encounter each other. In discussions of this scene, students have pointed out that the pattern can be distinguished from standard literary foreshadowing by its improvisational dimension. Clare's death is abrupt and unexpected—and if Irene is indeed responsible, she appears to act on the spur of the moment. Yet the imagery of the fall can also be interpreted as a resignification of the line that has been played throughout the novel, a variation in meaning that brings the narrative to its tenuous conclusion.

Reading Larsen's text as a blues narrative sheds further light on the novel's unsettling ending. In Eileen Southern's description of the three-line blues stanza, "two identical (or similar) lines are followed by a contrasting statement," which provides some kind of resolution either by answering a question posed by the first two or offering "a philosophical comment upon the situation" (335). As my students and I discovered by closely studying blues lyrics, death is a recurring trope of the third line. In several cases, for example, this line resolves with murder, either perpetrated against a woman (the fear of being poisoned by a man, for instance, in "Bo-Weevil Blues") or committed as an act of revenge in more empowering tunes such as Ma Rainey's "Broken Hearted Blues" and "Cell Bound Blues," which both sing of women accused of killing the men who treated them badly.[3] As I point out to my students, in black music, fatality has also historically signified a means of transcendence, even liberation, a motif derived from the spirituals in which crossing the river Jordan functions as a simultaneous metaphor for death and freedom. Read in terms of a musical tradition in which death provides a metaphoric means of acknowledging and addressing a variety of personal and social dilemmas, Clare's and Irene's fates in the final part of *Passing* become less confounding to students. They have come to see that the blues, in concurrently performing the cathartic acts of speaking pain and asserting determination in the face of it, offer a promise of triumphing over difficulty in order to emerge anew—whether by finding another man or independence. Thus death is often necessary in order to facilitate subsequent rebirth. It is this alternating trope of death and rebirth that Larsen adopted as the central pattern of repetition in her first novel, *Quicksand*.

While most students need considerable guidance to unpack the blues structure of *Passing*, once they have developed even a preliminary understanding of early-twentieth-century black musical forms and themes, they are able to run with this reading. In classes where I teach *Passing* and *Quicksand* together, I ask students whether the realization that Larsen has transcribed the classic blues into literary form changes the way they read *Quicksand*. Their answer is an emphatic yes. In what follows, I offer an analysis of *Quicksand* drawn from my experiences teaching the novel in the context of blues and jazz music. As my students and I discovered, the novel employs strategies of repetition and variation in at least two ways: first, by signifying on blues tropes to create call and response with female musicians; second, by adapting jazz-like structures and rhythms that achieve instrumental effects, such as improvisation and syncopation, in individual passages and across the narrative's span.

Like female blues singers, who used their music to express hardships derived from the limitations of race and gender, *Quicksand*'s mixed-race protagonist, Helga Crane, is consumed by a failure to achieve satisfaction in life and in love. In my experience, one of the challenges of teaching *Quicksand* has been students' inability to understand or sympathize with Helga's restlessness. The blues context provides them with a lens for interpreting her repeated pattern of unhappiness and her continual determination to seek a fresh start. As with *Passing*, I have found it useful to begin discussion of *Quicksand*'s musical elements by analyzing the opening of the novel. With Carby's essay in mind, my students are able to recognize that the initial chapters signify on themes central to women's blues: loneliness, resistance against the cage of domesticity, and migration.

Quicksand opens in the South, where Helga finds herself increasingly unhappy at Naxos, the black school that employs her as a teacher. From its notably prosodic first line ("Helga Crane sat alone in her room, which at that hour, eight in the evening, was in soft gloom"), the opening of *Quicksand* signifies on some of the blue singers' favorite subjects, as exemplified by the following lines from "In House Blues":

> Sitting in the house with everything on my mind.
> Sitting in the house with everything on my mind.
> Looking at the clock and can't even tell the time.

Walking to my window and looking outa my door.
Walking to my window and looking outa my door.
Wishin that my man would come home once more.
(Carby 476)

Like the persona of "In House Blues," Helga is sitting in her room with "everything on [her] mind." Carby argues that, in defiance of the content of the lyrics, the music and Bessie Smith's signature growl transform songs like "In House Blues" into parodies of feminine weakness (476). Larsen similarly sets up the theme of female confinement only to undermine, at least temporarily, women's supposed lack of power and mobility. By the end of the second chapter of *Quicksand*, Helga has decided to treat her dissatisfaction with one of the resolutions (in addition to death) most favored by the blues singers: travel.

Featuring a scenario in which a woman awaits the return of an unfaithful man who has likely deserted her, songs like "In House Blues" contrast male mobility with female confinement. This contrasting theme is picked up in numerous tunes that use trains as recurring images of migration. The following verse from "Freight Train Blues" is a case in point: "When a woman gets the blues she goes to her room and hides [Repeat] / When a man gets the blues he catch the freight train and rides" (Carby 475). "Freight Train Blues" depicts a historical reality for black women, who often did not have the freedom to travel on their own in the same way that their male counterparts did during the Great Migration. Yet Angela Davis discusses how, in contrast to "Freight Train Blues," many songs do depict women on the move, arguing that "blues presentations of traveling women constructed" an imaginary "site where masses of black women could associate themselves aesthetically with travel as a mode of freedom" (67). Unlike the woman of "In House Blues" who wishes her "man would come home once more," Helga sits in her room contemplating her own escape on a train, which will leave behind a man, her fiancé, James Vayle. Resolving not to sit in her room and hide, Helga Crane intends to catch the train and ride.

Adapting the tropes of the blues and the contrapuntal structure of jazz, the opening chapters of *Quicksand* set into motion a cause-and-effect pattern of dissatisfaction and movement that constantly circles back on itself to create the swirling effect of the novel's title. Like the rambling women of the blues imaginary, Helga travels from the South to the North, from Chicago to Harlem, from Harlem to Copenhagen and back again; she ends her narrative still unsatisfied, married to a preacher in the South but vowing to return North, only to find herself confined by the birth of her fifth child. In each scenario, Helga changes her location, her livelihood, and her male love interest. Symbolically rendered through recurring images of death and rebirth, sleeping and awakening, Helga's continual attempts to reinvent new lives for herself are invariably subjected to a kind of "changing same"; the different locations and characters operate as riffs on one another, and Helga, despite her attempts to break free, finds herself worrying the line, as the old patterns of her life are repeated in a stultifying cycle.[4]

Just as she saw the need to escape Naxos at the beginning, for example, she has a similar reaction to Harlem, declaring, "I can't stay in this room any longer. I must get out or I'll choke" (110). She expresses the same fear of suffocation when she vows once again to leave the South behind in the novel's conclusion.

In addition to improvisation, one of the most often discussed features of jazz composition is the openness of its ending. Just as the blues form of *Passing* compels reevaluation of Clare's sudden death, a "jazz" reading of *Quicksand* offers insight into the novel's ambiguous conclusion. The text's jazz form is encapsulated in a passage that uses the quicksand metaphor to portray the perpetual cycle in which Helga is stuck:

> For in some way she was determined to get herself out of this bog into which she had strayed. Or—she would have to die. She couldn't endure it. Her suffocation and shrinking loathing were too great. Not to be borne. Again. For she had to admit that it wasn't new, this feeling of dissatisfaction, of asphyxiation. Something like it she had experienced before. In Naxos. In New York. In Copenhagen. This differed only by degree. And it was of the present and therefore seemingly more reasonable. The other revulsions were of the past, and now less explainable. (134)

As my classes read this passage aloud, they note how Larsen alternates between complete sentences and sentence fragments, defying rules of written language to create a staccato effect. Thematically, the passage depicts the constant pull between Helga's determination to act, to improvise change, and her sense of being pulled under, or propelled, by forces beyond her control. (Helga's ambivalence is not unlike Irene's continual futile determination to be rid of Clare in *Passing*.) Helga admits to experiencing the same "feelings of dissatisfaction" in all of her homes while acknowledging a difference in degree, as if the music has gained in its intensity, or sped up in double-time. As in *Passing*, the cycle can only be subverted through death; as Helga finds herself trapped once again in a domestic cage, death presents itself as her only path to freedom, itself a kind of transcendence. The passage riffs on the trope of rebirth, here figured in the wordplay "Not to be borne. Again." These fragments intimate the finality of this death for Helga, but the text also maintains ambiguity about her fate in order to hold out the possibility that her demise is metaphoric rather than literal.

Like the nonlinearity of jazz, the ending of the novel persists in confusing temporality. Instead of building to a conclusive finale, it fades away like a jazz song, offering more than one ending in order to undermine the notion of progressive time. Trying to get the strength after childbirth to act on her decision to return North, Helga "dozed and dreamed in snatches of sleeping and waking, letting time run on. Away." While this final note, "Away," initially appears to bring the novel to a close, a single-sentence paragraph coda follows after a line break: "And hardly had she left her bed and become able to walk again without pain, hardly had the children returned from the home of the neighbors, when she began to have her fifth child" (135). The momentary silence of the line break supplies the anticipated ending, only to have the text take up again with "and" in an additional chord progression that further attenuates the conclusion. The fact that the text ends simultaneously with this recurring image of death (at least metaphoric) and birth (that of her fifth child) testifies to its refusal of neat closure.

In the liberties it takes with literary form, *Quicksand* conforms to the structures of jazz, a genre often associated with freedom and experimentation, one known for achieving the appearance of on-the-spot improvisation even when the music is not truly as spontaneous as it seems. Eschewing a progressive structure of linear narration for the circuitous effects of repetition, variation, improvisation, and syncopation, *Quicksand* mimics the meanings and rhythms of jazz, placing its author in direct dialogue with black musicians and writers such as Hughes and Hurston whose poetry and prose similarly took their inspiration from the African American vernacular. Although critics tend to ally her writing with white literary traditions, Larsen's use of black cultural forms in *Quicksand* and *Passing* demonstrates that she was not a writer to "run away spiritually from [her] race" (Hughes, "Negro Artist").[5]

Over the years that I have been teaching Larsen's novels, I have remained firm in my conviction that they sound blues notes. What enabled my discovery of the blues structure of *Passing* was the experience of teaching Toni Morrison's 1992 novel *Jazz* alongside Larsen's novel for a multiethnic literature course. In the foreword to *Jazz*, Morrison describes the literary experiment she undertook in applying the principles of jazz composition to her novel: "I had written novels in which structure was designed to enhance meaning; here the structure would *equal* meaning. . . . I didn't want simply a musical background, or decorative references to it. I wanted the work to be a manifestation of the music's intellect, sensuality, anarchy; its history, its range, and its modernity" (xix). Considering Morrison's stylistic experimentation and the notion of "structure equaling meaning," my students and I began to pay careful attention to the form of Larsen's writings, placing her work in a musical rather than solely literary tradition. Studying Larsen's novel in the context of the tropes and structures of blues and jazz enriched our reading experiences. By engaging critically with Larsen's formal strategies, we discovered the multitude of ways that her work becomes, in Morrison's words, "a manifestation of the music," which in turn allowed us to arrive at new perspectives on her mixed-race characters' lives and deaths.

NOTES

I thank Shilpa Davé, Kimberly Chabot Davis, Laura Tanner, and Katherine Adams for their feedback on this material. This essay could not have been written without the assistance of students at Boston College, Connecticut College, Harvard University, and the University of Pennsylvania who read Larsen's novels with me.

[1] In classes when time allows, I also include Ann DuCille's response to Carby. DuCille argues that Larsen's writing *is* an important alternative form of representation since the privileging of the folk elides the diversity of the African American experience and treats rural black expression as the only authentic mode. She proposes that Larsen's "bourgeois blues," as she calls them, challenges Houston Baker's "vernacular theory" of African American literature; according to DuCille, the critical investment in oral folk culture—a culture that, in Baker's theory, is dominated by the ideology of the blues—leads to the dismissal and condemnation of black female novelists who take middle-class black women's lives as their subjects (*Coupling Convention* 68). However, what Carby and DuCille share is a tendency to read Larsen's writing *against* the female blues singers: either the blues singers present an alternative to the sexually repressed representations of educated middle-class writers such as Larsen, or Larsen presents an option outside the romanticized folk roots that obscure intellectual urbanism. By introducing both sides of this scholarly debate, my goal is to get students to see that there is more common ground between Larsen and her musical contemporaries than these other critics have allowed for.

[2] Angela Davis's *Blues Legacies and Black Feminism* is another indispensable source for transcriptions of blues lyrics.

[3] Another famous example is "The Weary Blues," which Hughes cites in his famous blues poem of the same name; it ends with the musician's final declaration: "I ain't happy no mo' / And I wish that I had died" (29–30). This wish is fulfilled in the concluding line of the poem in which the musician sleeps "like a rock or a man that's dead" (35). Given the ambiguity created by the "or" between the alternative analogies, Hughes's use of death as resolution suggests why blues death should be taken figuratively rather than literally.

[4] On the notion of the "changing same" in black music, see Baraka.

[5] For recent examples of critics who ally Larsen with Western literary traditions, see Hutchinson, *In Search of Nella Larsen*; Labbé. Most discussions of Larsen's form consider how her textual ambiguities reverberate with and generate the indeterminate identities of her mixed-race characters. See, for example, Butler, *Bodies*, 167–85; Blackmore; Blackmer; Brody; Michie 147–54; Rottenberg; and my own essay, "Her 'Nig': Returning the Gaze of Nella Larsen's *Passing*." Cutter, *Sliding*, offers a particularly useful discussion of Larsen's narrative and textual strategies.

Nella Larsen and the Civilization of Images: Teaching Primitivism and Expressionism in *Quicksand*

Cristina Giorcelli

In a civilization of images like ours, it is of help to teachers of literature to tackle the relations between literary texts and the visual arts (and, when possible, the performing arts). The visual arts' iconic powers (and, eventually, the performing arts' gestures, sounds, movements, rhythms, images, and costumes) allow students to see—in the double sense of looking at and understanding—as well as to situate the cultural, synesthetic interplays among coeval artistic works. This appreciation will make them better grasp the significance and meaning of the books they read. Larsen's *Quicksand* bears definite traces of her knowledge and employment of the tenets of primitivism and expressionism: two major trends in European and American artistic media in the 1920s. She uses their techniques to further delve into her protagonist's awareness. In one instance, she shows how a scene can instantly summarize primitivist description/interpretation and expressionist judgment.

When teaching Nella Larsen's *Quicksand,* I first provide students with the art historical background concerning primitivism and expressionism by lecturing on their main characteristics, by showing pictures of the most important works of art, and even by listening to some pieces of music—all easily available in books, on DVDs, and on the Internet.

In Europe, primitivism, a set of Western interpretations of non-Western (mostly African) artifacts, inspired such masterpieces as Pablo Picasso's *Les demoiselles d'Avignon* (1907), Henri Matisse's *The Blue Nude: Souvenir of Biskra* (1907), Igor Stravinsky's *The Rite of Spring* (1913), and Constantin Brancusi's *Little French Girl* (1914–18), to mention but a few. Primitivism roughly encompassed the first two decades of the twentieth century.[1] This was a time when European artists and intellectuals, reacting against materialism in politics and science as well as positivism in philosophy, pillaged masks, statues, friezes from Africa, Oceania, and other remote locations to extract and absorb those modes of thinking and seeing believed to operate in them. By attributing a Western avant-garde artistic code to these works, European artists responded to them ethnocentrically. They took advantage of these exotic artifacts basically for their *enigmatic* qualities, for their iconographic and stylistic forms, for their plastic and sculptural structures—that is, for their aesthetic values assessed through idealizing (albeit also manipulative) conceptions.

Primitivist artists, "subjected to the Darwinian prejudices of the period, viewed the makers of this art as frozen within the 'childhood' or 'dawn of humanity' and paid scant attention to the diverse origins and functions of the works which they used as sources" (Behr 24).[2] They generally did not understand that such objects bespoke a "disciplined, abstract, laconic, fatalistic, and thus sophisticated" art (Ross 282). Totally decontextualized from their sociocultural frame, these artifacts could not but be debased to the status of commodified objects. There is, in fact, a profound difference between the primitive (as primeval) object and the primitivist artwork.[3] The former "always has a meaning which is accessible to all those who are part of that culture, and it is always dominated by a symbol which determines the structure of the work"; the latter, by contrast, is "an object for a collection or an exhibition. If it does have a symbolic significance, this is always arbitrary and individual" (Wentinck 10).

Within this primitivist context, I find it useful to draw students' attention to the 1920s European craze for the American soubrette Josephine Baker and to show them images of her costumes and postures. As the "Black Venus" and the star of the *Revue Nègre* (1925), she became famous in Paris for performing barebreasted, in a scene set in a jungle, the "banana dance," also called the "*danse sauvage*." Her body and its movements epitomized in her viewers' imagination the primitive (irrational, disorderly, uncivilized, uninhibited) and the exotic, par excellence. Presenting herself in extravagant attires (a G-string made of satin bananas) and wild-looking settings (foliage, vines, palm trees, cages), Baker "rolled her eyes, contorted her face, and swivelled her body in a deliberate parody of the blackface vaudeville routines and the conventions of the Negro minstrel show" (Martin 311). By exploiting the very tenets and forms that reified her, Baker became both an agent and a victim of primitivist race and gender stereotyping. While her entire body was turned into a medium of expression, some parts (breasts, pelvis, buttocks) were reduced to sites of racialized signification, "subjected to the intense gaze of a critical ethnography" (Sweeney 57). Furthermore, they were singled out and looked at as objectified parts, as artifacts, that bestowed on the body "a segmented stylization suggesting a strangely mechanical vitality" (Clifford 197–98). Notwithstanding or, perhaps, thanks to this exploitative fragmentation, Baker, with her abundance of bananas and feathers (later on also of furs and jewels), succeeded in appropriating "the collective image that Europeans had constructed of black female sexuality" (Lemke 100).

In more or less the same years, primitivism was assimilated by German and Austrian expressionism, which appreciated the primitivist hardness, simplifications, and incisiveness, while sharing the goal of attaining some sort of human and civil regeneration in a world perceived as irreparably old and spent.[4] In expressionism, by imitating exotic (but also medieval Gothic) artifacts, Western artists tried to mystically go back to the sources of integrity, piety, creativity, and truth and find their genuine selves beyond academic conventions, bourgeois values, and the dictatorship of rationality, which they saw as tools of repression. Expressionist painters—such as Ernst Ludwig Kirchner, Emil Nolde, George Grosz, Otto Dix, Egon Schiele—produced works intended to convey unmediated "expressions" of raw and harsh passions in order to make viewers realize how stifled they were by prevailing norms of conduct and thus reach out for some sort of spiritual renewal. These artists' aims were not to give form to mimesis or anecdote but to show the dark, violent, and beastly side of human nature (tellingly, their forerunners in France were called "fauves" ["beasts"]) and its deadly sins (mainly lust, sloth, wrath, gluttony), so as to unravel the mysteries of the unconscious (a purpose that would later—from the mid-1920s—be carried out especially by the surrealists). Not by chance, when Josephine Baker danced naked for a German count and his aristocratic friends in Berlin in 1926 (performing a quasi-parody of a primitive dance ritual), she was seen as "one of Grosz's mechanical dolls" (Sweeney 26).

In class, I specifically concentrate on the paintings that illustrate the expressionists' predilection for city scenes. Expressionists, in fact, thought of the city as a place of alienation in which people's inner agony could be displayed through horrid accentuations of physical features or of twisted and out-of-joint limbs (as with Schiele's works). Expressionists liked to paint the city's sites of entertainment (circuses, night halls, cinemas, variety theaters, amusement parks) because they saw them as emblematic of the brutality, degradation, perverted sexuality of modern humanity (in Kirchner's paintings, for example). Sexy, fashionable, and eroticized women often appeared in these works, not only as participants in or as victims of such a world but also as consumers, as part of a spectacle, as salable objects: "The concept of modernity became inseparable from artificiality and the commodification of the female body, transformed by the masquerade of display" (Behr 50). To present the dramatic content of life, its loneliness and despair, expressionist artists used distorted, grotesque, angular shapes; unnatural, strident colors; crude and unfinished brushwork. Like primitivism, expressionism had an impact on several cultural fields such as theater (August Strindberg's *Ghost Sonata*, Frank Wedekind's *Pandora's Box*), cinema (Fritz Lang's *Dr. Mabuse, the Gambler*), music (from Gustav Mahler's *Sixth Symphony* to Arnold Schoenberg's *Second String Quartet*), and architecture (from Antoni Gaudí to Walter Gropius and Mies van der Rohe).

Whereas black culture was "an exotic import" in Europe, in the 1920s in the United States African Americans, often seen "as barely civilized exiles from the jungle," became, for some, models "of 'natural' human behavior to contrast with the falsified, constrained and impotent modes of the 'civilized'" (61). The vogue of "the New Negro" postdated the birth of European primitivism, but it was likewise implicated in the prejudices inherent in the objectification of the other. In the United States (as well as in Europe), primitivism, in fact, ended up perverting the alleged black vitality, authenticity, and originality with which it intended to restock a depleted and decadent West.[5] Vitality frequently assumed wild and licentious innuendos, authenticity adopted barbaric colorings, and originality took on an atemporal and bizarre dimension. Primitivism supplied the other on whom to project what white people both desired and feared: a return to and a subjugation by "nature."

If, as some critics argue, primitivism helped make the Harlem Renaissance "by developing a receptive audience and by encouraging patronage" (65), it was especially jazz—misread as a transplantation of African ritual music—and jazz dances (the mooch, the black bottom, the shake, the shimmy, the mess-around), with their free movements and, according to some, indecorous contacts between partners, that represented for whites the essence of black culture: "Jazz fever and the primitivist euphoria supported each other throughout the 1920s in their mutual rise to celebrity" (Chinitz 63).

In the United States, expressionism—which, exception made for some precursors (like Marsden Hartley, Stuart Davis, George Bellows), properly started in the 1920s—shared the same narrative content (private fears, erotic obsessions, psychological scrutiny) as its European counterpart, but, according to Bram Dijkstra, its purpose was less individualistic. Dijkstra maintains that its focus was more "humanist" and communitarian in that it tried to create a "cultural bridge between the social classes" and the various ethnic groups so as to be "meaningful to those who had suffered the most from the excesses of early twentieth century capitalism" and from racist discriminations (11).

Primitivism and expressionism in both the United States and Europe adopted a critical attitude toward "civilized" norms, desiring resistance to, if not actual change in, society. Thus it is not difficult to see why both trends had an impact on African American artists of the Harlem Renaissance. If, as some critics state, the importance gained by African art in Europe gave African Americans a new perspective because they could see themselves "in relation to a dignified cultural past: a past in which the color black was the color of beauty" (Coleman 59), I contend that, from a "political" outlook, some of these artists' works indicate their conviction that in the United States the Negro vogue was but the latest manifestation of primitivist stereotypes of race and gender. They often employed expressionist distortions (especially in the scenes where urban crowds and places of entertainment are presented) to stress the sufferance inflicted by society on their fellow human beings. In class I show slides or photos of works by Aaron Douglas, Sargent Johnson, and Archibald Motley that exemplify the influence of primitivism and/or expressionism: for instance, Douglas's illustrations for the magazines *Opportunity* and *Crisis*, Johnson's sculptures of Elizabeth Gee and Pearl, and Motley's skin-tone portraits of women together with paintings like *Cocktails* or *Blues*.[6] When primitivism and expressionism entered the domain of literature, the writers who responded to them tried to achieve painterly and sculptural effects in their narratives through a radicalization of structure, essentialized forms, and, especially, plays of points of view.

In teaching *Quicksand*, I emphasize how Nella Larsen scathingly explores primitivist and expressionist modes *through* her protagonist's gaze (that elusive and complex visual exchange between subject and object, viewer and viewed, which, involving both the imaginary and unattainable desire, invites and discourages participation, involvement).[7] To properly approach Larsen's use of the gaze, it is important to convey to students what W. E. B. Du Bois—whom Larsen mentions explicitly in the novel (38)—had underlined when referring to the "unreconciled strivings" in African Americans' vision of themselves, their "double consciousness":

> [T]he Negro is a sort of seventh son, born with a veil, and gifted with second-sight in this American world—a world which yields him no true self-consciousness, but only lets him see himself through the revelation of the other world. It is a peculiar sensation, this double-consciousness, this sense of always looking at one's self through the eyes of others. . . . One ever feels his two-ness—an American, a Negro; two souls, two thoughts, two unreconciled strivings; two warring ideals in one dark body, whose dogged strength alone keeps it from being torn asunder (*Souls* 364–65).

From a different perspective, but on an analogous point, the art critic John Berger's observations regarding woman's dual vision of herself are extremely pertinent:

> To be born a woman has been to be born within an allotted and confined space. . . . A woman . . . is almost continually accompanied by her own image of herself . . . she comes to consider the surveyor and the surveyed within her as the two constituent yet always distinct elements of her identity as a woman. . . . Men look at women. Women watch themselves being looked at. . . . The surveyor of woman in herself is male; the surveyed female. Thus she turns herself into an object—and most particularly an object of vision: a sight. (46–47)

Because *Quicksand*'s protagonist, Helga Crane, is an African American, she is under the cross-fire of her own "double" (black and white) gaze, but, since she is also a woman, she has interiorized as well the gaze of her male (white or black) "surveyor." She is thus "gifted" with (or, better, damned by) what might be called a "striving" *threeness*. When she looks at herself, because of her "double" vision, white prejudices intrude and make her see herself as an exotic or a primitive entity; and when she is under the male (white or black) gaze, she knows and perceives that she is being turned into an erotic spectacle. By looking at herself through the socially imposed hegemonic white gaze, she comes to loathe herself; by being looked at by the male gaze, she is made vulnerable and becomes a commodity. In both cases there is an exercise of dominance that renders her powerless and thus inevitably defeated.[8]

Helga Crane is presented from a third-person narrative voice that, while it marks a distancing from her, gives access to her thoughts.[9] Thus, narratologically, Larsen succeeds in projecting, from the outside as well as from the inside, the difficulties that Helga, a mulatta (the daughter of a West Indian man and a Danish woman), faces in her quest for an ever elusive self-realization. Students must be made aware that they alternately look *at* her (thanks to the narrator's descriptions) and *through* her own eyes (where "double consciousness" and the "surveyor's" gaze converge).[10] Since modernism, with its insistence on self-consciousness, parody, self-referentiality, fragmentation, and disruption, intended "to probe the psychological depths of the individual through visual imagery" (Ross 293), sight and insight go appropriately together in *Quicksand*.

When the narrator shows Helga observing African Americans from the outside, she sees them *mainly* from a primitivist point of view as debased phenomena. In contrast, when in her thoughts Helga looks at African Americans (and herself), from the inside, she sees them (and herself) *mainly* from an expressionist point of view as grotesque, even as a nightmare. In some cases, however, these two somewhat contiguous approaches to presenting and representing inevitably overlap precisely because the narrative voice is so interlaced with the protagonist's thinking.

After laying out the art historical background and a summary of the textual strategies that characterize *Quicksand*, I generally single out five crucial instances in which, through the play of points of view and of intersecting and conflicting inner- and outer-directed gazes, the protagonist opposes or submits to her (American as well as Danish) society's supremacist and sexist commodifying gaze.

In the novel's opening scene, the young, beautiful, intelligent, cultivated, single Helga is seen from the outside. An omniscient narrator scrutinizes her while, alone in her room furnished with a Chinese carpet and oriental silks—objects that primitivists cherished—she reads a book of Arabic content.[11] To refer latently to Africa, otherwise absent from this list of exotica (Helga's being black has not yet been mentioned), the spot of light under which she sits is said to create "a small *oasis* in a *desert* of darkness"—a "darkness" of which physically and, as we will find out, emotionally she partakes (1; emphasis mine).

Helga stands out as a body, and a very sensual one at that. It has been remarked that "Helga's body is the event of the novel, whose plot consists of a series of descriptions of that event. Conflict arises with the question of who will have the authority of representing her body" (Gray 263). Although, by being black, her body is in fashion and attracts attention, she scornfully refuses to be appreciated on merely racist and sexist grounds. According to primitivist tenets, this body is described in terms of paintings or, better, of sculptures (like those of Johnson, for example): her arms and legs are "well-turned," her face is "sharply cut" and "distinctly outlined," while her ears are "delicately chiselled" (2).

Swathed in a "vivid green and gold negligée and glistening brocaded mules," her body is minutely looked at and described: each part (shoulders, arms, legs, face, brows, eyes, mouth, lips, nose, ears, hair) is accessorized by a wealth of adjectives (2). Yet this beautiful body is projected as a fragmented one: it is a body made of pieces (like that of Josephine Baker). Such discrete singling out and implicit enhancement help draw attention to its severed parts (as with some of Dix's paintings). Because its entirety, its wholeness, is lost, each of its parts might be liable to be turned into a fetish by voyeuristic observers.

But Helga's mind, too, is in pieces, angry as she is at both the white minister who preaches segregation at the Naxos school where she teaches and at her hypocritical, servile superiors and colleagues who do not rebel against such outrageous statements:

> [H]e had said that . . . [t]hey [Negroes] knew enough to stay in their places. . . . And then he had spoken of contentment, . . . pointing out to them that it was their duty to be satisfied in the estate to which they had been called, hewers of wood and drawers of water. (3)

Because Helga is painfully aware of prevailing, entrenched white stereotypes of oversexualized African American female bodies as objects of lust, she likes beautiful clothes not for the purpose of seducing anyone, but simply for aesthetic reasons. The novel's insistence on clothes and accessories is significant because, while providing another way of seeing and understanding Helga's physical and emotional self, it highlights the conflict between African Americans' resistance to primitivist white labelling and their legitimate demands for freedom of choice.[12] Helga thus dresses elegantly and would prefer vivid colors (as in Paul Gauguin's or Motley's paintings):

> [S]ome unanalyzed driving spirit of loyalty to the inherent racial need for gorgeousness told her that bright colors *were* fitting and that dark-complexioned people *should* wear yellow, green, and red. Black, brown, and gray were ruinous to them, actually destroyed the luminous tones lurking in their dusky skins. (18)

Yet in Naxos the conformist environment in which she lives recommends sober clothes. Helga consequently avoids strong colors and makes up for their absence by buying expensive fabrics, "soft, luxurious woolens or heavy, clinging silks" and sophisticated trimmings, "[o]ld laces, strange embroideries, dim brocades" (18). Her colleagues, however, detect in her many dainty garments her repressed aesthetic drive:

> [T]hey felt that the colors [of Helga's dresses] were queer: dark purples, royal blues, rich greens, deep reds. . . . Her faultless, slim shoes made them uncomfortable and her small plain hats seemed to them positively indecent. (18)

If Helga seeks the admiration that her clothed body prompts, she detests the reactions that her body arouses: because she denies desire and stifles her sexuality (Carby, "It Jus" 240), she is disgusted by her black fiancé's "quivering" lips and the "throbbing vein in his forehead" that she perceives when he is too near her: her own sexual desirability offends her (24). Given these troublesome circumstances, Helga abruptly decides to leave the South and her job, feeling deeply uncomfortable in both. With the unity of her body as well as of her mind lost, Helga, who, as a "new" black woman, is too critical and does not conform, is not only alone (she has no family to rely on) but also alienated from her social context.

In the second instance (ch. 5), after having been brutally thrown out of her white uncle's house by his white wife, Helga twice mingles in the Chicago crowds (Motley's paintings are very useful here). In the big and brash city, Helga is so isolated, afraid, and suspicious of the many people she does not know that her humanity seems to be eroded. The physical proximity and mental distancing of the urban crowds convey both their anonymity and their potential aggressiveness. On these two occasions, her being looked at and her looking at make her first exposed and then defiant. Both passages bear expressionist characteristics because of the implied ferocity in assuming pejorative characteristics in the other. In the first case:

> It was evening and much colder. . . . The wind cut her like a knife, but she did not feel it. She ceased her frantic running, aware at last of the curious glances of passersby. . . . Here a man, well groomed and pleasant-spoken, accosted her. On such occasions she was wont to reply scathingly, but, tonight, his pale Caucasian face struck her breaking faculties as too droll. Laughing harshly, she threw at him the words: "You're not my uncle." He retired in haste, probably thinking her drunk, or possibly a little mad. (29)

Helga's apparently nonsensical answer—"You're not my uncle"—vents her anger against the "Caucasian" man's inference and sexual overture. Taken by surprise by her aunt's treatment, Helga cries her rage at least at him (he too is humiliating her) in an oblique, somewhat disjointed way. When a (white) man looks at her—an African American woman walking alone in a street at dusk—according to bourgeois, racist, and sexist parameters, he cannot help mistaking her for a prostitute. In the second case:

> She stood intently looking down into the glimmering street, far below, swarming with people, merging into little eddies and disengaging themselves to pursue their own individual ways. A few minutes later she stood in the doorway, drawn by an uncontrollable desire to mingle with the crowd. . . . Looking at these, Helga caught herself wondering who they were, what they did, and of what they thought. What was passing behind those dark molds of flesh. Did they really think at all? (30)

Here Helga confrontationally looks at people (whites and blacks) and sees them as nothing more than "molds of flesh": odd, vilified creatures, drifting bodies, whose even having a mind, whose even being human remains in question.

In the third instance (ch. 11), Helga is in Harlem: the New York area that had come to be regarded as "the cultural equivalent of the American libido" (Martin 318). Upon entering a dance hall, she thinks that it is "one of those places characterized by the righteous as a hell" (58). This is what she sees:

> They [people] danced, ambling lazily to a crooning melody, or violently twisting their bodies, like whirling leaves, to a sudden streaming rhythm, or shaking themselves ecstatically to a thumping of unseen tomtoms. (59)

Helga is, at first, "drugged, lifted, sustained, by the extraordinary music, blown out, ripped out, beaten out, by the joyous, wild, murky orchestra" since the "essence of life seemed bodily motion," but, then, with a "conscious effort" (59), she turns into a spectator, and her knowledge of dominant white primitivist and racial stereotypes intrudes into her perception. Earlier, Helga had already been said to understand and sympathize with a white woman's (Mrs. Nilssen's) "point of view" (29), and the whites' outlook may also be included in that of the just-mentioned "righteous." Consequently, she now sees herself through their gaze and stops dancing:

> [A] shameful certainty that not only had she been in the jungle, but that she had enjoyed it, began to taunt her. . . . She wasn't, she told herself, a jungle creature. She cloaked herself in a faint disgust as she watched the entertainers throw themselves about to the bursts of syncopated jangle. (59)

Students might again be reminded here of Du Bois's concept of "double consciousness," which has taken over. Helga becomes endowed with a heightened capacity for scrutiny. Her refusal to go on dancing is informed by her awareness of racist stereotypes about the black body: its energy, its lithe movements, its lack of inhibition (Douglas's illustrations may come to mind). The vocabulary is tellingly primitivist. The reference to "tomtoms" and the echo between "jungle" and "jangle" cannot go unnoticed.[13] Immediately afterward, she heeds (and Motley's skin-tone portraits are particularly appropriate) the many different shades of color in the hair, eyes, faces of the people who belong to "this oppressed race of hers" (59), which are reflected (a *doubling* mirror-like effect) *in* her as she reflects (in the word's etymological sense of going and returning) *on* them. Here, once more, the body parts Helga sees spell out her divided self, which cannot imagine African Americans as a unity, not even a corporeal one. She sees as she is seen: in the partial, segmented way. In this dance hall Helga realizes how impossible her life in the United States has become, and, again abruptly, she decides to leave.

The fourth instance (ch. 15) is set in a Copenhagen vaudeville house—aptly called "the great Circus"—another place of mass entertainment, a meeting venue with the potential for sexual intimations. Dancing as a symbol of natural energy, of Dionysian release, had been a powerful force in expressionist paintings (for which Nietzsche's *Thus Spoke Zarathustra* had been an inspirational source). In this "Circus" Helga, who is not a participant but only a spectator, watches a minstrel show with the painter Axel Olsen, her white Danish suitor, and "some other young folk" (82). Two African Americans are singing and dancing: they are "pounding their thighs, slapping their hands together, twisting their legs, waving their abnormally long arms, throwing their bodies about with a loose ease!" while everybody around them enjoys this caricature of black bodies and gestures. "[T]he enchanted spectators clapped and howled and shouted for more!" (82–83). Helga, who had previously let herself be dressed spectacularly—as if she indeed were on a stage—knows that she too has been performing for those white people who are taking care of her because she is "different" (83). In effect, her Danish relatives had clothed her in strong colors ("indigo, orange, green, vermilion, and black"), in expensive fabrics ("velvet and chiffon"), even in "a leopard-skin coat" and—again like Baker—with "feathers and furs" (74). They had also bedecked her with "long" and "brightly enamelled" earrings, "glittering shoe-buckles" (69), "barbaric bracelets" (70), and enveloped her in "a nauseous Eastern perfume" (74).[14] Helga knows that she has let herself look like what white people consider "a veritable savage" (69). At the show, as "an ironical and silently speculative spectator,"

> she was filled with a fierce hatred for the cavorting Negroes on the stage. She felt ashamed, betrayed, as if these pale pink and white people among whom she lived had suddenly been invited to look upon something in her which she had hidden away and wanted to forget. (83)

By looking at the two dancers, she sees them in the way her accompanying suitor and friends cannot (she thinks) help seeing her: a grotesque embodiment of debasement. Because she had already realized that for those whites she was only a "pet dog" (70), a "decoration . . . curio . . . peacock" (73), it is as if she were transformed by their gaze into these animals, into these trivial and commodified objects. There is a convergence and a triangulation of gazes here: Helga looks at the dancers and at the audience that looks at the performers.

A confirmation of this debasement of her "self" follows immediately afterward when Olsen presents her with the portrait he has made of her: an objectified artifact of her "self" as he sees/understands her. The white, primitivist stereotype of the black woman's body as available dominates a depiction that in his eyes is "the true Helga Crane" (88): a woman who has "the warm impulsive nature of the women of Africa, but . . . the soul of a prostitute. You sell yourself to the highest buyer" (87). In Helga's eyes, on the contrary, the portrait is a complete misrepresentation: it "wasn't . . . herself at all, but some disgusting sensual creature with her features" (89).[15] Whereas in the first description, examined in the first instance, Helga's body might have been assessed fetishistically, voyeuristically, but was still rendered with objectivity, here the white painter's eye has appropriated *and* degraded it to the level of a prostitute's. This image tells *his* sight, presents *his* way of seeing, but also summarizes the sense of this book: how Helga is seen by others and how she sees herself through others. This image, however, is a deception in her own eyes both culturally (it relies on a stereotype) and individually (it does not represent who she is).[16] Helga, who walks the tightrope of sexual respectability, sees this portrait as a mystification and rejects it by violently turning down the painter's marriage proposal and, once more, abruptly leaving Europe—that too has racialized and sexualized her—to go back to the United States.

In the fifth instance (ch. 20), Helga enters, distracted and soaking wet, with a "clinging red dress," in a storefront Baptist church in Harlem. She has just been humiliated by the married Doctor Anderson's refusal to start a relationship with her, when she had finally decided to indulge her sexual desires. While, for the third time, her body is mistaken for that of a prostitute ("A scarlet 'oman. Come to Jesus, you pore los' Jezebel"), she sees herself through the eyes "of the men and women" (112) in the congregation and participates in a performance that, carried on by the "frenzied women" around her, "took on an almost Bacchic vehemence." She is first fascinated and then horrified by what she sees. She feels as if she were confronted with "rites of a remote obscure origin" (113). "[G]radually," however, she allows herself to become a participant, but one who observes (and judges) herself and those around her in the performing act:

> [S]he felt an echo of the weird orgy resound in her own heart; she felt herself possessed by the same madness; she too felt a brutal desire to shout and to sling herself about. . . . with no previous intention [she] began to yell like one insane, drowning every other clamor, while torrents of tears streamed down her face. (113)

While the women around her "dragged themselves upon their knees or crawled over the floor like reptiles, sobbing and pulling their hair and tearing off their clothing" (114), the trope of the primitive "orgy," with its overtones of bestiality and lasciviousness, sets in and creates an expressionist scene worthy of Strindberg's dramas. As noted "In the paintings of the German expressionists, women . . . are almost always primitive creatures . . . prone to wild, tribal dances and the physical distortions associated with African sculpture as in the work of Emil Nolde" (Dijkstra 45).[17] Helga's participation in this scene indicates that, in a moment of despair, she is no longer capable and willing to resist being absorbed and engulfed by "her people" in their most distorted, abject manifestations. In many expressionist paintings, "scenes of rape, murder and insanity in the city drastically questioned the prevailing order, substituting madness and anarchy in its place" (Behr 62).

Later, in rural Alabama, after having hurriedly chosen to marry the southern minister Pleasant Green, what she thought was a "primitive flock" (118)—she condescendingly employs whites' vocabulary and criteria—imposes on her the traditional roles of wife and mother, based again on the exploitation of her female body and personality. In the end, her body, deformed and debilitated by many pregnancies, will entrap and, perhaps, kill her—a body that is finally presented "in its least artificial, most biological, most 'given' terms" (Gray 268). With such a distressing conclusion, by dramatizing "the ways in which social forces impinge upon the individual psyche" (Monda 37), Larsen problematizes the primitivist vision, showing not only how exploited her protagonist's body and self are but also expressionistically deforming both of them.

Given this novel's denouement, Du Bois may have been only partially right when he praised Helga Crane for embodying the New Negro woman "on whom 'race' sits negligibly."[18] Although, at one point, Helga had affirmed that she cherished the "blessed sense of belonging to herself alone and not to a race" (64), her constant "double" vision as a Black and her subjection to the male distorting gaze as a woman prove how impossible this detachment, this freedom, is in the given historical and social circumstances. Her plight is not that of the "tragic mulatto" who could not be white and would not be black, but rather stems from the "unequal power relations" (McLendon, *Politics* 74) between men and women as well as between whites and blacks.

Larsen's troubling and troubled portrait of Helga (so different from the portrait of Helga by Olsen) and the sophisticated play of narrative and visual perspectives seem to demand a new mode of representation of race in which African American women would finally *see* and be *seen* with a combination of "naturalistic accuracy and individuality" (Ross 285). This combination would finally overcome notions of exoticism and licentiousness and reach out for what Alain Locke has termed "the psychology behind the physiognomy" (*New Negro* 653).

The reading of *Quicksand* I have here described invites ekphrastic responses from students. When I detect their enthusiasm, I ask them to compare in writing passages from the novel and the works of art we have discussed. I have been surprised by the insightful renderings they develop. As such cases evidence much creative thought, for their joy and mine, I sometimes gladly skip administering yet another formal exam.

NOTES

[1] One has to keep in mind, however, that in those years the West also believed that it had its own "primitives" (peasants, children, the insane). As primitivism was "informed by a multiple, complex and often chronologically overlapping" cluster of ideas (Rhodes 9), what is "primitive" was interpreted by different artists in different ways (Paul Klee and the Dadaists, for instance). In addition, let us also not forget that medieval art objects too were designated as "primitive." See Rhodes; Harrison, Frascina, and Perry.

[2] See also Bassie; Dube. Since expressionism is not an approach to reality confined to the twentieth century (painters of the past—like Grünewald, Hieronymus Bosch, El Greco, James Ensor, for instance—may legitimately be said to partake of the expressionist

mode), American writers before Larsen may also have incorporated expressionist tenets. Stephen Crane, who is generally praised for his impressionist stylistic qualities, drew a very expressionist scene in *Maggie: A Girl of the Streets*, and Larsen endowed her protagonist with the surname Crane!

[3] Alfred Jarry (1873–1907) made an earlier use of the primitive in *Ubu Roi* (1896), a parody of traditional realist theater.

[4] Contemporaneous with primitivism, expressionism began in Germany around 1905, and although its most authentic phase expired toward the end of World War I, in the United States it went on well into the forties with abstract expressionism.

[5] Without detracting from his assistance to and promotion of African American artists through his articles and book reviews, one has but to think of Carl Van Vechten's *Nigger Heaven* (1926).

[6] I mention some African American artists here, but there are, of course, a host of white ones in the 1920s; see Dijkstra.

[7] If students want to know more about this very important concept, they may study Jacques Lacan, *Seminar XI*.

[8] At the very beginning of the novel, Helga thinks that "she was powerless" (5).

[9] See McLendon, *Politics* (99–100). In many cases, the distance from Helga Crane is marked also by her being designated by her full name. See Barnett 582.

[10] As Dorothy Stringer has summarized, in the novel the act of looking is split into watching, being seen, watching oneself being seen, seeing oneself (70).

[11] To underscore how accurately chosen every detail is, in a "brass bowl" on the table near Helga, there are "nasturtiums" (1), exotic flowers of Indian (or Peruvian) origin.

[12] It may be worth recalling here that Larsen was the daughter of a dressmaker.

[13] After seeing Baker's performance, E. E. Cummings wrote that "we find ourselves remembering the jungle" (qtd. in Martin 311).

[14] For more on the clothes and accessories worn by Helga, see Roberts.

[15] Based on a reading of Sander Gilman's study, McLendon makes the observation that often in European paintings of the eighteenth and nineteenth century "black women (and men) were depicted . . . in order to sexualize the paintings" (*Politics* 73).

[16] Stringer observes that Helga here looks narcissistically at the painting, giving it, as it were, a life of its own (76).

[17] For the relation between Larsen and expressionist drama, see Hutchinson, *In Search of Nella Larsen*, ch. 13.

[18] On Helga as the "antirace race woman," see Posnock 85.

"Anything Might Happen": Freedom and American Identity in Nella Larsen's *Passing*

Beryl Satter

What is the meaning of freedom in a culture marred by racism and misogyny? One resource that my students use to unpack this question is Nella Larsen's *Passing*. We pay particular attention to one sentence from the novel: "If Clare was freed, anything might happen" (236). At the start of the class devoted to *Passing*, I write this line on the blackboard. For the remainder of the class, we spell out the forces binding Clare. We thereby infer the vision of freedom contained in Larsen's novel and articulate what Clare's destruction implies about 1920s America.

I teach *Passing* as the culmination of the first half of an undergraduate United States history course entitled The 1920s and the Great Depression. The students tend to be representative of the undergraduate population at Rutgers University, Newark. There are more than fifty languages spoken on our campus. Many students are either immigrants or the children of immigrants, and most are first-generation college students. African American, Caribbean, and African students are part of the mix, but no single race, ethnicity, or national group dominates. Given the diversity of backgrounds in the classroom, I make no assumptions about prior knowledge of United States history. I assume, nevertheless, a high level of analytic sophistication from the students, as long as I provide adequate context and guidance.

Historical Context: The Culture Wars of the 1920s

My students learn that 1920s America is best understood as a period of "culture war" between Victorian and modernist values. Most of them already know that nineteenth-century Victorian culture was famous for its sexual repression (women wearing floor-length dresses, censorship of sexual language, etc.). I explain that Victorian sexual repression also had economic implications. Victorians assumed that people who controlled their sexual desires would also control their desire to spend money. Men who saved their money, in turn, would ultimately achieve economic independence. Finally, the economic independence of middle-class Americans was seen as a cornerstone of United States democracy; supposedly, economically independent voters would make political choices based on virtue and logic, not economic desperation. Victorian sexual repression was about economics and politics, therefore, as much as it was about sexuality. Victorians were particularly adamant about the importance of female sexual control. Their ideas about women's natural purity resolved the problem of how to have a society based on competition and individual assertion, on one hand, and morality and virtue, on the other. Men could compete, Victorians believed, because their wives encouraged their morality; tamed their aggressive, sexual natures; and raised their children to be virtuous, self-controlled, and hardworking.

The Victorian worldview was overtly racist. Drawing on Gail Bederman's work, I explain that late-nineteenth-century white Protestants believed that the world's peoples were divided into races such as the "Anglo-Saxon," "Celtic," "Hebrew," "Slavic," or "African." They believed that these races had competed for thousands of years and that white Anglo-Saxon Protestants had emerged as the "fittest." Anglo-Saxons then passed their superior competitive abilities and greater sexual and self-control to their descendants, who were uniquely qualified over all other "races" to be Americans.

I explain how the early-twentieth-century shift from a producer to a consumer economy, as well as massive immigration and urbanization, challenged the Victorian worldview. By the 1920s, competition between hardworking individuals rarely led to economic independence. Instead, this era saw the rise of massive corporations that crushed competition and relegated even white-collar workers to routinized labor and dependence on employers. New technologies enabled mass production, which in turn required mass consumption. Mass consumption would produce prosperity only if older Victorian values of saving and self-denial were replaced with modern values of spending and self-expression. This became the job of new forms of advertising. Immigration from southern and eastern Europe brought Catholics and Jews to the United States in large numbers, people whose values challenged those of white Anglo-Saxon Protestants. Cities housing immigrant populations as well as African Americans fleeing southern racism became incubators of a new popular culture that challenged older Victorian values of self-denial and sexual self-control.

The result was a cultural battle between older Victorian and new modernist values. Victorians trumpeted Anglo-Saxon superiority, thrift and saving, emotional and sexual repression, female purity, and a single standard of "Christian" behavior. Their modernist opponents believed in cultural diversity, emotional expression, female sexuality (within limits), and the expression of desire, all of which eased the way for a new culture of spending and consumption. Drawing on Ann Douglas's work, I explain that while Victorians believed in guarding speech to promote "higher" values, modernists heralded "terrible honesty"—that is, the frank discussion of life's realities. In place of purity and patriotic racism, modernists valued "sophistication" and cosmopolitanism. We examine the 1920s youth revolt, Prohibition, the Ku Klux Klan, fundamentalism, and immigration restriction, in the light of the battle between Victorian purity and Anglo-Saxon superiority on the one hand, and modernist diversity on the other.

Finally, I provide the students with a basic history of the Harlem Renaissance by drawing on the work of Nathan Huggins and George Hutchinson. I explain that in the 1920s, some "sophisticated" whites embraced African American artists because of their primitivist fantasies. They assumed that blacks were in touch with primitive emotions—feelings lauded by a modernist culture that opposed Victorian purity and self-control. Black Harlem Renaissance authors saw their contributions in a more complex light. Many modernists felt that the United States failed to develop a distinctly American culture. "Anglo-Saxons" copied the British, while newer immigrants remained too close to their native countries. African Americans, however, had been a presence here since the 1600s, and the harsh conditions of their importation had stripped them of their native culture. At a time when many believed that a nation's identity was found in its folk culture, some African Americans pointed out that black southern farmers were the United States peasant class. Therefore, their music, folklore, and art could uniquely reveal America's soul. Black intellectuals also argued that we must explore what was truly distinctive about political culture in the United States—namely, its racism. Those best situated to explore this phenomenon were those who lived it: African Americans.

Passing and 1920s America

This leads us to the class session on *Passing*. I prepare the students by explaining that while the book seems to be about the decay of a marriage, it is actually about race relations and American identity. I remind them that Irene Redfield is an unreliable narrator. I warn them to note the names of the characters, since these give clues to what each represents.

I also say a few words about "passing" itself, citing the historical example of Philippa Schuyler. By this point in the semester, the students have read black writer George Schuyler's "Our Greatest Gift to America." This scathing essay argues that racism artificially elevates ignorant immigrants, oppressed factory workers, and exploited southern whites. All are "buoyed up . . . by being constantly assured of their superiority to all other races and their equality to each other" (1615). This "gift" of an inflated racial ego, Schuyler says, encourages them to ignore their reality—that they are nobodies who are brutally exploited by bosses and "cheap grafters" alike—and instead "blame it all on the dark folks" that society in the United States has trained them to believe are "without exception [their] inferiors" (1613, 1614). The students are therefore shocked to learn that Schuyler's own daughter Philippa, a brilliant musician, felt compelled to pass as white to escape the racist barriers she faced. I also tell them about Adrian Piper's powerful 1988 performance piece *Cornered*. In it, Piper pushed "white" Americans to consider the privileges they receive from passing, despite the likelihood of their having miniscule African ancestry and thus being defined, by racial conventions in the United States, as black.

We begin our class on *Passing* by discussing the novel's lesbian subtext. The students note Irene's adoration of Clare's beauty. I point out Clare's flirty behavior. For example, 1920s women greeted one another with a kiss on a cheek, not, like Clare greets Irene, by kissing her "dark curls" or "bare shoulder" (194, 233). When the women meet in New York, both imagine freedom from their husbands: Irene fantasizes her husband "dead before her," while Clare says, "Damn Jack! . . . I could kill him!" (196, 200). Because the students have already read excerpts from George Chauncey's *Gay New York*, which describes a new 1920s cultural visibility for homosexuality, they accept *Passing* as another contribution to that "sophisticated" context.

Next, the students break into groups. Each group is asked to do the following:

List every issue, emotion, or event that Irene attempts to evade.
List as many adjectives describing Clare's character as you can come up with. Describe Irene's characterization of Clare. Decide if you agree with it or not, and why.
List Brian Redfield's wishes or desires.
List adjectives that describe John Bellew.
List adjectives that describe Fred Martin (husband of Gertrude Martin).
Determine the message that Larsen is signaling by the names of the following characters: Irene ('Rene) Westover Redfield, Clare Kendry Bellew, John Bellew, Hugh Wentworth, Felice Freeland.

We then regroup as a class. To situate the novel within the 1920s Victorian/modernist debate, we first look at Clare's great-aunts, Grace and Edna. The students note that the aunts are described as "good Christians," who value "morals and thrift and industry" (158, 159). They are racists who insist that Clare perform menial labor because of her tainted "Negro blood" (158). They forbid Clare to mention her racial background. In short, they epitomize Victorian racism and hypocrisy. Larsen's critical depiction of Clare's aunts situates the book as promoting modernist values.

We next turn to Irene. I make a list on the board of all the things that Irene evades: her attraction to Clare, her dislike of her husband, her discomfort with marital sexuality, her desire to control others, risk and danger in any form, and, perhaps most significantly, the effects of American racism. We note Irene's pride in her "outward sinking of self"—that is, her false self-image as self-sacrificing (193). In reality, Irene prevents Brian from escaping the "monotony" that he hates and works to keep Brian's discontent with United States racism "smothered" (190, 188). We also look at Irene's struggles to keep her children "free from the knowledge" of sexuality and racial violence (231).

Irene's character makes perfect sense in the light of an article the class reads earlier in the semester, Christina Simmons's "Modern Sexuality and the Myth of Victorian Repression." Simmons provides a critical analysis of the 1920s sexual revolution. She explains that young women of the 1920s had been raised with the Victorian belief that their role was to uplift morality, in part by controlling their husbands' sexuality. They entered adulthood at a time of changing norms, when female sexual "prudery" and control within marriage were attacked as outdated and even pathological. Sexual modernist values were expressed in three new, negative images: the independent career woman, the controlling wife, and the lesbian. All were denigrated because they sexually withdrew from men. Only the flapper was valued—the sexually available woman who became a dutiful and sexually compliant wife.

Irene's self-image as self-denying, her desire to control and "protect" her husband and children, and her sexual withholding from Brian all mark her as the 1920s modernist stereotype of the prudish, controlling wife (189). Understanding Irene in the light of "Modern Sexuality and the Myth of Victorian Repression" also casts Irene more sympathetically, however, since Simmons shows that the 1920s lauding of sexually charged marriages pressured women to cater to men sexually while undercutting their previous status as guardians of morality.

We then look at the characters' names, starting with Irene ('Rene) Westover Redfield. Why the name 'Rene? 'Rene looks and sounds like *rein*, or "the ability to control." 'Rene is also close to *reign*, "to rule." Both meanings fit 'Rene's character. And if one wants to push it, there are also French words that sound like 'Rene: *rien* ("nothing") and *reine* ("queen"). Is she a queen who has become nothing, or the reverse?

What about her maiden and married names, Westover and Redfield? Did 'Rene come "over west" to a "bloody" ("red") land? The students assume this means that 'Rene's ancestors came from Africa, west over the Atlantic to the red field / blood-soaked land of the United States. Maybe there she was a queen and here she is nothing. I point out that given 'Rene's light complexion, some of her ancestors came west, over to a violent new land, from Europe.

We turn next to Clare Kendry Bellew. The students identify the name Clare as "light" and "clarity" and Kendry as "kin" or "kindred." Clare's "kin," like 'Rene's, are both black and white, but only Clare acknowledges this fact. Her husband is named Bellew, as in "bellows" (invoking hot air, inflaming fires), "bellow" ("roaring," "shouting"), and "below" (with its attendant sense of "lower")—all appropriate for a ranting racist.

Our discussion of Clare's character is usually contentious, but we agree that she's 'Rene's opposite. She is more open about her desire for 'Rene. She is flirty and sexually provocative with men as well as women. She embraces risk and danger and does not claim to be self-sacrificing. She even makes the radical statement (for a woman) that "[c]hildren aren't everything" (210). Clare rejects the loyalty to "race" that 'Rene claims to possess and instead fights racist restrictions by passing. Yet Clare still feels emotionally drawn to black people. Far from denying racism's existence, as 'Rene does, Clare pushes her husband to express his racist ideas in front of 'Rene and Gertrude.

The students are often critical of Clare, judging her to be a sexy, selfish woman, but I push the students to consider all sides. They know from Simmons's essay that sexually self-possessed women were denigrated in the 1920s. Should we join in that condemnation? Clare admits that she lacks Irene's "proper morals or sense of duty," but we've already seen that 'Rene's "sense of duty" and "morals" are mostly a cover for her anger and denial (210). Is Clare's lack of duty necessarily a bad thing? 'Rene recalls that as a child, Clare risked her father's wrath by saving some of her own earnings to purchase material for a dress. Is this behavior selfish, or is it an example of the courage and drive that many Americans value? Clare describes herself as someone who "wanted things" (159), and 'Rene describes Clare's "having" nature three times (153, 174, 210). Given the context of the rampant consumer culture of the 1920s, the students see that this makes Clare a typical American.

I point them to the line where Clare explains that she wanted "to be a person and not a charity or a problem" (159). This line echoes a section of Anzia Yezierska's "How I Found America," a short story that the students read earlier in the semester. Yezierska describes the experiences of an immigrant who hoped that America would give her a life of intellectual and personal freedom but who instead found bigotry and soul-killing work conditions. In one section, Yezierska vehemently rejects "charity" and insists, "I came to America to make from myself a person" (123, 115). This positions Clare's desires for "personhood" and independence as larger, widely shared American values. Finally, 'Rene notices that Clare was "capable of heights and depths of feeling that she, Irene Redfield, had never known" (195). The students know that while Victorians valued self-control, modernists valued "heights and depths of feeling" as expressions of authentic selfhood. If we favor modernist over Victorian outlooks, should we favor Clare over 'Rene?

The question of Clare's "having" nature leads to the issue of economics, and to John Bellew. They see that John Bellew, Mr. Hot Air, is a racist who is, not surprisingly, completely ignorant of actual black people. The students usually remember that Bellew is an "international banking agent" who "turned up from South America with untold gold" (166, 159). Thus the wealth that Bellew shares with Clare was appropriated from what he calls "the niggers" in South America (173). I remind them that this is the same South America where Brian Redfield imagines he can escape American racism. Bellew's "work" of draining "gold" from South America, however, suggests that racism can't be so easily escaped, given the "international banking" system that profits from it.

We then move to a discussion of Brian Redfield and his links to various races or nations. Redfield sees the United States as a bloody land, a "hellish place" where blacks are hated, feared, and lynched. He wants to escape to Brazil. He feels similarly connected to Haiti, since he decorates his upscale Harlem home with a "marvelous" but "hideous" object (perhaps a mask or religious object) that he obtained there (232, 218). Yet for all his affiliation with nations that he imagines as black, Brian is also connected to the whites of the southern United States.

I remind the students that Brian's link to southern whites is described through an object—the teacup that Irene shatters at her party. Irene explains to her friend Hugh Wentworth that the broken cup was the "ugliest thing" ever owned by the "charming Confederates," and that it belonged to "Brian's great-great-grand uncle" (221, 222). Thus we learn that Brian, like many African Americans, is partially descended from southern whites. Irene tells Wentworth that she hated the ugly cup—and, we assume, the "hoary history" of slavery and racism that its existence in her family implies—but only now realized that "I had only to break it and I was rid of it for ever" (222). But can the United States be free of its "hoary history" simply by casting it aside? The description of the cup itself—which shatters into "white fragments" and "dark stains"—implies not (221).

Irene also identifies these same "charming Confederates" as "ancestors" of Hugh Wentworth, a sophisticated white writer who attends black parties (222). Thus Redfield and Wentworth are "kindred." Wentworth is another signifying name—one whose "worth" has "went," or passed. I remind the students that Clare describes Wentworth as a cynic who "despised everything and everybody" (198). When I ask the students what writers we've read that fit this description, they easily identify Schuyler, and also H. L. Mencken, whom we read earlier in the semester. Mencken's caustic essay "On Being an American" mocked Americans as provincial bigots and ignorant hustlers. Is Larsen implying that the savage, above-it-all attitude toward America's racism and provincialism that Mencken and Schuyler (and Brian Redfield, to some extent) express is now passé? That a new approach is needed?

I point out that Brian's dreams of escaping to Brazil, like Irene's dreams of protecting her son from "queer ideas" about sex by sending him to Europe (189), are part of a bigger web of connections—personal, ancestral, economic, cultural—that the novel draws between Europe, Africa, and the United States. The book's characters, "white" and "black," are actually mixed-race "kindred" (even Bellew has a "black" child). Even Brian admits this, referring to his Anglo compatriots as "so-called whites" (186). Brian and Irene Redfield, Clare and

John Bellew, and Hugh Wentworth also share economic and cultural connections to both Europe and "black" nations. Bellew extracts wealth from South America and practices business in Europe. Wentworth's very successful writings are drawn from his experiences living "on the edges of nowhere in at least three continents . . . in all kinds of savage places" (198). Clare acknowledges her black and white relatives, loves Harlem, but speaks in a "voice remotely suggesting England" (151).

This puts the novel in dialogue with the broader questioning of American identity typical of the early twentieth century. For example, *Passing* challenges modernists like Randolph Bourne. His radical essay on "Trans-national America," read earlier in the semester, encouraged Americans to break their slavish dependence on Britain and embrace a "cosmopolitan" culture that included the homelands of immigrants from all of Europe—but excluded any mention of Africa and South America. The students see that *Passing* instead reveals an American people, economy, and culture entwined not only with Europe, but with Africa, Brazil, and Haiti.

These complex relationships are not without violence. I read out loud one of the book's small, subtle images of violent white privilege. It occurs in the scene on the roof of the Drayton Hotel, when Irene observes Clare, whom she still believes is a white woman. She watches "the silver spoon in the white hand slit the dull gold" of a melon—an image of whiteness ("white hand"), privilege ("silver spoon"), and violent extraction of wealth ("slit . . . the gold") (149).

From here, we move on to another character with a signifying name: Felice Freeland. Ms. Happy Free Land shows up at moments in the narrative when truths are revealed. She's at the tea party where Irene concludes that Brian is in love with Clare. She's arm in arm with Irene when Irene encounters Bellew on the street, thus enabling Bellew to recognize that Irene is "black." Bellew's final, fatal confrontation with Clare occurs at her home. Felice is described as having "[l]ooks and brains" (216). Her color is "golden" (226), and, fittingly enough, she loves to shop (seeing Irene depressed, she advises her to "buy yourself an expensive new frock" [219]). I push the students to consider why the novel would associate this character with a "free land." Is the novel making a sarcastic comment on "freedom" as freedom to consume? Or is it arguing that a happy free land is one in which those with "looks and brains," and those who know the truth, can be "golden" and thereby partake of the free land's abundance?

The final character we discuss is a minor one, Fred Martin. An ordinary man with an ordinary name, Martin is the "white" owner of a meat market. Fred is married to Gertrude, a light-skinned "black" woman. Irene is horrified by Gertrude's meaty appearance, but despite her snobbery, she finds that Gertrude's husband is a decent man. Fred Martin married Gertrude although he knew that she was "black." He didn't dream of having a son, as most men do—on the contrary, he wanted a daughter. He values all skin tones equally. As Gertrude observes, "he actually said he didn't care what colour [his child] turned out." Fred's indifference to racial and sexual hierarchies does not extend to religion—he pronounces an African American man who converts to Judaism "crazy" (168, 169). Still, Fred Martin seems to hint at the possibility of a new era in which racism and sexism no longer constrict the actions of the nation's common people.

To conclude, I bring the students back to the sentence I'd written on the board at the start of class: "If Clare was freed, anything might happen" (236). What is the "anything" that could happen if Clare was "freed"? Irene fears that Brian would leave their loveless marriage and go off with Clare, but the novel implies that if "Clare was freed," much more than a marriage would be overturned. Clare pursues the love of women and men alike. She values black people but refuses to be limited by racism. She is as indifferent to boundaries of age and class as she is to those of race: as Irene notes, Clare will just as happily visit with Irene's young sons or with her servants as with Irene herself (208). Clare feels deeply, takes risks, and will not sacrifice herself for her marriage or her children. If "Clare was freed," she would drop Bellew, the bellowing racist, and become Clare Kendry—that is, clarity about the kindred that Americans share across our obviously artificial racial boundaries. Irene's reflection is true. If such a woman could be "freed," a woman who refused containment by ideologies of race, class, gender, or sexuality, then, as Irene observes, "anything might happen. Anything" (236).

In the novel's conclusion, Clare is not "freed." Instead, the dizzying possibilities that she represents are snuffed out. We are left with 'Rene Westover Redfield. Instead of the uncertainties and transformations represented by Clare's freedom, we will have the "security" and deadly stasis that Irene craved to the point of being willing—in her fantasies if not in reality—to kill for it (235). Repression, control, and denial, as well as lovelessness, sexual hypocrisy, and quiet domestic misery, triumph over freedom. This, Larsen seems to imply, is 1920s America. As Larsen describes Irene, "She was an American. She grew from this soil, and she would not be uprooted" (235). It's a bitter yet radical vision of the limits of American freedom and the meaning of American identity, one every bit as harsh as Schuyler's yet far deeper in its critique.

Teaching *Passing* as a Lesbian Text

Suzanne Raitt

At the end of a semester teaching an upper-level course called Lesbian Literatures, I always ask students to talk about which texts they recommend keeping the next time I teach the course. They mostly love Virginia Woolf's *Orlando*; they usually dislike Radclyffe Hall's *The Well of Loneliness*, but they see why it should be in the course; and, almost to a person, they tell me I should drop *Passing*. It's not about lesbians, they complain; the lesbian interpretations we developed were far-fetched; the novel deals with racial passing, and not with passing as a heterosexual. In this essay, I explore several ways of teaching *Passing* in a course on lesbian literature and suggest some reasons for student dissatisfaction with it in such a context. Much of their resistance, I believe, grows out of their inexperience with and potential reluctance to accept the socially and culturally constructed nature of racial and sexual identities, or the ways in which such identities are mutually constitutive—what Kimberlé Crenshaw has called "intersectionality." In my Lesbian Literatures classroom, I encourage students to reflect on the historical and cultural contingency of identity categories and on the multivalence of literary writing. The ambiguous nature of much of the language of *Passing* encourages students to think about how their assumptions about the social and cultural configuration of race, sexuality, and gender shape not only the ways they read written and visual texts but also their own identities and their experience of the world around them. Perhaps it should go without saying that their resistance to reading *Passing* as a lesbian text has not deterred me from including it in the course. Rather, knowing how intensely students deny the novel's engagement with lesbian erotic experience has allowed me to experiment with different ways of using the book to help them question their habits of reading and of analysis.

Context in Lesbian Literary History

I teach Lesbian Literatures at a small research university with a liberal arts focus. Lesbian Literatures is an upper-level course in English, cross-listed with women's studies and often with literary and cultural studies, with a maximum of thirty students, most of whom are white, and several of whom usually openly identify as lesbian, gay, bisexual, or queer. The course is organized chronologically, so that students develop a sense of the historical evolution of contexts and languages for lesbian identities and experiences in Britain and the United States. Students usually encounter *Passing* about halfway through the semester, after they have read selections from the work of the seventeenth-century poet Katherine Phillips, the eighteenth-century novelist Sarah Scott, the Victorian writers Christina Rossetti and Sheridan Lefanu, and the critics Martha Vicinus,

Judith Butler, and Sue O'Sullivan. Immediately before reading *Passing*, students study Hall's classic lesbian tragedy *The Well of Loneliness* and Woolf's fantasy biography of her lesbian lover Vita Sackville-West, *Orlando*.

Students are prepared to read *Passing* in the sessions that precede our study of the novel by discussion of how literary texts sometimes anchor their representations of lesbian experience in an essentialist, usually masculinized, version of what a "lesbian" is, and how they sometimes use imaginative language to release lesbianism from the constraints of definition altogether. *The Well of Loneliness* is an example of the first strategy. Students learn about the "congenital invert" by reading and discussing excerpts from Carl von Westphal, a German doctor, who wrote a case study in 1869 about Fraulein N., a woman who dressed as a man and felt attracted to women (qtd. in Zimmerman 102–03); Karl Heinrich Ulrichs, a German lawyer, who wrote of gay men being "women trapped in men's bodies" and who worked to liberalize the German antisodomy laws in the 1860s (Zimmerman 688); Richard von Krafft-Ebing's *Psychopathia Sexualis*, which describes homosexuality as an "inherited diseased condition of the central nervous system" (Zimmerman 331); and Havelock Ellis's magisterial *Sexual Inversion*, which notes that "[t]he commonest characteristic of the sexually inverted woman is a certain degree of masculinity or boyishness" (Ellis and Symonds 94). Havelock Ellis wrote a brief foreword to the first edition of *The Well of Loneliness*, and its central character, Stephen Gordon, fits Ellis's description of the inverted woman almost exactly. *The Well of Loneliness* is thus rooted in the new science of sexology, dramatizing its theories of lesbian sexuality as a function of gender identity.

However, there is one character in the novel whose desire confounds such an easy correlation between masculinity and attraction to women, and students are always attracted to the ways in which she slips beneath the radar in most readings of the book. Mary, Stephen's devoted wife, is ultrafeminine, but nonetheless she has overwhelming and passionate sexual feelings for Stephen. The book resolves with her seeking solace in the arms of a man after Stephen pretends to betray her in order to save her from her tragic life as the wife of an invert. Mary's desire is apparently aroused by masculinity whether it inheres in the body of a woman or of a man, but the novel is uninterested in the complexities of this anomalous, more fluid configuration of erotic feeling. However, Mary is a useful context for discussion of *Passing*, since she is an example of someone who could and sometimes does "pass" in the sexual sense. Her confusing presence in a novel that is apparently so confident about its own explanatory paradigms inadvertently reveals some of the shortcomings of identity politics, shortcomings that are at the center of *Passing*'s interrogation of racial and sexual identities.

Identity politics are also challenged in the next book the students read, *Orlando*. Its central character, based on Woolf's lesbian lover Sackville-West, lives for over three hundred years and changes sex from male to female at the beginning of the eighteenth century. Students learn about the biographical context of the novel in the relationship between the two women and about the place of the novel in the literary history of biography. They view slides of some of the more resonant passages in Virginia Woolf's diaries and letters while she is working on *Orlando*, observing that Woolf never identified herself as lesbian. She was wary even of attaching the label to Sackville-West, who was a well-known lesbian. Woolf, however, preferred to revel in the linguistic possibilities opened up by her lover's erotic splendor: "I like her & being with her, & the splendour—she shines in the grocers shop in Sevenoaks with a candle lit radiance, stalking on legs like beech trees, pink glowing, grape clustered, pearl hung." Woolf saw no contradiction between Sackville-West's womanliness and her attraction to other women: she described her in her diary as "what I have never been, a real woman" (*Diary* 52) while still recognizing her as a "Sapphist" (51). After her sex change, Orlando, though biologically female, is an androgynous figure, frequently cross-dressing and retaining the attraction to women she felt as a man: "She was man; she was woman; she knew the secrets, shared the weaknesses of each" (Woolf, *Orlando* 117); "as all Orlando's loves had been women, now, through the culpable laggardry of the human frame to adapt itself to convention, it was still a woman she loved" (119). Thus *Orlando*, even while it recalls sexological theories of sexual inversion in locating the origins of lesbian eroticism in a heterosexual encounter, also undermines their assumptions, reflecting on the tenuous relation between gender and sexuality and on the fluidity of identity. The question of the legibility of identity is at the center of both *Orlando* and *Passing*.

Editions and Critical Contexts

Since 2007, when it was published, I have used the Norton Critical Edition of *Passing* edited by Carla Kaplan in my course. I do not require students to read the supporting materials in the volume, but I do on occasion cite them to support a particular interpretation, and I encourage students to browse through any critical articles or other texts that interest them in the second half of the volume.

Interracial and Same-Sex Marriage

Because *Passing* is a relatively short novel, I usually spend only one week (two class sessions) on it. During the first session, I present a brief lecture-style set of remarks, based on a series of *PowerPoint* slides, to frame our study of the text. In my lecture, I focus on the broader context of the issues raised in the novel and allow students to develop their own specific literary-critical readings of the text itself in the discussions that follow my remarks.

I have found it most useful in the contemporary context to start by outlining the history of the miscegenation laws in the United States and encouraging students to compare the legal and social histories of interracial and same-sex marriage in the United States today. I focus on marriage for two reasons: first, because in *Passing*, interracial marriage is key to Clare Kendry's vulnerability as a passing black woman married to a racist white man and, second, because discussion of marriage in *Passing* can frame a discussion of how lesbian or bisexual women can pass for heterosexual in the context of marriage to a man. Comparing the histories of interracial and same-sex marriage in this country pushes students to think about the specific terms in which discrimination is debated in American culture, allowing them to reflect on the similarities and also the differences between the civil rights and the LGBTQ rights movements. For example, I ask them why interracial marriage has been legal in all fifty states since 1967, whereas same-sex marriage was not federally recognized until 2015.

I open with a slide documenting the gradual passage of miscegenation laws in the majority of American states, giving specific information about Virginia, the state in which I currently teach.[1] Students learn that the first American miscegenation law was passed in Virginia in 1661, that in 1924 the Racial Integrity Law in Virginia made it illegal for a white person to marry anyone with "a single drop of Negro blood," that by the 1920s marriage between whites and blacks was illegal in thirty-eight states, and that by the 1950s many miscegenation laws had been extended to include marriage between whites and a range of ethnic groups, including Mongolians, Malayans, and Native Americans. I then discuss the specific states relevant to *Passing*: Illinois, where Clare and Irene grew up, and New York, where they are living at the time of the action of the novel. Students learn that New York never enacted a miscegenation law and that Illinois enacted laws in 1829 banning whites and blacks from marrying and repealed them in 1874. At the time of writing, then, Larsen and her characters are living in states in which whites and blacks are free to marry. Clare's peril comes not from her legal situation but from ingrained attitudes and feelings; the novel is about prejudice, not about civil rights.

Partly because, as I have noted, I teach in Virginia, I then spend some time on *Loving v. Virginia* (1967) and the subsequent nullification of the miscegenation laws that were still on the books in sixteen American states (most states repealed their laws during the 1950s and early 1960s). I show slides of Mildred Jeter and Richard Loving, who married in Washington, DC, and were arrested at their home in Virginia in 1967. Chief Justice Earl Warren wrote in the Court's decision: "Under our Constitution, the freedom to marry or not marry a person of another race resides with the individual and cannot be infringed upon by the State" (*Loving v. Virginia*). Discussion of this opinion usually leads to a discussion of the terms of the same-sex marriage debate and of why race has been treated differently from sexual orientation in the marriage laws of so many American states.

Contemporary Cases of Racial Passing

My remarks on interracial and same-sex marriage are usually followed by a series of slides and comments on two famous contemporary cases of racial passing, at least one of which was certainly on Nella Larsen's mind while she was writing *Passing*. My aim in introducing students to some of the specifics of the history of racial passing in the United States is both to encourage them to understand the severity of the consequences of being exposed as a passer in the late nineteenth and early twentieth century in the United States and to invite them to reflect on the historical and contemporary instability of markers of racial identity in our culture. An understanding of this instability allows students to make a connection between women's sexual passing (where a woman adopts a heterosexual identity despite her sexual attraction to women) and their racial passing (where a woman of color adopts an identity as white). Questions of intent and consciousness inevitably come up during this discussion. If a white woman does not know she is black (for example, if she has black ancestry of which she is unaware), can she still be said to be "passing" as white? If a woman who thinks of herself as heterosexual finds herself attracted to another woman, is she now "passing" as straight? If she never consciously acknowledges her lesbian feelings, how might we describe her sexual identity? Students talk about the peculiar qualities of literary writing, which allows an author to manipulate narrative voice to intimate that a character has feelings but lacks language to describe them.

The two case histories I use to frame this discussion are the story of Anita Hemmings, who was revealed to be black a few weeks before she was due to graduate from all-white Vassar College in 1897 (Mancini; Perkins; Sim), and the *Rhinelander* case, an unsuccessful but heavily publicized lawsuit filed by Leonard Kip Rhinelander in 1924 in which he accused his wife of deceiving him about her African American identity (Madigan; Thaggert). Students view slides of Anita Hemmings and associated images and learn that she was admitted to Vassar College in 1893, that in 1897 her roommate's grandfather hired a private investigator to look into her family background and discovered that her parents were interracial, and that Anita Hemmings appealed her dismissal from Vassar and was allowed to keep her diploma but not to participate in graduation ceremonies. In 1903 Hemmings married Andrew Love, an African American physician, and moved to Manhattan, where the couple successfully passed as white. Their daughter, Ellen Love, did not learn about her ancestry until she met her grandmother for the first time in 1923. She never told anyone, including her own daughter, Jillian Sim, about the meeting, and Sim did not discover that her grandparents were African American until 1994.

The *Rhinelander* case is specifically referred to briefly in *Passing* (228) when Irene, fearful that her husband and Clare are having an affair, starts to worry that if Bellew finds out that Clare is only passing as white, he will divorce her. Leonard Kip Rhinelander, who had married his African American maid, Alice Jones, in October 1924, filed a suit for annulment a month later, claiming that he had married her thinking she was white and that she had lied to him about her racial identity (he alleged that she told him her father was Cuban). The case dragged on for a year and involved Alice Jones in numerous humiliations, including being forced to remove some of her clothes in the jury room so that members of the jury could decide for themselves whether Rhinelander's claim that he thought she was white was credible. In 1925 the New York State Supreme Court finally ruled that Alice had never deceived her husband as to her race. Alice filed for separation in 1927 on grounds of desertion and cruelty.

I follow these painful accounts of the dangers of passing with some slides and discussion of contemporary environments in which interracial social relationships were viewed more positively, telling students a little about Larsen's involvement with the Harlem Renaissance and about the interracial gatherings hosted by Carl Van Vechten and his wife, Fania Marinoff, which Larsen attended.

In-Depth Discussion of Specific Passages and Themes

Passing is full of highly suggestive language describing Irene's obsession with Clare's beauty and her longing for her: "the woman . . . had for her a fascination, strange and compelling" (161); "What was it about Clare's voice that was so appealing, so very seductive?" (165); and so on. Toward the end, the novel opens up the possibility that Irene displaces her erotic feelings onto a fantasy that Clare is sexually involved with Irene's husband, Brian. I open our discussion of three key passages in the text (the first chapter, the encounter between Clare and Irene in the Drayton Hotel, and the tea party at Clare's house with Gertrude) by drawing students' attention to the erotic and obsessive nature of Irene's feelings about Clare.

In discussing the opening chapter, students respond to the intensity of Irene's reaction to the "mysterious," "furtive" letter Clare sends her (143) and to the passionate language of the letter itself. What expectations does the opening set up in the reader? Close reading of the vignette of Clare as a girl sewing her frock on the sofa (143–44) reveals the ambivalent nature of the narrator's perspective on Clare, who is treated with tenderness and compassion as well as with exasperation. This oscillation in the narrator's feelings echoes Irene's confusion about how to feel about Clare.

Discussion of the Drayton Hotel episode in chapter 2 explores Irene's narcissistic identification with and repudiation of Clare's actions. Students analyze the complex erotic dynamics of passages such as this one:

> Her lips, painted a brilliant geranium-red, were sweet and sensitive and a little obstinate. A tempting mouth. The face across the forehead and cheeks was a trifle too wide, but the ivory skin had a peculiar soft lustre. And the eyes were magnificent! dark, sometimes absolutely black, always

> luminous, and set in long, black lashes. Arresting eyes, slow and mesmeric, and with, for all their warmth, something withdrawn and secret about them.
>
> Ah! Surely! They were Negro eyes! Mysterious and concealing. And set in that ivory face under that bright hair, there was about them something exotic. (161)[2]

The free indirect style here suggests that these are Irene's thoughts as her gaze moves slowly over Clare's face. Clare's blackness is revealed bit by bit, and as it is revealed the atmosphere of exoticism and mystery associated with her intensifies: first the "ivory" skin, then the "absolutely black" eyes, and finally the discovery: "they were Negro eyes!" Students talk about whether Irene is attracted to or discomfited by Clare's feminine beauty or her blackness or both, explore the distancing effect of words such as "exotic" and "mysterious" to describe Clare's blackness, and reflect on the interpellated reader in the passage and think about whether the reader is asked to identify with Irene as a passing woman: is the reader experiencing herself or himself as white or black? heterosexual or lesbian/gay? Does it matter?

Conversation about the tea party episode (165–76) centers on Irene's disgust at Gertrude's appearance and explores whether Irene's repudiation of Gertrude is linked to her knowledge that Gertrude—described as "white" (167)—identifies as African American and to her jealousy at Clare's friendship with Gertrude. The complex social and erotic dynamics between the three women are intensified by the arrival of Clare's husband and Irene's rage and mortification at his racist remarks. Forced to pass as white, Irene notices a "look for which she could find no name" on Clare's face as she says good-bye and feels a "recrudescence of . . . fear" (176), perhaps at the idea of what she herself is capable of. Indeed, one of the ironies of the novel, as Jennifer DeVere Brody points out, is that on occasion—for example, in the taxi on the way to the Drayton—Irene herself passes easily and without a second thought (Brody). Irene's sense of transgression and danger in visiting Clare can be linked to violation of both racial *and* erotic norms, so that the "passing" of the title takes on an ambiguity that is never fully resolved in the novel. Unknowingly echoing the conclusions of Deborah E. McDowell, one of my students once remarked that *Passing* itself passes as a novel about race, when in fact it is about the hidden lives of lesbians.

After the close reading exercise is over, students form small groups to identify key moments in the book that relate to Irene's marriage. They then return to the full group to share and reflect on what they have found. During this exercise, students always comment on the distance between Irene and Brian and his contempt for her, as well as on his desire to escape his marriage and what the novel calls his "queer, unhappy, restlessness" (178). Irene's craving for security—"to her, security was the most important and desired thing in life" (235)—is an implicit acknowledgment that identity can never be secure, that people are frequently not what they seem, and that the price of taking advantage of the ambiguous status of one's own identity is a sense of "impermanence" (229) that Irene finds both alluring and unbearable.

The Ending

The ending of *Passing* is notoriously ambiguous. Readers who believe that Clare committed suicide or was pushed by Bellew probably see her story as continuing the tradition of the "tragic mulatto." Readers who think that Irene pushed her are likely to view Irene's sexual turmoil—whether over her attraction to Clare, her sexual jealousy of Clare, or both—as central to the dynamics of the text. Or they may see Irene herself as the "tragic mulatto," increasingly uncomfortable with the ways in which she has chosen to live out her racial identity, and perhaps revealing of Larsen's own ambivalence (Washington). Readers who see Clare's death as an accident may feel that the novel deliberately holds open a range of possible interpretations of its central themes, as may readers who feel that the cause of Clare's death is deliberately left unresolved.

To encourage students to explore all these different ways of reading the final pages of the novel, I ask them to stage either a debate over the ending or a mock trial of Irene. In the debate, different teams represent different readings of the ending (Clare killed herself, Bellew killed her, Irene killed her on purpose or by accident, etc.) and quote passages from the novel as evidence for their interpretations. In the mock trial, I play Irene, on trial for the murder of Clare, and the students divide themselves into a prosecution group and a defense group. They take it in turns to present their evidence (in the form of quotations from the texts) and to question me. I respond in character, using quotations to support my answers. Eventually, the class forms a jury, deliberates, and votes on my guilt. We then discuss the implications of our decision as a class for our reading of the text, along the lines I have suggested above.

The final exercise (debate or trial) forces us to address the possibility that the text is deliberately ambiguous about the nature of Irene's attraction to Clare. In the course as a whole, we talk at length about available languages for lesbian desire in different historical and cultural contexts, and we allow for the possibility of coded or censored languages of love. During our discussions, I often emphasize the relatively open nature of Harlem Renaissance society and the number of lesbian or bisexual women associated with it (McDowell). This helps students understand that Nella Larsen moved in a world in which lesbianism was visible and somewhat accepted. But students are still often very resistant to the idea that Larsen is encouraging her readers to imagine an attraction between Irene and Clare based not just on their race but also on their shared femaleness. I believe this resistance is in part a resistance to the qualities of literary language itself: its capacity to hold open a number of different readings simultaneously, to allow *Passing* to be more than one text at once. Students' discomfort at this lack of fixity is related to the broader questions engaged in the novel and in our course about the fluidity of racial and sexual identities, which can also be unresolved for a lifetime and even beyond. I often point toward Claudia Tate's defense of her refusal to adopt any single reading of the ending as a way to help students accept their own uncertainties.

If I can encourage them to see the connections between their anxieties and the anxieties so painfully explored in the novel, I feel I have done my duty as a teacher. A text that invites readers into the longings of one woman for another is inevitably unsettling for a number of students, even those enrolled in a Lesbian Literatures course; one that engages their discomfort about race at the same time is even more troubling—and this goes for students who are lesbian or heterosexual, white or people of color. My role in the classroom is to provide a safe space in which they can learn to articulate both their pleasures and their anxieties as readers and to understand that those pleasures and anxieties have a long and painful history in American culture and society.

NOTES

[1] Information in the lecture comes from Pascoe.

[2] Cheryl A. Wall, in *Women of the Harlem Renaissance*, has written most persuasively about this passage (361).

Approaching Gender in *Quicksand*

Beth Widmaier Capo

Nella Larsen's novel *Quicksand* is an ideal place for undergraduates to examine how the social construction of femininity is shaped by race and class. Complex classroom discussions can evolve from examining appearance, behavior, sexuality, relationships, and identity as gendered constructions when race, class, and sex constrict and occasionally empower the protagonist of the novel, Helga Crane, and other female characters.

I have primarily taught the text in upper-level undergraduate literature seminars cross-listed with gender and women's studies. The text can be covered in a week, although more time may be allotted depending on the level and class size. At my small, private liberal arts college with a primarily white Midwestern student demographic, white female students dominate in literature courses. As a white feminist college professor, I foreground the importance of our own raced, gendered, and classed positions to literary analysis before discussing the text. Reminding students that our experiences, physical and intellectual, are grounded in our bodies and situated in social systems that determine meaning and experience helps students identify with authors/protagonists different from them while discouraging readings as strictly representational (as in, "Well, I'm not a mixed-race woman so I have nothing in common with Helga Crane" or "Helga Crane represents all mixed-race women").

Quicksand raises critical questions about the social construction of gender and the intersection of gender, race, and class, thus making a feminist theoretical approach ideal. To establish the focus on gender, I preface our discussion of the text with an overview of feminist theory. Although our literature students have *The Bedford Glossary of Critical and Literary Terms* (Murfin and Ray), its overview of the development of feminist theory is less useful in understanding how theory is used to approach a text. "Using Concepts from Feminist Theory to Understand Literature," chapter 6 of Lois Tyson's *Using Critical Theory: How to Read and Write about Literature*, provides an excellent explanation of feminist theory and its basic concepts while providing example analyses in clear and direct language. We can take as a starting point to *Quicksand* Tyson's explanation that "[f]eminist theory asks us to examine . . . the ways in which our personal identity is formed by our culture's definitions of what it means to be a man or a woman" (139). Once students understand key terms (e.g., patriarchy, gender, sex, sexuality, and intersectionality), we can identify the use of gender in the text as it delineates how patriarchal ideology shapes identity development. Explicitly articulating the theoretical approach provides undergraduates a stronger sense of English as a discipline and the various approaches available to them.

Gender, as the socially constructed traits appropriate to masculinity or femininity, is always historically and culturally contextual. Since students must understand that appropriate appearance and behavior denoting femininity change over time, it is important to briefly contextualize *Quicksand.* Students can be assigned brief biographical presentations on Larsen, on the Harlem Renaissance, and on topics such as the "modern girl," black clubwomen, or eugenics and birth control. For instance, Larsen confronts readers with the inevitable result of female sexuality without legal contraception (Capo 76, 102). Students could investigate the American birth control movement under Margaret Sanger, W. E. B. Du Bois's and the NAACP's support for the Harlem Clinic in 1930, and eugenic theory within both the birth control movement and "talented tenth" philosophy. Excellent resources are plentiful, including online access to the Margaret Sanger Papers Project and the Image Archive of the American Eugenics Movement, as well as historical and literary scholarship (see English, *Unnatural Selections*; Hart; McCann).

Successful pedagogy gives students guidance on sources and encourages them to go beyond facts to explore significance (Why? So what?) while they are empowered by sharing their "expert" knowledge with classmates. Reports can be staggered throughout the class periods assigned to the text. Deborah E. McDowell's introduction to the Rutgers edition of *Quicksand* is an excellent resource for this assignment. The purpose of this assignment is to engage students with background material and to consider how novels are cultural artifacts revealing social attitudes. For instance, they discover the congruities between Larsen's biography and her protagonist, Helga Crane.

From its opening, *Quicksand* lends itself to reading for gender. The first paragraph luxuriates in the material details of Helga's domestic surroundings at Naxos, followed by a paragraph literally fleshing out her attractive physical form. Aesthetics are foregrounded, as is the importance of materiality for Helga and for her social gendering. What do these details, of color, clothing, decoration, and appreciation for beauty, tell us about the character of Helga? How is she judged by others based on her physical appearance? Does this reflect the symbolic iconography of the female body in the Western tradition? How does it shape reader expectations? Do we still have gendered stereotypes about women and shopping? about physical appearance and moral value? The focus on her fragmented body and surface appearance are reinforced by a lack of narrative interiority that sets the reader's position as voyeur (Barnett 581–82). The narrative's structure provides repeated opportunities for students to identify how a gendered identity is constructed and shaped by race and class. For instance, at Naxos Helga's love of bright colors is inappropriate for the "machine" that "tolerated no innovations, no individualisms" (Quicksand *and* Passing 4 [1994]) but rather enforced a form of "good taste" that "knew enough to stay in their places" (3), like plain and proper Miss MacGooden. But Helga "could neither conform, nor be happy in her nonconformity" (7). It is her appearance that introduces us to the gendered bind. Her body also performs according to gender stereotypes, displaying weakness. (Following Tanner, instructors can point to passages showing Helga's body as swaying [*Quicksand* 8, 105], dizzy [115], shivering [24,

27], shuddering [23], trembling [21, 28], shaking [29], quivering [28, 39, 49], or faint [8, 49, 123]). This can be contrasted to other female characters, the unattractive Miss MacGooden, the unkempt bulk of Mrs. Hayes-Rore, and the hard strength of Clementine Richards, to encourage discussion of gender roles.

Helga is judged by her outward appearance in each location she inhabits, and she constantly struggles against the limitations of those categories. A compelling comparison can be made between her episode at Naxos and her time in Denmark, where her love of beauty is indulged by relatives who decorate her body for their own social gain. Helga's attractive youth and dark skin are emphasized to objectify her as an exotic, sexual primitive. She is aware of being stared at as "exotic" (68, 70), "savage" (69, 70), like a "foreigner" (68), "pet dog" (70), "curiosity," "stunt" (71), "decoration," "curio," and "peacock" (73). She is prized as a sexual object, which is made clear by Axel Olsen's portrait of her: he contends that it is "the true Helga Crane," while she can only see "some disgusting sensual creature with her features" (88, 89). The servant calls it "wicked," voicing the way overt female sexuality is judged. For all their beauty, the colorful low-cut dresses sexualize Helga at the expense of subjectivity. Indeed, Axel's offer of marriage comes mixed with his statement that she has "the soul of a prostitute" (87). If at Naxos the appropriate gender role was virgin/lady, here she is "whore." Indeed, Larsen repeatedly shows the limited options for women: Helga is mistaken for a prostitute when walking in Chicago (29, 34), and she is called a "scarlet 'oman" and "pore los' Jezebel" after entering a storefront church in a later scene (112). A focus on gender initiates discussion of this (hetero)sexual double bind, as well as the female body as commodity in both prostitution and marriage.

These scenes also establish the gendered limitations for occupation. How are Helga's choices and behaviors constrained by society's rules for gender, race, and class? Her love of material goods is often confounded by lack of independent wealth and available jobs. Helga begins as a teacher, a respectable job for a single, educated woman, but she works at a school where education reinforces racial subservience. In Chicago, she is too well-educated to do the domestic work assigned to other black women, but her lack of references precludes her from the few professional jobs available. Her employment as "traveling companion" to Mrs. Hayes-Rore, who is eminently respectable yet in her description much less classy than poor Helga (35, 38), leads to work for a black-owned insurance company in New York. But none of these positions provide Helga with a sense of fulfillment or identity. In Denmark, her job is to be admired by men as a possible wife, and, after returning to America, she marries and becomes a preacher's wife in rural Alabama. It is important to remind students of Helga's advantages—education, beauty, wealthy friends—and the role of individual agency when discussing her "career" trajectory and the gendered appropriateness of her occupational options.

The novel's structure highlights Helga's pattern of brief periods of contentment followed by "growing dissatisfaction," "growing restlessness," and "discontent" that push her to flee to a new environment (81). Students often comment on this "annoying" pattern, this "flightiness." Do we judge Helga's instability through a gendered lens? That is, student readers often assess Helga's movement as volatility, a personal flaw. Would they read a male protagonist this way, or are they unconsciously slotting the character into the "feminine" role of hysteric? Students can empathize with Helga's plight when they identify the ways social expectations insistently limit her options by policing her behavior. Her instances of "flightiness" can then be read as attempts to escape social proscriptions, to use mobility as resistance and for the purpose of identity negotiation (Scheper 682). Each location expects conformity; Helga "tries on" these roles but finds nothing that fits. If the problem is not in Helga herself, can we identify it in society, widening the lens to make the "personal" more "political"? This search for self-definition in the face of conflicting messages can resonate with contemporary students.

What is at the root of Helga's discontent? Helga must come to terms with her sexuality in a culture that enforces the general dichotomy virgin/whore, as well as the further constraints of black middle-class clubwomen's crusade for social respectability opposing the legacy of slavery's sexualization of black female bodies. Her desirability can be both a powerful and destructive force. Helga first realizes her power over men with James Vayle: "[H]is mute helplessness against that ancient appeal by which she held him pleased her and fed her vanity—gave her a feeling of power. At the same time she shrank away from it, subtly aware of possibilities she herself couldn't predict" (8). Helga is frightened by the power of her desire and fights becoming a "jungle creature," the uncontrolled physical pleasure of immersing herself in music, dance, and bodies in the cabaret scene (59). She has internalized the sense that there is something "shameful" about such behavior, or of being too comfortable with her sex appeal, as Audrey Denney is. Anne, who serves as an alternative model of appropriate black femininity, is disgusted by Audrey's sensuality and her willingness to mix with white men. Already a widow, Anne marries Robert Anderson, modeling proper female behavior of sex within marriage and restrained elegance, with her "face of a golden Madonna" and manner of "queens" (45).

Helga struggles with the dichotomy of sexual "jungle creature" or desexualized "lady." When Robert Anderson, to whom she always felt an inchoate attraction, kisses her at a party, Helga's desires are ignited. Her dreams are filled with "uncontrolled fancies" as she relives the "ecstasy" of that kiss (105). Anderson's polite and proper rejection of her at a subsequent meeting crushes Helga. How can she be a woman and fulfill her desires? What will society allow? Marriage is the institution for sanctioning female sexuality, the only script Helga finds to understand her desires. Students are intrigued by the storefront church scene where Helga meets the Revered Mr. Pleasant Green. The scene's language approaches orgiastic tones, as Helga is first mistaken for a prostitute, then gives herself over to the uncontrolled religious fervor surrounding her. Why does she seduce Green, who is physically unattractive and unlike any of her previous suitors? Students often eagerly dissect the language of power: "How could he, a naïve creature like that, hold out against her?" (115). They debate what happened in that single night that would then induce their marriage, and they question how marrying Green, a preacher, doubly legitimates Helga's sexuality. Why does she "settle" for this unwashed, uneducated, unattractive man?

Marriage is an excellent topic for extended discussion, both for its role in *Quicksand* and for its larger role in heteronormative patriarchy. At earlier points in the narrative, Helga contemplates marriage in an economic rather than romantic sense, as a means to financial security:

> Some day she intended to marry one of those alluring brown or yellow men who danced attendance on her. Already financially successful, any one of them could give to her the things which she had now come to desire, a home like Anne's, cars of expensive makes such as lined the avenue, clothes and furs from Bendel's and Revillon Frères', servants, and leisure. (45)

When she breaks the engagement to James Vayle in an early chapter, she is aware of the loss of his family connections, and in Denmark her aunt and uncle encourage her to marry a man who will advance their own social strivings. But *Quicksand* offers the complication of race, both the specter of miscegenation and the psychological displacement it has generated in Helga. In Denmark, she rejects the idea of marriage to the white Olsen as representing a sale (87), but she also rejects the idea of marrying a black American because the result would produce children who would suffer in a racist society: "How stupid she had been ever to have thought that she could marry and perhaps have children in a land where every dark child was handicapped at the start by the shroud of color!" (75). After returning to New York from Denmark, she denigrates marriage with comments like "if a person wanted only to be married" and "if mere marriage is all one wants" (99, 98).

Why, then, marry Pleasant Green? By this point, students have tracked the narrative trajectory and Helga's geographic and psychological journeys, examining her bouts of compliance with and struggles against pervasive gender dictates. Students can see it as a "rebound" relationship after Anderson's rejection, as a sign of exhaustion ("It was a chance at stability, at permanent happiness" [117]), or as a calculated compromise to express sexuality within social boundaries. The decision is consistent with her pattern of quickly acting to escape growing discontent. She initially embraces her new position in Alabama as a preacher's wife:

> Every minute of the day was full. Necessarily. And to Helga this was a new experience. She was charmed by it. To be mistress in one's own house, to have a garden, and chickens, and a pig; to have a husband—and to be "right with God"—what pleasure did that other world which she had left contain that could surpass these? (120)

And yet, predictably, and despite the opiate of religion, Helga soon grows restless, a feeling compounded by a "sensation of shame that she should be less than content" when living what society says should fulfill her as a woman (125).

Helga tries on another sanctioned gender role, that of wife and mother (having passed through and discarded "young single teacher," "respectable bourgeois race woman," and "exotic eye candy"). As Helga says, "Marriage—that means children, to me" (103). In the space of a few pages, Helga is an exhausted young mother: "The children used her up. There were already three of them, all born within the short space of twenty months" (123). Students can examine the gendered objectification of Helga as an exotic sexualized other and, in the next class, her embodiment as a sexed and reproducing body. Without access to reliable birth control, Helga is quickly and repeatedly pregnant, leading to her physical and emotional exhaustion. Students can discuss the ideal formation of the "wife" and "mother" in conflict with the social forces shaping its impossibility. She loves her children but is not magically fulfilled, and she feels only relief when the newest baby dies (131). It is this final gender role from which Helga cannot flee. Any hope of escape is absent in the novel's final line, a metaphoric death sentence: "And hardly had she left her bed and become able to walk again without pain, hardly had the children returned from the homes of the neighbors, when she began to have her fifth child" (135).

The end of the novel is usually read as a tragedy. But why? And who is at fault? How are women complicit in maintaining gender norms? The tragedy Larsen presents goes beyond Helga to offer a social critique, a depiction of the unwinnable construction of gender. Helga has at times, at least briefly, tried to conform to gender expectations. She tries to "play the part" assigned to her in Denmark—for instance, dressing for attention while intentionally keeping her language ability low and not forming close relationships to maintain the aura of mystery that buoyed her social cachet, but at the expense of personal growth or relationships. When she does act on her sexual power to seduce Green, she wastes herself on an unworthy man, and her power is short-lived (124). At the novel's end, she recognizes her complicity in "the quagmire in which she had engulfed herself" (133). Her journey is not progressive, her actions not strategic, but how much agency does the individual have within prescriptive systems such as gender?

Examining *Quicksand* through a gendered lens leads to lively conversations about the text, about its characterization and narrative development, and about larger social issues. I encourage students to examine their reactions and to consider how those reactions are influenced by changing social expectations. Does the double bind of virgin/whore still apply to women today? How are women still defined by their appearance, and do they receive a mixed message that they must always appear desirable to men (heteronormativity remains)? Can we identify gender norms that we chafe at, are passive accomplices to, or actively support? Students who find Helga frustrating can be asked to consider the effects of Larsen's narrative choice of limited point of view, which denies access to interior thoughts and motivations—they can be asked to write and compare speculative diary entries or rants from her point of view, unpacking their assumptions. This is especially interesting in a class with both male and female students.

Focusing on gender and race may lead to uncomfortable moments in classrooms without much diversity. The single student of color in a recent seminar was a mixed-race woman who was very uncomfortable with discussions of Helga's sexuality, feeling as though other (white) students were looking at her throughout a discussion during which she remained silent. In predominantly homogeneous classrooms, it is necessary to preface discussions of texts by or featuring minorities (be they sexual, racial, or other minorities) with the reminder that no student can be a "spokesperson" for any group. There is no universal "female" or "male" experience, no correct "black" or "white" position. *Quicksand* reveals the socially constructed limitations of race and gender that students can apply to their own awareness of identity.

The novel also lends itself to comparisons surrounding the importance of gender roles and sexuality in other texts. For instance, in a course on Japanese and American modernism, I pair it with Jun'ichirō Tanizaki's *Naomi*; in modern American courses with Djuna Barnes's *Nightwood* and James Baldwin's *Giovanni's Room*; and in courses on women writers with Kate Chopin's *The Awakening* and Zora Neale Hurston's *Their Eyes Were Watching God*. Thematic discussion can be enriched with assignments such as the biographical and contextual reports discussed earlier or reports summarizing scholarly articles on the text. Helga's struggle to define herself as an individual is a struggle with and within gender norms. Students are often both unsettled by and engaged with the novel's depiction of the explicit limitations that gender, race, and class impose on the protagonist, and they are encouraged to consider the current forces impinging on their own identities.

From "My Old Man" to Race Men in *Quicksand*

Riché Richardson

Nella Larsen's novel *Quicksand* has been critically acknowledged as a groundbreaking work of the early twentieth century in part for its straightforward engagement of black women's sexuality.[1] The complex discourse on masculinity and femininity that the novel offers underscores its relevance for areas such as feminist studies and masculinity studies, making it a work germane to the broader field of gender studies. Yet *Quicksand*'s discourse on masculinity has typically been given short shrift from a critical standpoint and as a topic of teaching. Because the major transitions of the character Helga Crane in the novel are intimately tied to a series of male characters that catalyzes her movements in both national and transnational contexts, it seems important to scrutinize Larsen's thematic emphasis on masculinity in a bit more depth, beginning with men in Helga's family. Therefore, to supplement the teaching approaches to this novel that routinely emphasize feminine subjectivity, this essay reflects on a pedagogical approach related to masculinity. The teaching strategy that I outline frames male figures in Helga's family as a backdrop for pondering the male characters she later encounters, including James Vayle, Robert Anderson, Axel Olsen, and the Reverend Mr. Pleasant Green. This teaching approach clarifies Larsen's critique of the concept of the "race man" and highlights the marriage plot that frames all these encounters. Larsen delineates and critiques several types of masculine models in the novel, including white patriarchs and black "race men."

While whiteness was perceived to be the normative category of identification within the emergent critical scholarship on masculinity during the 1980s, the impact of race in constituting masculinity was emerging as a critical concern (e.g., Stecopoulos), to the point of bringing about "critical black masculinities" as a field of study. My own pedagogical perspective on this novel is grounded in this scholarship. In African American literature courses that I have developed at the graduate and undergraduate levels, I have often explored Nella Larsen's *Quicksand* by emphasizing masculinity, a strategy that also reinforces students' skills in close reading, along with their critical and theoretical understanding of masculinity as a topic.

For purposes of teaching, I suggest that the best starting point for a productive analysis of masculinity in *Quicksand* is with the men in Helga's family. The men in Helga's family are important to consider because they have a bearing on some of the earliest patterns of movement and migration that she experiences, which frame her later geographic movements that a range of other masculine figures in the novel also helps catalyze. For example, after being deserted by Helga's father in a Chicago slum, Helga's destitute mother escapes it with Helga, a mixed-race girl, by marrying a white man, who neglects Helga.

Helga's low sense of self-worth and feeling of having been unloved while growing up are linked to what the narrator describes as "the jealous, malicious hatred of her mother's husband" (23). Similarly, after her mother dies, Helga escapes from this situation when her Uncle Peter enrolls her in a school for blacks:

> Her rescue by Uncle Peter, who had sent her to school, a school for Negroes, where for the first time she could breathe freely, where she discovered that because one was dark, one was not necessarily loathsome, and could, therefore, consider oneself without repulsion. (23)

The "old man" mentioned in the epigraph to Larsen's novel, taken from Langston Hughes's poem "Cross," might even be identified for students as a symbolic figure who anticipates the deep-seated psychological impact of a range of male relatives on Helga's consciousness, beginning with her father. The passages of the novel that identify her father as a "gambler" and "gay suave scoundrel" (26) who deserted her Scandinavian mother also notably establish the groundwork for the theme of flight recurrently linked to Helga as a character. In analyzing her, it is additionally useful to acknowledge biographies of Larsen and critical perspectives that have linked the paternal background of fictive characters such as Helga Crane to the background of Larsen's own black and Caribbean father (T. Davis, *Nella Larsen*; C. Larson; Hutchinson, *In Search of Nella Larsen*). Moreover, it is worth mentioning that Helga's absent father is a figure who ironically recasts the situation typically described at the outset of many African American slave narratives in which slaves, who were often the offspring of white slave-master fathers and black mothers, expressed uncertainty about their paternity. Indeed, though she is a Chicago native and though her father is a black man, it is particularly significant that Helga registers this uncertainty about her background when she is in the southern United States, at Naxos, given the region's intimate links to the history of slavery. In this sense, her urgent migration to the North evokes the escape to "freedom" associated with this traumatic history.

However, in discussing the masculine contexts for the character Helga's development in the classroom, I point out for students that her Uncle Peter is the most ubiquitous masculine figure in her family background. In helping students understand the significance of male family members to her development, it is therefore useful to encourage them to reflect on Helga's relationship with her Uncle Peter and the assistance that he gives her at age fifteen when she loses her mother, his favorite sister. For while the novel most ostensibly critiques the white philanthropy that supports Naxos, a closer look at the financing of Helga's education by her wealthy white uncle through his patriarchal privilege will help students think about the levels of subjection that she experiences on the basis of race, gender, class, and sexuality.

In my focus on masculinity in teaching *Quicksand*, I also frame the paternalism foundational to Uncle Peter's interactions with Helga in relation to the "benevolent patriarch," a typology traceable to the system of antebellum slavery. Helga's sense of abandonment and rejection on the basis of her color is fully underscored by her Uncle Peter's new wife's callous assertion that he is not her uncle, which thrusts Helga out onto the brutal urban landscape in Chicago as a young woman. This moment not only recasts the "jealous mistress" motif of antebellum slave narratives but also links Helga to the trope of the "fallen woman" that had emerged in Victorian literature of the nineteenth century, a trope that resonates profoundly with the novel's use of quicksand as its overarching metaphor.

To develop the themes related to Uncle Peter's masculine construction as a benevolent patriarch further, I use close reading to explore additional textual evidence that frames him as a symbolic father for Helga in the novel. Helga's white mother and black father is a raced and gendered pairing that contradicts and in effect deconstructs that of white father / black mother, which the novel's epigraph (taken from the Hughes poem) emphasizes. However, a close reading of the letter from Uncle Peter that frames the tenth chapter helps students make the link between the mention of the "old man" in the epigraph and Uncle Peter's reference to his "old man's advice," which he shares in order to remind Helga not to make the same mistakes that her mother made, urging her to go abroad. Highlighting such continuities in the novel's prose makes the idea that Uncle Peter serves as a symbolic father for Helga more plausible. This exercise also allows students to examine more closely the diverse genres that shape the novel's rich narrative economy. In this vein, when considering the death motif of the epigraph ("my pa died in a fine big house"), it is significant, too, that the letter's envelope includes the money that her uncle had intended to bequeath her, culminating his role as her benefactor and his symbolic fatherhood. While his absence during the time of her aforementioned visit suggests to the audience that his new wife is the primary reason that he becomes alienated from Helga, this letter underscores his complicity with the cruel decision to cut off contact with her. His rejection is particularly hurtful when considering that, for Helga, he was "the one relative who thought kindly, or even calmly, of her" (6).

Significantly, financial support from her Uncle Peter enables Helga's travel to Copenhagen to see her aunt Katrina and uncle Herr Dahl, extending the themes of patrimony and the critique of patriarchal masculine types to transnational contexts, which the novel most elaborately develops in relation to Uncle Peter as a character. I draw students' attention to how ominously marriage surfaces as a motif in alienating Helga in her earliest years by acknowledging both her mother's and uncle's marriages to people who reject her because of her black ancestry; similarly, I acknowledge that the marriage that never occurs between her parents lies at the root of some of her deepest insecurities. In teaching the novel, it is useful to connect this childhood background to the ostensible marriage plot that is traceable in Helga's adult life as she encounters major masculine figures, drawing on criticism related to the "coupling convention" that the scholar Ann DuCille has linked to black women's writing. After exploring the family foundations related to masculinity on which Larsen develops the subtext of *Quicksand*, the class is well positioned for a fruitful exploration of the novel's central economy of male characters and the larger theme related to marriage and geography that constitutes her encounters with all of them.

James Vayle, Helga's first fiancé, from the world of the black elite, is the first major male character that Helga encounters. Looking more closely at him helps us understand the complex discourse on masculinity that Larsen presents from the beginning of the novel. Larsen links their relationship to the novel's overarching marriage plot. Inasmuch as the novel critiques the ideologies of black racial uplift and, particularly, the notion of the "race woman" through the scripting of the protagonist Helga Crane, it unsettles the romanticism typically associated with the "race man," most saliently through a critique of the character James Vayle. To introduce the race man, I frame the race man as a raced, classed, and gendered figure within black uplift ideology associated with promoting black social advancement while I acknowledge feminist critiques of this concept, from Zora Neale Hurston's ("Art") to Hazel V. Carby's (*Race Men*), which have acknowledged its implications for black female subjectivity. Whereas James fits in at Naxos, Helga feels herself to be as much of a "black sheep" at Naxos as she felt in her family as a lone mixed-race girl growing up among whites. By emphasizing that James Vayle and Helga were engaged from their first semester at Naxos, the novel underscores how superficially he knew her even when he proposed marriage. Significantly, the novel establishes his character as the major binary point of contrast for a character such as Helga:

> He was liked and approved of in Naxos and loathed the idea that the girl he was to marry couldn't manage to win liking and approval also. Instinctively Helga had known that secretly he had placed the blame upon her. . . . Naxos pleased him and he had become content with life as it was lived there. No longer lonely, he was now one of the community and so beyond the need or desire to discuss its affairs and its failings with an outsider. (7)

That Vayle's comfort at Naxos strikingly contrasts with her sense of alienation points to how much his acceptance there is conditioned by his masculine privilege and elite class status. Significantly, he eventually becomes the school's assistant principal. Tacitly, he endorses the colonialism at the heart of its philanthropy and has thoroughly internalized a model of black uplift ideology that conflates whiteness with notions of civilization, along with an elitist view of black masculinity that is primarily grounded in Anglo-Saxon culture and values.

In reading the character James Vayle, it is useful to acknowledge the possible wordplay on his last name, which rhymes with "veil." In the classroom, it helps to ponder that his name may allude to the concept of the veil invoked by W. E. B. Du Bois in *Souls of Black Folk* or to the masking invoked in Paul Laurence Dunbar's "We Wear the Mask," a poem that critiques the superficiality of the black middle-class culture in which Vayle is rooted. For example, such a critique of the black middle class is resoundingly clear in a passage such as the following:

> Negro society . . . was as complicated and as rigid in its ramifications as the highest strata of white society. If you couldn't prove your ancestry and connections, you were tolerated, but you didn't "belong." (8)

It also seems that Vayle's vision is blurred, or that he is wearing a veil, since he views Naxos superficially enough to overlook the very qualities that prove to be suffocating and stifling for Helga.

As the narrator mentions in the first chapter, when Helga plans to flee Naxos and leave her fiancé:

> The family of James Vayle, in near-by Atlanta, would be glad. They had never liked the engagement, had never liked Helga Crane. Her own lack of family disconcerted them. No family. That was the crux of the whole matter. For Helga, it accounted for everything, her failure here in Naxos, her former loneliness in Nashville.

The narrator goes on to mention that for Helga to leave

> James Vayle would most certainly be social suicide, for the Vayles were people of consequence. The fact that they were a "first family" had been one of James's attractions for the obscure Helga. She had wanted social background, but—she had not imagined that it would be so stuffy. (8)

Here, the very mention of the term "first families" invokes the concept as it emerged in the seventeenth century and played out in colonial America in the Virginia families headed by white male planters, a patriarchal, insular cohort of subjects privileged on the basis of race, gender, and property ownership and positioned at the top of the class hierarchy; slave-owning English colonists who descended from the Jamestown colonists and who typically married among themselves constituted this landed aristocracy. This angle helps us understand the deeper and ironic implications in the name "James" Vayle and provides further contexts for the novel's discourse on masculinity. Helga rejects a marriage to a man who embodies values and legacies associated with whites of the antebellum South as much as the black bourgeoisie, a man who also argues that it is urgent for the elite class of blacks to have children (104). In general, just as Larsen's father may have informed the development of the character Helga's father, it is conceivable that a character such as James Vayle also provides a veiled commentary on Larsen's husband and his family. That is to say, we know from her biographies that Larsen's marriage to the elite and middle-class physicist Elmer Imes was troubled, blighted by infidelity, and ended in divorce.

These biographical details, particularly when considered in the context of the early twentieth century's attitudes toward male privilege and patriarchal authority, influence the representation of masculinity in the novel. In general, themes related to marriage and its instability saturate Larsen's writing, especially her novels, *Quicksand* and *Passing*.

If the early chapters establish the groundwork for this thematic trajectory related to his character, it comes full circle when Helga encounters him again in Harlem, and as he reacts with shock and outrage over her indifference to having children:

> But Helga! Good heavens! Don't you see that if we—I mean people like us—don't have children, the others will still have. That's one of the things that's the matter with us. The race is sterile at the top. Few, very few Negroes of the better class have children, and each generation has to wrestle again with the obstacles of the preceding ones, lack of money, education, and background. I feel very strongly about this. We're the ones who must have the children if the race is to get anywhere. (103)

In a classroom discussion, as a background for analyzing the dialogue between Helga and Vayle, it will help to provide an overview of the nineteenth-century ideologies of black uplift that still carried weight in the early twentieth century. Similarly, it will also be important to give students an understanding of eugenics to contextualize Vayle's comments. In the typical readings of Larsen's works that focus so much on femininity and sexuality, we can easily miss the novel's profound commentary on marriage, masculinity, and sexuality so poignantly implied in passages such as the one above.

The novel also critiques the discourses of black racial uplift and the concept of the race man in relation to Dr. Robert Anderson, the new principal at Naxos. Like James Vayle, Dr. Anderson emerges as a quintessential model of the black race man so fundamental in constituting black-uplift ideology. His credentials and top administrative position further set him apart and position him at the very top of the social hierarchy at Naxos. Dr. Anderson describes Helga as a "lady" with "dignity" and "breeding" (21), a reading of her that reflects an internalization of the ideological efforts of the emergent black middle class to associate black women with domesticity and respectability to counter the pathologies that had shadowed the black feminine body within slavery, including stereotypes of lasciviousness. Her retorts that acknowledge her birth in a Chicago slum to an unmarried black father who gambled and a white immigrant mother confront and critique his elitist presumptuousness about her background and social status, as well as his offhand appropriation of her as a model of the feminine ideal that he most reveres. It seems ironic that his description of her as a "lady" helps her finalize her decision to leave Naxos. As Helga muses, "She didn't, she told herself, after all, like this Dr. Anderson. He was too controlled, too sure of himself and others. She detested cool, perfectly controlled people" (22–23).

While this dispute regarding the definition of a "lady" throws into relief profound contestations related to gender, they are all the more incendiary for Helga in the light of the kind of man that she perceives Dr. Anderson to be. A reading of these early passages about Helga's "breeding" within a lesson on masculinity might link them to James Vayle's family background and commentary on the importance of reproducing the black elite.

Significantly, the wedding of Dr. Anderson and Anne Grey brings Helga back to the United States from Copenhagen. Anderson's dignified, staid demeanor and his status as a paragon of black masculinity and model (race) man are belied by internal struggles with his sexuality that his spontaneous kiss with Helga, notwithstanding his status as a newlywed, throws into relief. Indeed, Anne herself is aware of this dimension of his personality, which makes him far more complex than one might perceive at first. Her estimation of his sexuality foreshadows his encounter with Helga, and, in its aftermath, seems amazingly prescient:

> Anne had perceived that the decorous surface of her new husband's mind regarded Helga Crane with that intellectual and aesthetic appreciation which attractive and intelligent women would always draw from him, but that underneath that well-managed section, in a more lawless place where she herself never hoped or desired to enter, was another, a vagrant primitive groping toward something shocking and frightening to the cold asceticism of his reason. (94–95)

The marital coupling of Anne and Dr. Anderson surfaces as the most likely if ironic context in which Vayle's rhetoric about the reproduction of the black elite might be realized and further extends the novel's marriage plot. While the novel develops its discourse on black middle-class masculinity primarily in relation to James Vayle and Dr. Anderson, the fact that they both end up in Harlem links them to the migration theme on which *Quicksand* relies in developing its protagonist, Helga.

It seems significant, too, that Harlem emerges as the primary setting for Larsen's critiques of black uplift and of the masculinity associated with the black elite. Larsen's novel highlights migrations across a range of geographies from national to global. Indeed, one good exercise, to help students follow the complex and multilayered geographic movements and to make those more visceral and dynamic, is to provide students with a blank map of the United States and Europe and ask them to pinpoint and trace Helga Crane's various geographic movements, along with those of primary male characters such as Vayle and Anderson. Such an exercise, which will be very straightforward for students who have done the reading, might also be useful as a pop quiz in teaching the novel at the undergraduate level. To help students further understand the shifts and developments in Helga's identity formation, I emphasize that her movements are correlated with a range of masculine figures with whom she is romantically linked, from James Vayle at the beginning to the Reverend Mr. Pleasant Green toward the end.

The racialized gaze of the white and male Axel Olsen, which is directed toward Helga in Copenhagen, serves as a counterpoint to the black race men that she encounters in the United States. Furthermore, he serves as a primary site on which Larsen sustains the marriage plot that underpins the novel. Olsen's painting of Helga represents the crux of Helga's objectification and humiliation in Copenhagen as a woman of African descent, a work that also symbolizes his ownership and possession of her in a way that marriage would further compound. The painting draws interest in the art marketplace and casts Helga as a symbolic slave for bid and sale. Significantly, he remarks:

> You have the warm impulsive nature of the women of Africa, but, my lovely, you have, I fear, the soul of a prostitute. You sell yourself to the highest buyer. I should of course be happy that it is I. And I am. (87)

Her rationale for not accepting his marriage proposal, which relates to reservations about marrying a white man and her concerns that he would perhaps someday come to dislike dark people, is also grounded in her memories of her mother's rejection of blackness. Her rejection of Axel's proposal marks the climax of her time in Copenhagen, gravely disappoints her uncle and aunt, and sets the stage for her eventual return to the United States. Helga's rejection of Olsen by extension disrupts patterns of white male control that have shadowed her life, following the example of her uncle Peter, who had assumed the role of patron in relation to her, inasmuch as it reflects a panic about the possibility of reproducing mixed-race children who might experience the anguish that she has encountered. Just as Olsen threatens to commodify her on the art market, Uncle Peter uses the bequest of a financial windfall to preclude further contact with her. Essentially, he buys her off. Indeed, scrutinizing characters such as Uncle Peter and Olsen can help students grasp how assertively the novel's commentary on white masculine patriarchal types mirrors its investments in analyzing black masculinity. This approach has the added benefit of encouraging comparative methodologies within masculinity studies. The commodification of the black body within the photography of a white male such as Carl Van Vechten and the primitivist view of Harlem that his artistry often advanced is a useful framework on which to draw while examining a character such as Olsen. Furthermore, in discussing the sections on Copenhagen and the politics of Helga's sexualized objectification under Olsen's masculine gaze, I outline contexts related to Josephine Baker, Sarah Baartman's portrayal as the Hottentot Venus, and black artists and expatriates in Europe during the Jazz Age of the 1920s.

Yet if we recognize the relationships associated with Helga across a range of geographies, then it becomes evident that the Reverend Mr. Pleasant Green embodies the most abject and reprehensible masculine model in the novel, and the one that proves to be most inimical to Helga. Significantly, the novel relates the pathology associated with him to its running marriage plot. In a Dantean kind of journey across geographies and through a range of love relationships, it is significant that Helga Crane encounters the most objectionable model of masculinity in the rural South as she navigates across a very complex geography of relationships. The novel also reveals that her affective response to this character is most negative and extreme. Her downfall, as symbolized by her miring in quicksand, is intricately linked to her fateful coupling with him. These penultimate passages about the Reverend Mr. Pleasant Green are also useful for reinforcing students' skills in close reading when considering that the novel associates Green with animal imagery and dirt and marks him as pestilential. The narrative describes him as a "fattish yellow man" (115) with body odor and dirty clothes. It also likens him to a rat, an image foreshadowed, along with her entrapment in the symbolic quicksand, at the end of the third chapter where Helga's angry thoughts "scurried here and there like trapped rats" (24). The irony in his naming, as in James Vayle's, speaks volumes. Indeed, in the attempt to camouflage and offset his lack of literacy with bombastic speech, Green replicates and mirrors the kind of superficiality that Helga found to be so off-putting at Naxos, enacting a symbolic veiling that ironically recasts that of James Vayle. In his view of Helga primarily as a sex object, Green's gaze upon her mirrors that of Dr. Anderson, registering a theme of masculinity and sexuality intricately tied to the groundbreaking treatment of sexuality and black femininity that made *Quicksand* so revolutionary at the time of its publication. Green's leadership over "a scattered and primitive flock" reflects a paternalism that lies in the continuum with Uncle Peter's and constitutes him as a race man in the rural South.

Yet Helga's marriage to Green unsettles romantic notions of black uplift and marriage and the concept of the race man. Her excitement about being a "helpmate" (120) in the rural South for her husband, Rev. Green, gives way to looming despair. The irony is that, whereas she and Green marry and produce several children, marriage proves to be inimical to Helga's well-being, and the effect of reproduction for her is not uplift, contrary to the arguments and rationales that James Vayle had articulated in Harlem about the urgency of reproduction within the black middle class. Instead, childbearing brings Helga down, literally, to the point of sinking into the quicksand symbolically invoked in the novel's title. Her ironic internalization of the very ideologies of blackness that she had critiqued at earlier stages of her life, when they were articulated by Vayle and Anderson, are tested with Green as a masculine model in their move South and quickly unravel:

> For she had to admit that it wasn't new, this feeling of dissatisfaction, of asphyxiation. Something like it she had experienced before. In Naxos. In New York. In Copenhagen. This differed only in degree. (134)

This passage synthesizes her journeying through a range of geographies, which stages her multiple encounters with masculine figures framed by the marriage plot in which it also initially grounds its narrative background on her family, and links her final decline to Green as a rural black masculine subject.

Just as the models of masculinity in her family fall short, the novel associates unfavorable qualities with all the men that Helga encounters in her adult life. James Vayle is a puppet and mouthpiece for the conventional uplift ideologies of the black middle class. Robert Anderson lacks integrity and the courage to pursue his desires. Axel Olsen is condescending and lustful and seems to view Helga through the pornographic gaze at the black feminine body established within the white patriarchal slave system of the antebellum South. Yet it is intriguing that her encounters with them shape her more profoundly than her encounters with women and point to *Quicksand*'s complex discourse on gender. That the novel links both black and white masculine types to Helga, from the race man to the patriarch, also mirrors her conflicted interracial identification with both categories from childhood on. A teaching standpoint that meditates on masculinity in a sustained way helps students appreciate Larsen's complex and multilayered approaches to character development and learn from the rich discourse on masculinity that the novel presents.

NOTE

[1] Larsen, Quicksand *and* Passing, ed. McDowell (1987). All subsequent references in this essay are to this edition.

The Matter of Beginnings: Teaching the Opening Paragraphs in *Quicksand* and *Passing*

Steven B. Shively

> [The poem] assumes direction with the first line laid down.
> —Robert Frost

When I dare to ask students what they think of a book, all too often their reply is, "It took a long time to get into it." Nella Larsen's novels *Quicksand* and *Passing* rarely bring such a complaint. It would be easy to conclude that a likely reason is the shortness of these books. I believe, however, that students "get into" these novels not because the novels are short but because the opening paragraphs contain features that immediately engage readers. Indeed, Nella Larsen offers enough intrigue and mystery, enough puzzling descriptions, enough evocative images to grab the attention of most student readers. The beginnings of these novels, however, are important for more than their ability to gain attention; they introduce themes, forecast plot, and offer compelling uses of language.

While students often find literary endings more powerful—and more frustrating—than beginnings, the privileged position of opening paragraphs calls for careful attention to their details and their nuances. This is especially true in the undergraduate American literature survey courses in which I often teach *Quicksand* or *Passing*, courses that include more poetry, short stories, and essays than long novels. I have also had good experiences using such an approach in an upper-division course focused on the Harlem Renaissance, which includes several novels.

Elaine Showalter stresses the importance of beginnings in *Teaching Literature*: "Beginnings are important in twentieth-century fiction, especially American fiction, which can't hang around to work out all the genealogical and historical details but has to grab the reader's attention right away" (98). Showalter's comment places responsibility on authors, but it also suggests that readers have the responsibility to fill in gaps and discern meanings from inherently limited information. It is worth noting that this responsibility extends to teachers whose classes are filled with students who are often naive, even ignorant, about matters of race and gender, which are important in understanding Larsen's novels.

An approach that focuses on beginnings grows out of Larsen's emphasis on beginnings in the lives of her characters. Although *Quicksand* begins when Helga is an adult teaching and living at Naxos, experiences from her early years have shaped her: her mother's death, the stepfather "so instinctively resented by Helga even at the trivial age of six," the "poverty, sordidness, and dissipation" of her childhood (23), and the saving generosity of her Uncle Peter shaped her character and influenced her choices. "The tragic cruelties of the years," Helga realizes, "had left her a little pathetic, a little hard, and a little unapproachable" (23). Likewise, in *Passing*, childhood experiences have established certain parameters for the relationship between Clare and Irene. For Clare, in particular, the period of her early years, spent living as the daughter of the unique Bob Kendry, his death, and her removal from the neighborhood to be raised by her white aunts explains—and in some ways dictates—the woman she becomes. Beginnings matter in life, and they matter in literature.

Larsen herself notes that the right opening is crucial: near the end of chapter 1 of part 2 of *Passing*, Irene blames herself for a conversation with her husband Brian that goes badly; she chastises herself for "having chosen . . . so clumsy an opening for what she had intended to suggest" (190). Fortunately, the openings Larsen chooses for her novels are not clumsy; they effectively garner students' attention as they offer rich possibilities for teachers seeking to help their students "read figurative language and distinguish between literal and metaphorical meanings" (Showalter 26).

Technically speaking, Larsen does not begin either *Quicksand* or *Passing* with an opening narrative paragraph; both novels begin with a dedication and an epigraph. These dedications and epigraphs, especially when combined with close readings of the early paragraphs, offer useful paths for exploring the novels and their meanings; in particular, the epigraphs introduce the topic of race, which is notably missing from the opening paragraphs of the texts.

Quicksand

The dedication for *Quicksand* reads "For E.S.I."—referring to Larsen's husband, Elmer S. Imes, whom she had married in 1919 and would divorce in 1933. A noted physicist with deep connections to Fisk University, Imes was part of the national black elite. The marriage broadened Larsen's world considerably, and George Hutchinson notes that husband and wife shared an affinity for "challeng[ing] boundaries" (*In Search* 122); nevertheless, their dissimilar backgrounds and divergent goals made for a troubled relationship. While it would be unfair to read the dedication as a suggestion that Helga's depressing marriage in the novel was similar to Larsen's own doomed marriage, the vexed nature of marriage is an important theme in the novel.

Larsen prefaces *Quicksand* with the last four lines of Langston Hughes's 1925 poem "Cross." The mixed racial heritage of the speaker, first stated in the beginning of the poem—"My old man's a white old man / And my old mother's black"—and repeated in the last line of Larsen's epigraph, establishes racial origin as a significant interest of the novel. While Larsen reverses the racial identity of Helga's parents (Helga's mother is white and her father is black), students could profitably discover connections between the two literary texts: a concern for wealth and poverty, changing loyalties, literal and metaphoric references to death, and confusion about where a mixed-race individual belongs. Hughes's title, "Cross," packed with its multiple suggestions of religion, burdens, and intersections, forecasts important themes of the novel. The meanings in Larsen's dedication and epigraph become richer and more apparent after students have read the novel; a return to them at that point can underscore the value of researching such allusions while creating an awareness of the ways that authors embed meanings that readers perceive only gradually, unconsciously as well as consciously.

The first sentence of *Quicksand* gets students' speculative juices flowing. Why is Helga sitting alone? By the end of the paragraph, we know her isolation is intentional (though I often have students who are skeptical of that claim, and I have found that such skepticism from the beginning serves them well in the rest of the book). Discussion of possible reasons can lead students to several of the novel's major concerns: Helga's search for meaningful companionship and company, her psychological isolation even among groups, her response to her own otherness, the vexing behavior of Helga's associates. The first sentence's pointed location of Helga "in her room," which is reinforced by the words that close the opening paragraph—"Helga Crane never opened her door"—introduces the novel's emphasis on interiority and points to the end of the novel, which, as Thadious Davis points out, finds Helga "much as she begins in Naxos, isolated in a small room" (*Nella Larsen* 272). Students can be surprised to find themselves interested in knowing more about Helga despite the lack of any real action in the opening paragraph; indeed, Hutchinson, drawing on Larsen's own words, notes that "'the psychology of the scene' and the 'poetic conception of the character' count more than actions and words" (*In Search* 226).

Larsen is a master at expressing the complex, often contradictory, nature of her characters and the circumstances in which they find themselves. For example, she mixes words that suggest light with words that suggest darkness. Words like "gloom," "dimmed," "shadowy," "drawn curtains," a "single shaded light," and "desert of darkness" communicate the literal setting of "eight in the evening," a time that will inevitably proceed to night, but also the more symbolic meanings of darkness, shadows, and gloom, which at times describe Helga's circumstances and personality as much as they describe her room. Such words, however, are countered by the similarly connotative yet contrasting words "pool of light," "bright," "white," and "flooded with Southern sun." Larsen uses particularly odd language to describe the effect of the sole source of light in Helga's room, a "single reading lamp, dimmed by a great black and red shade." Surprisingly, this lone, shaded lamp (descriptive details Larsen mentions in the second sentence and then repeats only two sentences later) casts "a pool of light," and Larsen emphasizes in five consecutive and drawn-out prepositional phrases that there is enough light to illuminate the carpet, a group of books, the particular book Helga is reading, a flower-filled brass bowl, and a silk-covered stool. The repeated, detailed, and contrasting treatments of light and darkness illustrate the complex ways these terms suggest race, understanding, happiness, and imprisonment. From the beginning, Larsen establishes that darkness and light coexist, that Helga's world is not sharply defined, and that the boundaries between black and white, happiness and sadness, freedom and imprisonment are blurred and imprecise.

As they read beyond the opening, some students argue that Larsen's words might be misleading. Yes, Helga sits "alone," but the label hardly fits a woman who is engaged and who lives and works in a place where she is surrounded by colleagues and students. The dullness of the opening, with its emphasis on loneliness, gloom, and dimness belies the attractiveness of Helga's room, which holds several fine things. With a bit of discussion, they recognize that being alone is not synonymous with being lonely and that material possessions, which make a place "attractive" and "comfortable," do not ensure happiness; this is a "homey" place, but it is not a "home." Such understandings are important thematically, but they also help students realize that the language of this book is destabilized from the start. The meanings of words like *happiness*, *success*, *white*, *foreign*, *successful*, and *spiritual* are difficult to pin down. Students do not, then, readily accept Helga's conviction after she marries the Reverend Green that for once "she had not clutched a shadow and missed the actuality" (118).

Students readily acknowledge the conflicted meanings of the "drawn curtains" of Helga's room: they block light, create shadows, and reinforce a sense of isolation; yet they also ensure privacy and create a sanctuary. Later in the novel, Larsen reiterates the conflict with the wonderful phrase "that tantalizing oppression of loneliness and isolation" (45). The curtains might well remind students of W. E. B. Du Bois's famous assertion that he counts himself as one "of them that live within the Veil" (*Souls* 42). The likely allusion is reinforced when Larsen later mentions Du Bois (38); furthermore, Cheryl Wall argues that the name of Helga's fiancé, James Vayle, "evokes the 'veil' of Du Bois's famous metaphor" (*Women* 97). Du Bois's veil asserts racial identity as it suggests division and separation. His phrase, however, also has biblical connections, where it is more positive in marking a place that is holy (see, e.g., Leviticus 16, where "within the veil" appears three times, and Hebrews 6.19 [*Holy Bible*]).

Larsen's first paragraph of *Quicksand* is heavy with adjectives: "*soft* gloom," "*bright* covers of books," "*long* shelves," "*shining* brass," "*low* table," "*oriental* silk, "*rare* and intensely *personal* taste," "*small* oasis," and others (emphasis added). While students might profitably consider the ways modifiers (including participial and prepositional phrases) communicate meaning, a more striking observation is that only one adjective in the paragraph describes Helga, and that one seems rather innocuous: "her slim feet." Larsen calls attention to the room and its possessions, to its appearance and its effect on Helga, an emphasis that will reappear later in the novel. Helga, for example, will approve of the "aesthetic sense" of Anne's home and its furnishings, which are described with words like "dignity," "luxurious," "gleaming," "fine," and "precious" (44). So caught up does Helga become in her desire for material things that she intends to marry one of the men who "could give to her the things which she had now come to desire, a home like Anne's, cars of expensive makes such as lined the avenue, clothes and furs from Bendel's and Revillon Frères', servants, and leisure" (45). The early focus on material things, particularly fine things, helps readers appreciate Larsen's later comment that, contrary to what Helga concludes, the Reverend Green's mind is not spiritually focused but is "at home amongst the mere material aspect of things" (116). Readers are prepared to receive with considerable skepticism Helga's conclusion that "things . . . hadn't been, weren't, enough for her" (116). Appearances and things matter a great deal in this novel.

Teachers can alert students to watch for ways that specific words, images, and ideas are introduced in the opening paragraph and then reappear in significant ways later in the novel. Alternatively, after completing the novel, students can be sent on a treasure hunt of sorts to find places where key words or images reoccur (I have students complete this exercise in small groups). Then they can derive conclusions from their findings. For example, the words "Chinese" and "oriental" both appear in the opening paragraph, announcing that one of the novel's interests will be exoticism, that which is foreign, mysterious, special, and different. "Chinese" is later used on pages 15, 44, 56, 68, and 120, and there are additional suggestions of orientalism such as when Helga chooses to read Marmaduke Pickthall's *Said the Fisherman*; in a note, Deborah McDowell suggests that "Larsen intends an ironic contrast to the dull sobriety and sterility of Naxos" (243). Students might look for mentions of flowers, comparing in particular the "many-colored nasturtiums" that crowd the brass bowl of Helga's room at Naxos with the "unceasing litter of half-dead flowers on the table" beside her sickbed in Alabama (124). Even the specific time of the first sentence, "eight in the evening," is repeated in the climactic scene when Helga slaps Dr. Anderson (106–07); significant references to evening occur in several places in the book. One of the more substantive and revealing aspects of the opening paragraph is the use of colors: four different colors are mentioned (black, red, blue, white), as well as the "many-colored" flowers and the suggested yellow of the sunlight and gold of the brass bowl. Larsen reveals that color is a significant source of Helga's conflict with Naxos (17–18), and references to color appear throughout the book until the last chapter, when only the colors black and white are used; not even Green, the colorful last name of her husband—and surely of Helga herself—is mentioned in the stark conclusion. Among other words my students have enjoyed finding in repeated uses are "darkness," "tranquility," "curtains," "Southern," "gossip," and "door."

Sometimes I have students read the opening paragraph in class, and then I stop them from reading further. I ask them to think of the novel as a mystery. I am prompted, in part, by Helga's assertion that her life is not a mystery (39) and by the questions she asks herself about the anonymous people of Chicago (30). I alert my students that clues to the ending will unfold if they can discern them, but I caution them that everything will not be tied up in a neat package with all of their questions answered. The first step in dealing with a mystery, of course, is to ask questions. At first, my students struggle, for they find the opening paragraph straightforward; they do not consider Helga odd for wanting to be alone at the end of a hard day. Their questions usually fall into two categories, questions about the school (their word for an "educational community") and questions about Helga:

> What kind of school is it? (Many assume it is an institution for troubled children because of "the strenuous rigidity of conduct required.")
> Why are the teachers so unkind, especially to one another?
> Why does Helga live at the school?
> Why do the teachers behave immaturely, like students (gossiping, seeking information and favors, bothering others)?
> Is something wrong with Helga?
> Is Helga a neat freak? Why?
> How old is Helga? (They think she is old because she needs rest, keeps her room orderly, and seems boring.)
> What is the real cause of Helga's intentional isolation? Rudeness? Some reason she is different from the others? Something she once did to make others dislike her?

The exercise pulls some students into the story, giving them a reason to read on. As they read, they become attuned to ways that their questions were sometimes presumptuous, but more important, they come to understand that such questions don't have clear answers, that their questions were, in fact, rather trivial, that they should be alert to new questions, that logic and clear reasoning rarely inform human behavior, and that Helga, like all good literary characters, is complex and conflicted.

Passing

As with *Quicksand*, Larsen's dedication and epigraph work with the novel's opening paragraph in both covert and overt ways to prepare readers for the novel's themes. *Passing* is dedicated to Carl Van Vechten and Fania Marinoff, the flamboyant Manhattan socialite couple well known for their fixation with Harlem culture. While too much attention to Van Vechten and Marinoff, especially before reading the novel, could overshadow Larsen's text, teachers may wish to help students see ways that the dedication announces certain of the novel's themes. The fact that the two people named in the dedication were married, a reality not readily apparent to most students, tells readers to pay attention to married couples in the novel. The dedication to Van Vechten and Marinoff focuses attention on the cultural interplay between white and black worlds that will be important in the novel. Hugh Wentworth, a character in the novel, seems closely modeled on Van Vechten. Many aspects of cultural politics, especially patronage and language, might be provoked by giving attention to Van Vechten and Marinoff and their relationship to Larsen.

For the epigraph to *Passing*, Larsen selected four lines from Countee Cullen's long poem "Heritage," lines that Cullen repeats as something of a refrain in his poem. While the entire poem offers a rich comparison to Larsen's novel, most teachers will find it adequate to call attention to the theme of exoticism expressed in the epigraph ("three centuries removed," "spicy grove, cinnamon tree") and to the profound question, "What is Africa to me?" The poem's speaker, not unlike Clare, Irene, and Brian in the novel, is vaguely aware of a rich heritage yet unable to make it meaningful in a modern world. Teachers might alert students to consider "Africa" literally as well as symbolically—that is, as representative of how characters will use geographic and cultural distance both to escape their heritage and to connect to it.

Nella Larsen masterfully captures her readers with the opening paragraph of *Passing* and its "mysterious and slightly furtive" letter (143). Details of the letter predict most of the major issues of the novel; it becomes a metaphoric map of the characters and their actions and a path to the novel's themes. The "Italian paper" of the envelope, the "foreign paper" of the letter, and the "alien" appearance foreground the novel's attention to difference and otherness. The "purple ink" announces that color will be important. Words like "betray" and "furtive" communicate that there is something sinister about the letter; indeed, acts of betrayal (real and assumed) reveal character and move the plot along. The "almost illegible scrawl" suggests difficulties in communication (intentional and unintentional). The word "mysterious" suggests that students be alert to the novel's puzzling secrets (those that are revealed and those that remain mysteries). Working in small groups, students can search for examples of these issues—otherness, color, betrayal, communication, mysteries—and track their development through the novel.

Larsen's illogical yet meaningful description of the letter as both "furtive"—she uses the word twice in the first the paragraph—and "flaunting" calls for discussion. Students will understand that the words seem to be opposite, with "furtive" meaning hidden or secretive, and "flaunting" indicating open defiance, even exhibitionism. Students will see these paired adjectives become accurate character descriptors of Clare as much as they are of her letter. In a broader sense, they also describe the practice of racial passing (as well as other manifestations of passing). If readers view the letter as inextricably connected to Clare and as anticipatory of her appearance in the novel, then they would do well to follow Kathleen Pfeiffer's call to "look at the passer as a figure who values individualism, who may be idiosyncratic, self-determining, or inclined toward improvisation" (2).

As important as the strange letter, however, is the telling detail that Irene saves it to open last. My students notice that she "immediately [knew] who its sender was" and that she had received a similar letter two years earlier. They speculate why she might save it until last: perhaps she suspects what it will say and dreads the news; perhaps she is uncertain of its contents and wants to deal with her other mail before a potential distraction; perhaps she wishes to savor expected good news. By focusing initial speculation on Irene, teachers can ensure that she becomes part of students' consciousness before Clare inevitably takes over. The shifting of attention from Irene to Clare then becomes purposeful.

The passivity of *Passing*'s opening paragraph is crucial to understanding Irene's character and to preparing readers for the end of the novel. The dull opening words "it was," the heavy use of weak verbs, and the fact that four of the sentences in the paragraph contain no verb suggest that Irene is indecisive and reactive. Larsen's use of limiting modifiers to qualify and tone down descriptive words reinforces the idea that Irene is tentative and noncommittal: "*almost* illegible scrawl," "*slightly* furtive," "*a little* flaunting" (emphasis added). Readers soon learn the truth of such a judgment when Irene's memory of a trip to Chicago reveals that she was too exhausted to do anything when a man beside her crumpled into a heap on the concrete, and she can barely summon the strength to hail a cab, indecisively telling the driver, "I guess . . . it's tea I need. On a roof somewhere" (147). Her tentativeness continues in her lack of response to the offensive comments of Clare's husband, both in Chicago when he makes them (173) and later when she unexpectedly meets him in New York City; in disgust, she thinks to herself, "I had my chance and didn't take it" (227). Furthermore, her practiced avoidance of unpleasant subjects when speaking with her own husband reinforces the idea that inaction is a regular pattern of behavior (186). Such passivity, planted in readers' minds in the opening paragraph, heightens the ambiguity and uncertainty of the novel's ending; readers question what seems to be Irene's complicity in Clare's death by pushing her out the window. The cloudy ending illustrates one of Larsen's major themes: the instability of commonly accepted meanings of race, gender, sexuality, marriage, and happiness.

Teachers can use the opening paragraph, then, to enhance readers' understanding of either Clare (through her connection to the letter) or Irene (through the ways she echoes the paragraph's passive structures and vocabulary), or both. A reading that probes meaning for Irene and Clare, both individually *and* collectively, matches the complex nature of this text and the ways Larsen destabilizes personal identity, human relationships, and cultural practices.

This essay demonstrates that teachers who pay significant attention to the prefatory material and opening paragraphs of *Quicksand* and *Passing* can give their students experience with close textual reading, reader-response approaches to the study of literature, and psychological and cultural criticism.

After they have finished a novel, students should be able to recognize and weigh the relative merits of Larsen's choice of a starting point for her narrative. J. Hillis Miller perceptively notes that "any beginning in narrative cunningly covers a gap, an absence at the origin." In an example that becomes startlingly ironic when applied to *Passing*, Miller points out that "[i]f the novelist begins abruptly, with one character throwing another out the window, sooner or later he will have to explain who threw who, and why" (58). Storytellers consciously fill in some gaps and leave some empty. Since both *Quicksand* and *Passing* have flashbacks that cover earlier years, students should be able to discern questions about those years that remain unanswered, and they should be able to argue that a different starting point—Helga's first day at Naxos, for example (would she be filled with hope or dread?), or a domestic scene in Clare's home with her husband (would it reveal why she initiated contact with Irene?)—would be better or worse (or both) than Larsen's actual beginnings.

The endings of Larsen's novels have received much more critical comment than her beginnings, and they should not be ignored, even in an approach that emphasizes beginnings. Students can consider how the opening paragraphs prepared them (or did not prepare them) for the endings. They can perceive ways that characters changed—for better or worse—from their starting points. They should be able to translate Larsen's endings into starting points for a new narrative without falling into clichés or personal wishes: Will Helga ever free herself from her tragic circumstances? What details of the novel predict your answer? What kind of marriage will Irene and Brian have after Clare's death?

Ultimately, understanding comes neither from beginnings nor endings but from the conversation between the two.

Versions of *Passing*

John K. Young

From its retrospectively ambiguous title that conjoins Clare Kendry's racial identity and death to its reflections on the muddled notion of "race" in the 1920s United States to its famously open-ended final scene, Nella Larsen's *Passing* appeals directly and powerfully to undergraduates' engagement with textual instability. Indeed, to the above list most readers would add questions about the nature of Irene Redfield's apparent desire for Clare, doubts about the accuracy of Irene's anxiety about an affair between Clare and her husband, and other more local gaps and cruxes. These are all important hinges on which interpretation turns, and they have been addressed extensively, in this volume and elsewhere. But most of Nella Larsen's readers—whether students or teachers—miss an equally irresolvable textual conundrum: *which* version of *Passing* to read and how to read it.

As Mark J. Madigan first pointed out in his 1989 essay, the novel's third printing in 1929 (the first two were simultaneous) omitted the closing paragraph, in which a "strange man, official and authoritative" (241) judges the death to have been "by misadventure." Thus the third printing transfers the novel's closing words from a (presumed) white police officer back to Irene's consciousness, or rather her loss thereof, with the now final line, "Then everything was dark" (242), a description that obviously resonates with Larsen's representations of racial identity as well. Gaps in the historical record make it impossible to know exactly why this textual change occurred—whether it was an authorial revision, an editorial imposition, or even a printing error. As George Hutchinson concludes in his magnificent recent biography, the "final paragraph mysteriously disappeared. No one knows why" (*In Search of Nella Larsen* 310).

As a teacher of textual scholarship and African American studies, my goals for teaching *Passing* are both to introduce students to the text's material instability (and, by extension, to the broader instabilities that manifest themselves in almost all published works) and to link this material mystery with the narrative's thematic and structural uncertainties. I have developed this learning objective through a variety of methods, including in-class writing on how to read each version of the ending and broader discussions of each closing paragraph in relation to those ending the book's earlier parts, "Encounter" and "Re-encounter." But the most effective strategy, I have found, begins before the class proper, when ordering texts from the bookstore.

Conveniently for my purposes, both versions are in print and in paperback. The Rutgers and Griot editions of *Quicksand* and *Passing* use the third printing's ending, acknowledging the original final paragraph only in a footnote in the Rutgers and not at all in the Griot, while most other current paperbacks (e.g. Penguin, Modern Library, Norton, and the Anchor volume of *Complete Fiction*) follow the first printing. Thus I have ordered, for example, the Rutgers edition for half the class and the Penguin for the other half, only informing students on the first day of class that either copy is acceptable (and reassuring them that they are not required to purchase both). Even absent this mild trick, I would assign a response in advance of our closing discussion on what happens at the end of the novel, which of course leads most students to focus on the question of how and why Clare dies at the Freelands' party. The ensuing discussion of Irene's culpability leads eventually to the narrative's final lines, when I ask for someone to read the last two paragraphs aloud. Depending on which student volunteers, this recitation will feature "[t]hen everything was dark" as either the middle or ending line, immediately yielding confusion and discussion of why some students have read one ending and some another.

It is certainly possible to introduce the novel's textual history without going to the trouble of ordering multiple editions, and elsewhere in my teaching I incorporate other material examples either online or as paper handouts, such as the manuscript version of the Marabar Caves scene in E. M. Forster's *A Passage to India*, in which Adela Quested definitely is assaulted; the changes between Virginia Woolf's British and American editions of *To the Lighthouse*; or the original publication of Thomas Pynchon's story "The Secret Integration" in the *Saturday Evening Post*, of all places.[1] Such documents serve as valuable starting points for discussion, but I have also found that the material form of their presentation as digital references or as handouts tends to reinforce undergraduates' perceptions of these documents as supplementary, as detachable from the "main" or "real" text that is otherwise under discussion. Discovering that the person sitting next to you has read a different ending to the "same" book, on the other hand, brings home the uncanniness of books' material instability in ways that seem to students to be more real precisely because these documents originate outside the boundaries of the classroom and thus seem to transform that admittedly artificial space into a site that connects more immediately to the social and cultural histories behind it.

Once *Passing*'s different endings have been discovered, I provide a brief outline of the relevant textual history, noting that we cannot finally explain the change even if we can imagine its possible causes. Because most undergraduates are either firmly entrenched in reading for authorial intention or learning how to disengage themselves from such assumptions, the idea that a text could be changed without its author's consent, tacit or explicit, is disturbing, but it also leads productively into conversations about other interpretive connotations of textual ownership. As Jacqueline Foertsch explains of her strategies for teaching different editions of *Frankenstein*,

> That students may be required to buy and study and even be tested on not one but *two* versions of the 'same' novel can lead them to questions that their teachers ask as well: Is there only one "right" text? . . . Can there be two "right" versions of the same story? What else am I reading "out there" for which a radically different version exists? (698)

(The answer to this last question, incidentally, is quite a lot, as evidenced by Joyce's *Ulysses*, Dickens's *Great Expectations*, Woolf's *The Voyage Out* and *To the Lighthouse*, Wright's *Native Son* and *Black Boy / American Hunger*, Wordsworth's *The Prelude*, Fitzgerald's *Tender Is the Night*, Moore's "Poetry" and many other works, Melville's *Typee*, Raymond Carver's stories, or Eliot's *The Waste Land*, to cite but a smattering of well-known nineteenth- and twentieth-century British and American examples.)

At the level of plot and narrative structure, the question of which last paragraph to read in *Passing* intersects productively with discussions of the final scene leading up to either ending. While we might not be able to establish beyond a reasonable doubt that Irene has pushed Clare out the window, most of my students (and I) are in this interpretive camp. And while the narrative is ultimately ambiguous on this point, it is uncertain within specific limits; that is, we can enumerate the possible explanations without lapsing into the "anything goes" analytic chaos that many of my students seem to fear from theoretical readings. For the most part, these possible causes for Clare's death comprise the following: Irene has pushed her out the window, Bellew has pushed her, Clare has deliberately thrown herself out the window, or Clare has accidentally fallen. While a close reading of the final pages quickly annotates Irene's guilt and presumed culpability, occasionally a few students will suggest that Clare's fall is in fact not Irene's fault but that she reacts as if it were because she has subconsciously desired Clare's death and is now reacting to the sudden manifestation of this suppressed wish.

In any case, while the narrative may point us in a particular direction (or then again may not; over the years I have encountered some artful student readings that rest the proximate cause with Clare), there is no smoking gun, as it were. As my more capable students quickly discern, this evidentiary lack is a deliberate feature of the narrative's focalization through Irene, especially as our readerly confidence in her perspective has already been thrown into doubt with the earlier unanswered question of Brian Redfield's relationship with Clare. Furthermore, while the action of Bellew's abrupt entrance and Clare's fall is generally narrated as if it were happening in the immediate present, we actually find these events to be mediated through Irene's retrospective reluctance to see them clearly: "What happened next, Irene Redfield never afterwards allowed herself to remember. Never clearly" (239). This announcement of a narrative filter creates what Robyn Warhol has termed a "narrative refusal," a "strategy for addressing the unnarratable in fiction, rather than simply keeping quiet about it" (259). As Warhol observes, however, "Paradoxically, narrative refusal does not block narrative transmission. It opens up alternative stories . . ." (259). This is certainly the case with the end of *Passing*, as attentive readers will immediately wonder what we would know of Clare's death were Irene to allow herself to remember the scene clearly.

Similarly, an awareness of the text's materially unstable ending compels consideration of how this change might have occurred and how each version of the ending might generate revised conceptions of the narrative globally. Below, I outline the pedagogical implications for each of these problems. Depending on the level and type of class in which I am teaching *Passing*, I may include a supplementary handout charting the types of explanations scholars have suggested for the original final paragraph's omission. These include the assumption that Larsen authorized or at least did not oppose the change; that someone at Alfred A. Knopf was responsible for the excision, with or without Larsen's knowledge; or (as seems least likely to me) that a printer's error occurred, as in Charles R. Larson's supposition that we have "a matter of a dropped plate" (218n129).[2] Strikingly, Thadious M. Davis has reached opposing conclusions in her capacities as Larsen biographer and *Passing* editor, first hypothesizing that Larsen "may well have been responsible for dropping the final paragraph of the novel after the second printing in order to suspend the action before a verdict is reached on Clare's death and Irene's fate" (*Nella Larsen* 322), but then justifying her inclusion of the original last paragraph in her Penguin edition because "there is no indication that Nella Larsen herself recommended, sought, or approved the excision of the final paragraph" ("Note").

For undergraduates, this evidence of confusion among professional scholars can be amusing and enlightening, authorizing them to settle for their own tentative conclusions when a lack of evidence calls for hesitancy, instead of rushing to judgment whatever the available textual support. This is an especially worthwhile lesson in a case like that of *Passing*, where the readerly problem of experiencing only what Irene perceives complicates our sense of the plot and of its thematic resonances in such areas as suppressed or unacknowledged lesbian desire or in the narrative's representation of race itself—as in Brian's remark, for example, that if he could explain why blacks passing as white "always come back," then "I'd know what race is" (185).

Along those lines, the material instability of the final paragraph(s) resonates with the novel's larger pattern of redirecting narrative patterns at the end of its earlier two parts, "Encounter" and "Re-encounter." While part 1 has focused intensively on Irene's chance meeting with Clare at the Drayton Hotel and her subsequent reactions, the final paragraph shifts toward a different set of concerns: "She dropped Clare out of her mind and turned her thoughts to her own affairs. To the home, to the boys, to Brian," and especially "that old, queer, unhappy restlessness [that] had begun again within him" (178). This narrative turn carries forward into the opening of part 2, when Irene and Brian share breakfast and a ride to the printers, all the while debating Clare and the practice of passing generally. Much of "Re-encounter" presents Irene's perceptions of her husband and her erstwhile friend and so appropriately concludes with Irene's inability to read Clare clearly; as their conversation about the risks of Clare's marriage becomes more intensely emotional, the section ends, "But Clare Kendry had begun to cry, audibly, with no effort at restraint, and for no reason that Irene could discover" (210). Larsen's readers, of course, may well feel that, unlike Irene, they can discern the cause of Clare's tears, and so the privileged position of this closing moment highlights the growing gap between what Irene experiences and what readers believe of Irene's perceptions, a pattern that will only accelerate in part 3. The opening of "Finale" jumps forward in time and thus reinforces this epistemological gap, compelling readers to attribute retrospectively what has happened in Irene's and Clare's lives in that narrative space.

Such moments of close reading generate productive discussions of the novel's two endings, as my students and I consider the broader effects of each final paragraph. (In contrast to McDowell's claim that the first printing's last paragraph "does not seem to alter the spirit of the original in any way" [246n10], my students have found substantial differences in each ending, and I certainly agree.) As Davis notes, the third printing leaves Irene's legal fate more open, and ends the novel with a "sentence doubly evocative of female unconsciousness: 'Then everything was dark'" (*Nella Larsen* 322). The ironies and ambiguities of Irene's lapsing into darkness at the end of a novel about cultural misreadings of blackness and whiteness are (usually) readily apparent to my students, as are the narrative implications of the first printings' shift away from Irene's focalizing perspective to a voice of white male authority speaking the novel's last words. At the same time, the police officer's decision to "go up and have another look at that window" suggests the need for an interpretive return as well, for a rereading of the final scene that can expand easily into a reconsideration of the narrative as a whole.[3]

Just as I am careful to refrain from authorizing a particular interpretation of Clare's death as absolutely correct, I make sure to emphasize the unknowability of the textual question posed by the two endings. As Hutchinson explains, the decision by Knopf to issue a third printing was spurred not by strong initial sales but rather the lack thereof: in a May 1929 letter to Carl Van Vechten, Alfred Knopf notes sales of only about 3,500, "confined almost entirely to New York," with a "small third printing" ordered (Hutchinson, *In Search of Nella Larsen* 328). This biographical context might support an assumption that Larsen, presented with the opportunity to revise her novel for an audience that had not found it initially, chose a more ambiguous, if more thematically coherent, ending. Or perhaps the change was initiated by Alfred or Blanche Knopf, or routed through Blanche by Van Vechten in his capacity as unofficial press adviser on New Negro renaissance literature; there is no way to know, and unlike the case of *Passing* itself, no direct evidence to consider. Given this editorial undecidability, the proliferation of both versions in print is an effective, if unintentional, solution to the problem of which version of *Passing* to prefer: neither is the "correct" edition (even if the standards by which they are edited vary substantially), and so both versions should be available. Indeed, we might even think of *Passing* as a materially queer text—that is, in addition to its thematic resonances along those lines, the book refuses to settle into one edition or the other.[4]

Such analyses should lead students to see the term *text* as both more prominent and more complicated within the author-reader-text triangle. As Peter L. Shillingsburg notes, any physical document represents "a patchwork of mixed authorities" (183). By extension, documents reflect as well the social and cultural pressures behind such mixed textual authorities, the kinds of messy "considerations of the gender- , race- , and class-inflected facts of life" that manifest themselves in "texts as social instruments," as Martha Nell Smith writes (4). In cases like *Passing*, such considerations include a publishing system that marked "white" (which is to say, especially in the 1920s and 1930s, non-Jewish) fiction as the cultural standard and "black" literature as defined in contrast to that racialized norm. While the cultural practice of passing and the extensive body of passing fiction in the early twentieth century should demonstrate the falsity of categories premised on a *Plessy v. Ferguson* view of racial identity—the most accurate designator for Clare and Irene, after all, would be mixed race—literature of the Harlem Renaissance, including Larsen's writing, was consistently marketed as offering windows (often for white readers) into the black "condition," despite the resistance to such advertising rhetoric by Jean Toomer, among others (C. Larson 25).

In works like *Passing*, then, textual instabilities encourage discussions about *race* in America as an unstable term, one that has been premised not only on misreadings of bodies as physical texts but also on a social construction that often has inescapably real consequences. Such a contrast between material and ostensibly immaterial notions of race should flow organically from the class's discussions of textuality, but to bolster it, I juxtapose related examples, such as Glenn Ligon's pair of identical photographs, entitled *Self-Portrait Exaggerating My Black Features / Self-Portrait Exaggerating My White Features* (see Fusco and Wallis), and a Massachusetts Institute of Technology study that found significantly higher rates of response for résumés from applicants named Emily and Greg versus otherwise identical materials with the names Lakisha and Jamal. When teaching African American fiction, this approach leads to discussions that illuminate and historicize the specific terms through which culturally dominant images of blackness have been produced, marketed, and resisted.

NOTES

[1] On Forster, see Levine; Fordham; and Restuccia. On Woolf's simultaneous publication of the British and American editions of *To the Lighthouse*, see Briggs; Gabler. On Pynchon, see my "Pynchon in Popular Magazines."

[2] I explain my reasons for doubting Larson in *Black Writers, White Publishers* 49–50.

[3] For other readings focusing on the importance of the last paragraph (though without always realizing the significance of reading one edition versus another), see Carr; Harrison-Kahan; Kawash; and Sullivan. I discuss these examples in *Black Writers* 52–55.

[4] I am indebted to Erica Fretwell for suggesting this point to me.

The Uses of Biography

George B. Hutchinson

Despite the low prestige of biographical criticism, we all use biographies. We want to know where people are from, how old they are, and usually by whom they were raised. Virtually all criticism, including criticism by poststructuralist critics, has a crucial biographical component that helps frame interpretation. We routinely situate authors in space and time before any interpretation begins and read them in relation to other authors to whom they may have been responding. Moreover, biographical sleuthing turns up evidence sometimes of such import that it completely changes our notions of a text or of an author. Where, for example, did scholars situate *Incidents in the Life of a Slave Girl* before Jean Fagan Yellin proved that the author was black?

When biographers informed us that Nella Larsen, contrary to her consistent claims, probably never visited Denmark and that her mother may have placed her in an orphanage in early childhood, it changed not only our perspective on Larsen, suggesting that she lied in order to "play up" her whiteness, but also our reading of *Quicksand* and of other aspects of her career. When we learned, on the other hand, that Larsen did live in Denmark after all—not once but twice, and for a substantial portion of her early life—her whole career looked different again.

Arnold Rampersad has urged the value of biography in getting at questions of racial guilt and racial shame in the Harlem Renaissance. He urges scholars to take seriously the problem of racial confusion during the renaissance, the many different ramifications of racism and "the ways, admittedly impossible to map, in which the black mind reconstituted and reconstitutes itself in the face of the repeated woundings inflicted by racism" (32). Acknowledging the importance of such projects, my emphasis here will be different, having more to do with the surprises in biographical research and how those surprises help us and our students gauge the shape of our own, often unconscious, expectations.

In thinking of the lives of Harlem Renaissance authors generally, one is struck by their liminality. Whether thinking of class, sexuality, racial background, even national identity, many key authors of the Harlem Renaissance—including, especially, Larsen—straddle the thresholds of social difference. The liminal positions of the authors have much to do with their choice of vocation—and may be screened out when their texts are read as functions of a "tradition." This is not to argue against the value of traditions or group identities but to suggest that the most compelling responses to the forms of oppression that create a sense of collective identity emanate from the boundary where individual consciousness encounters the experience of group subjection. Artistic identities are not often forged at the center of a group tradition but on its ever-moving edge.

Many readings of Nella Larsen's novels rely on situating her first in relation to black women's fiction generally, and in the process make convincing claims about how she felt constrained by stereotypical treatments of black women's sexuality, primitivism, and so forth. As one popular argument would have it, she slyly "subverted" the paradigms exploited, above all, by Carl Van Vechten in *Nigger Heaven*. The fact that Larsen personally praised *Nigger Heaven*, not just when it first came out but often, over a period of several years, has failed to convince some of those who continue to regard her work in this way. After all, one can simply argue that she was wearing a "mask" for a powerful white intermediary, one in a position to aid her career. The fact that Larsen dedicated *Passing* to Van Vechten and his wife, Fania Marinoff, does not make any difference for this argument. Perhaps it was just a gesture of thanks for his help in getting Larsen's first novel accepted at Knopf—an indication of how black writers had to negotiate the perilous waters of white patronage and thus either succumbed to cooptation or wore a mask of accommodation while subversively skewering the masters.

But what about the fact that one of Nella's and her husband Elmer's close African American friends, Lillian Alexander, who nominated Larsen for literary awards and hosted literary discussions in Harlem, wrote Elmer to apologize for criticizing the book before she had read it, based on what other people had said, because after finally reading it she realized how "dumb" the criticism of it was?

> Really the book is an epic—to me—(and I rarely rave over anything or anybody) and is revealing in every line of Negro wants, needs, failures and why, aspirations and the vicious circle that prevents their realization. And it is true at the same time. Most folks choke over the prologue but I just drank it in because you know how well I know my Lenox and Seventh Avenues and how I walk up and down them drinking in the magnificent comedy and the dire tragedy and woe encountered in every block. Except for some of his obscure slang, Carl knows Nigger Heaven almost (?) as well as I![1]

There was nothing obsequious or duplicitous, then, in Larsen's appreciation of the novel, nor in her dedication of *Passing*—which is not, I hasten to add, to say anything for or against Van Vechten's novel as we read it today.

Moreover, one can still argue that aspects of Larsen's texts undermine aspects of Van Vechten's; nothing requires us to read either Van Vechten's or Larsen's novels the way Nella Larsen did. It may be impossible to do so. But what does the need or desire to position Larsen's work against Van Vechten's reveal about the (biographical) assumptions with which we approach literary history and intertextual relations, and what might Larsen's unexpected response to *Nigger Heaven*, if we take it more at face value than in the past, do for us, even if as a purely heuristic exercise? A text that looks—indeed, is—stereotypical today and continuous with white writers' racist depictions of black culture often looked quite different in the 1920s. Students can learn from this that what counts as a stereotype shifts over time as new forms remake the literary field; one work helps open a path by which new experiments ultimately retire that very work to the dust heap. Biography is one of the best ways, although not the only way, of getting at this dynamic. Perhaps its most important use, pedagogically, is to teach about the strangeness of the past, the way it can perpetually surprise us.

After completing her first novel, *Quicksand*, Larsen wrote Van Vechten: "God forbid that I should ever be bitten by the desire to write another novel! Except, perhaps, one to dedicate to you. For, why should Langston Hughes be the only one to enjoy notoriety for the sake of his convictions?" (Imes [7 Mar. 1927]). Hughes had just been roasted in the black press for *Fine Clothes to the Jew* and his relationship to Van Vechten (to whom *Fine Clothes* was dedicated). And he had responded with a two-page essay in which he attacked his critics for being, among other things, nouveau riche snobs lacking in real "culture." Such people often complain, he noted, that the young writers don't write about the "best" colored people. He truly wished that someone would do so; it would be worth doing:

> But I fear for them if ever a really powerful work is done about their lives. Such a story would show not only their excellencies but their pseudo-culture as well, their slavish devotion to Nordic standards, their snobbishness, their detachment from the Negro masses and their vast sense of importance to themselves. A book like that from a Negro writer, even though true and beautiful, would be more thoroughly disliked than the stories of low-class Negroes now being written. And it would be more wrathfully damned than NIGGER HEAVEN, at present vibrating throughout the land in its eleventh edition. ("Those Bad")

Larsen believed that *Quicksand*, the novel she had just turned in to Knopf, was precisely such a book. Both Larsen and her husband expected her book to be reviled in the fashion that Hughes predicted. As Larsen wrote to Van Vechten, "Elmer says that if I do get the present one published that 'your people' will run me out of these United States. (He didn't use the word 'your people' either, in referring to them)" (Imes [7 Mar. 1927]). Larsen identified the cultural politics of her work completely with that of Van Vechten and Hughes.

As a matter of fact, in the late 1920s Nella Larsen was considered by many to be on Van Vechten's side of the culture wars. Her friendship with him was well-known, not least because she attested to it in interviews and frequently went with him to the theater and nightclubs. Attacks on *Nigger Heaven* were, as often as not, attacks on Larsen and her crowd. On 1 September 1926 appeared Hubert Harrison's extensive screed in the *Amsterdam News*, "Homo Africanus Harlemi." "The author of this breach of the peace," he began,

> has been well and favorably known to Harlem's new and nocturnal aristocracy of "brains" and booze. . . . "Nigger Heaven"—the title and the theme should be highly appreciated by Van Vechten's dusky hosts—and hostesses—over whose bottles he imbibed the conception of Harlem, which is here exhibited. The futile footling of our "intellectual" ephemeridae is fairly well indicated in the character of Byron Kasson, which is (like the other chief characters), a composite of elements to be found in the real Harlem. . . . One thing, however, Van Vechten has achieved and we thank him for it—he has risen up like a German submarine to throw the fear of "Nigger Heaven" into "the whole crowd of timorous and flocking birds" who hover around in Harlem dreaming that they are writing "Negro" literature, because Van Vechten's kind has coddled them at pink-teas and literary contests. (20)

Floyd Calvin in the *Pittsburgh Courier* also used *Nigger Heaven* as an occasion to attack Van Vechten's African American friends:

> It is clear that Mr. Van Vechten tried to give a faithful picture of the set he associated with. His descriptions are at least accurate, for one can see he was writing what he saw. . . . But we do not blame Mr. Van Vechten for the wave of "Niggerism" which this book has caused. We rather blame those really responsible, the Negroes who backed the volume from the start; who lent it their moral, if no other support, and who attempted to justify its appearance when it was first published. We blame those Negroes who were practically Mr. Van Vechten's guides in Harlem while gathering his material, who were in position to stifle the influence of the work on its initial appearance, had they had the courage and interest of the race at heart as they have so often claimed.

In the late 1920s, no woman (except Fania Marinoff, Van Vechten's wife) spent more time in cabarets and at dances with Carl Van Vechten than Nella Larsen Imes, often without her husband or Van Vechten's wife present.

What use could such information be in teaching Larsen in relation to the Harlem Renaissance? For one thing, the positions of Calvin and Harrison are related to those of later commentators on the movement as a whole, exemplifying institutional as well as ideological continuities between today's debates and those that informed the renaissance itself. For another, it throws a wrench into a lot of assumptions about the various "camps" of the movement and their interrelationships. For decades Larsen's work was perceived as focusing on "middle-class" and light-skinned characters because of her supposed rear-guard "uplift" philosophy; she wished to prove to white folks, so the argument went, that there were Negroes just like them who ought to be allowed into their churches and homes. "It is all rather banal," Hoyt Fuller wrote in his introduction to the 1971 edition of *Passing*, the classroom standard for fifteen years; "In the tradition of mulatto writers since William Wells Brown . . . Miss Larsen dwells on the 'white' traits of her 'society Negro' characters" (19). It doesn't take much research into her life to discover the irony of such charges, although charges of class bias against Larsen are not entirely off-base. Still, the nature of the bias may look different when we realize how humble were her own class origins. Although Fuller's dismissal of Larsen has long been superseded in literary scholarship, one still finds related views among general readers and students. Her life story helps explain why she would find it difficult to write about the people Zora Neale Hurston did. On the other hand, it also helps explain why she was able to write fictions that no one else of her period could about the psychology of the color line.

In her novel *Passing*, appropriately enough, Larsen herself includes a remarkable set of reflections on the near inescapability of biographical constructions in daily experience. When Irene runs into Clare in a Chicago rooftop restaurant at the beginning of *Passing*, the chief reason she cannot at first remember her old friend is that she thinks of the woman confronting her as white—that is, she leafs through her "white" Rolodex, so to speak, and comes up with nothing. More to the point, Irene is constantly speculating about Clare Kendry's life story, and in her speculations one notes the constant influence of Irene's notion of her own self-identity, which she attempts to stabilize in part through her assumptions about Clare. Yet Clare uncannily knows exactly what Irene's thoughts and suspicions about her are. Thus, she is aware that Irene and other childhood friends speculated that she was a prostitute or concubine during the twelve years since she "disappeared"—and during which she was in fact married. Again and again, Clare trips up Irene's biographical presumptions, those presumptions with which Irene attempts to make "sense" of Clare. These sense-making attempts, rather like the attempts in later years to make sense of Nella Larsen herself, reveal the racial/sexual intricacies of what counts as common sense.

One way of using biography, or portions of biography, in the classroom is to examine it critically. Where does the biographer seem to be fudging evidence or covering gaps with speculation? Where might an excessive reliance on a particular source be shaping the narrative into a pattern worth questioning? And is it ever possible to completely escape such problems? Are these not in fact problems we encounter in everyday experience, almost as a matter of course? In biography, the careful reader is perpetually brought up against the hard fact that the past is not only a prologue but at the same time a function of the present and that much can never be known.

Larsen's life story, much like her fiction, helps make visible the structure of identity expectations and the continued force of color-line culture in the institutions of knowledge. More specifically, the suppression and "disappearance" of interracial families is part of the background of the misunderstanding of Larsen with which we must struggle today and is a major point of both of her novels. As I argued in my own "biography of the color line" and of Larsen, this does not have meaning merely for that still small minority of people sometimes termed "biracial." The subordination of "family" to "race," the attempt to ensure that families would always serve to reproduce race, is one of the great constants in the legal, social, cultural, and spiritual history of the United States. Thus biographical detective work provides a very practical way of getting at important theoretical and historical issues and making them seem very real and immediate to students.

In addition to the theoretical implications—for notions of black diaspora, for example, or of racial identity and its articulation with nationality, gender, and sexuality or for the type of black feminism Larsen represents—students' engagement with archival and biographical materials brings out the excitement of research and critical engagement with both primary and secondary sources. These are valuable qualities for any adult citizen to develop. But that's not all, because one inevitably is brought up against the limit of the archive, the things that printed records do not record, what gets lost—the bailiwick of prose fiction, which can be as "true" as biography and frequently takes the form of fictional biography.

Larsen's fiction reflects on how the map of an absence reveals something about the structure of what is present and what suppressions its presence is built on. Yet precisely because of the suppressions—inevitable in the story of any life but especially of those whose experience brings shame and guilt—much is irrecoverable. For all the "eureka" moments, one is left with a sense of humility and incompletion; there is nothing "definitive" about the reconstruction of a life or the living of one.

NOTE

[1] Elmer Imes sent the letter to Van Vechten to cheer him up over the vituperative response to the novel in Harlem. He was a lifelong fan of Van Vechten's fiction and read Van Vechten's *The Blind Bow-Boy* on his hospital deathbed in 1941.

"In Some . . . Determined Way a Little Flaunting": Teaching with Nella Larsen's Letters[1]

M. Giulia Fabi and Jacquelyn Y. McLendon

Famously dubbed the "mystery woman of the Harlem Renaissance" by Mary Helen Washington in the early years of her critical rediscovery, Nella Larsen remains an intriguing figure to this day. Despite the ever-increasing number of critical volumes and essays devoted to her work, the portrait of this woman as an artist remains rather elusive. Even the multiple biographies that have significantly broadened our knowledge of her life continue to differ on several important points and have not dispelled completely the aura of mystery that surrounds her brilliant, meteoric, far too short literary career and the literary silence that envelops the last decades of her life.

In the scholarly effort to shed greater light on the life and work of this major figure of American modernism, Larsen's correspondence has proved of great importance for biographers and critics alike. In this essay, we discuss how Larsen's correspondence can play an important role in the classroom as well, helping to introduce students to the complexity of Larsen's art, guiding them beyond the immediacy of biographical approaches to her fiction, challenging the documentary bias that often intrudes in the analysis of African American literary works, and encouraging the class to have a greater appreciation of Larsen's sophisticated use of modernism's unreliable narrative voice and limited point of view.

A selection of five or six letters, like the ones presented or discussed in this essay, can be used during the first class devoted to Larsen as an effective method of introducing her life and times and simultaneously foregrounding her artistic sensibility and writing style. Further references to Larsen's epistolary comments on reading and writing can then be made in subsequent classes focusing on her fiction, in order to emphasize her literary self-awareness and identify her intertextual allusions. In conjunction with the biographical information derived from the volumes of Thadious Davis (*Nella Larsen*) and George Hutchinson (*In Search of Nella Larsen*),[2] Larsen's letters offer an enlivening element of immediacy: they exert the fascination of the "authentic," add the excitement of seeing the handwriting of a famous author, and conjure up the "realness" of the writer as a person. Larsen's references to contemporary events (such as the grand wedding of W. E. B. Du Bois's daughter, who married Countee Cullen), national organizations (e.g., the NAACP), writers and other prominent figures (including Du Bois; James Weldon Johnson and his wife, Grace; Carl Van Vechten; Gertrude Stein; Langston Hughes; Walter White; Claude McKay; Rudolph Fisher; Roland Hayes; and Ethel Waters) create a vivid sense of the intellectual and social context of the Harlem Renaissance and of Larsen's active involvement in it.

Larsen's letters also point to her wide-ranging readings, which represent a crucial component of her modernist sensibility as a writer, as has been explored in various critical essays that focus on the rich intertextuality that characterizes her fiction (e.g., Brickhouse; Dittmar; Fabi, "To Fashion"; Giorcelli; McLendon, "Double Nature"). At the same time, the liveliness and wittiness of her epistolary style stand in striking contrast to the more sober, analytic, and introspective quality of her fiction. With their aura of seemingly greater immediacy, Larsen's letters provide a useful strategy to draw students into a more direct and personal engagement with her powerful individuality, stimulating a participatory response to the ironic, sometimes condescending, and often irreverent comments on contemporary figures and concerns such as Du Bois, Walter White, or the "uplift."

Larsen's letters are an invaluable pedagogic resource for more reasons than one, since her fiction and her correspondence illuminate each other. In an early essay entitled "The Letters of Nella Larsen to Carl Van Vechten: A Survey," which is still one of the few literary critical pieces devoted specifically to her correspondence, William Bedford Clark argues convincingly that Larsen's letters "provide us with an implicit portrait of their author" and that they yield rare insight into the creator of characters like Helga Crane and Clare Kendry, for the letters bear the unmistakable personality of the woman who penned them and cover the vital period leading up to and immediately following her brief career as a writer of fiction (193).[3]

While Clark prefers to focus on the letters in order to answer the question, "But what was she like as a woman?" (195), Larsen's correspondence may be usefully analyzed in the classroom to discuss what she was like as an artist. The close reading of her letters, in fact, affords great, if characteristically "oblique" (McDowell, Introduction xxxi), insight into her poetics, her negotiations with a cultural context where the "Negro" may have been in vogue but the publishing industry was certainly white-dominated, her strategies to navigate race and gender inequalities, and especially her careful, brilliant modulation of her own writerly voice even in the supposedly more private epistolary medium.

The shift from approaching these letters as informative historical sources to analyzing them as texts in their own right, ones that possess high intrinsic value and require careful close reading, accomplishes at least two important goals in teaching Larsen's work. First, this shift problematizes the documentary bias that tends to inhibit an appreciation of the artistry of African American literature, thereby stimulating a more analytic reading of Larsen's novels. Second, it draws attention to how Larsen constructs her first-person epistolary voice to negotiate her precarious space as a black woman writer vis-à-vis her literary sponsors, other writers, her friends, and even her spouse. This analytic approach to her epistolary voice prepares students for the subsequent approaching of her novels and short stories by making them more critically wary of reading her works as a direct reflection of her life and by discouraging automatic identification of the narrator or characters with Larsen.

In her fiction, Larsen gestures repeatedly toward the interpretive, rather than simply informative, significance of letters and to the need to analyze them as texts within the text. In her works, letters lend insight into the psychology of her characters even when they seem to function mostly as devices to advance or twist the plot, as in the case of the note that panicked Mrs. Romley (aka Julia Hammond) sends to "the wrong man" in the eponymous 1926 short story. In *Quicksand*, notes and letters change the course of Helga's life more than once, revealing her insecurities, her priorities, and her attempts to find less confining social contexts for self-definition and self-expression. For instance, the short note from the YWCA employment office not only leads to her departure for New York in the company of Mrs. Hayes-Rore but also changes her relationship with the YWCA employees who write the note, revealing how Helga's previous dislike of them derived from her unwillingness to acknowledge her needy condition and from her self-protective tendency to anticipate and preempt the possibility of rejection. And when the shock of rejection has already been felt, as in the case of her traumatic visit to her uncle Peter, Helga's reaction to the letter that formalizes the severance of their relationship with a check shows her equally self-protective attempt to blot out the memory of pain and humiliation by focusing on the novel potentialities of a move to Copenhagen.

In *Passing*, letters function even more evidently as tools of characterization and psychological exploration. Larsen masterfully illuminates the complex inner landscapes and conflicted relationship of her heroines by characterizing the unreliable limited point of view that dominates her novel. She accomplishes this through the initial detailed description of how Irene perceives the envelope of Clare's "mysterious," "slightly furtive," "thin sly" letter (143) almost as an objective correlative to her friend's personality, an interpretation that to the reader of Larsen's novel reveals much about Irene's own fears. As becomes most clear in the case of *Passing*, exposure to even a few of Larsen's letters engenders a different reading experience of the novel because of the writer's "[a]lternately witty, cynical, and self-effacing" epistolary style (Clark 193), which is very different from the intense pensiveness of her fiction's third-person narrative voice and at times makes the reader of her fiction experience some of the surprise and impatience that, when confronted with Irene's irritation toward Clare's letters in the novel, we tend to blame almost automatically on Irene's fastidiousness and jealousy. Larsen's correspondence complicates that reaction and challenges any easy identification between the writer and her heroines, shifting the students' attention to how they function as each other's double.[4]

If Larsen's correspondence sheds light on the complexity of her fiction, the reverse is equally true. Irene's unreliability as the novel's central consciousness makes readers aware of the superficiality of face-value, documentary readings even of primary documents like letters, defying students to interpret Larsen's correspondence as a direct, unmediated reflection of her personality. Gossipy, at times condescending, and at other times seemingly sycophantic, "determined," and also "a little flaunting" in their emphasized assuredness (*Passing* 143), upon first reading, Larsen's letters seem to reveal little of that impressive ability for psychological exploration that characterizes her fiction, nor do they provide many direct statements on her poetics and artistic goals. However, her comments on the work of other writers may be fruitfully read as indirect elucidations of her own poetics or, to question even further her level of indirectness, at the very least as reflections on artistic concerns that emerge also in her work. The reasons she offers in praise of *Nigger Heaven*, for instance, evoke qualities of her own fiction and provide interpretive clues that guide students to a more sophisticated reading of it. In a letter to Van Vechten, she lauds his novel's "air of deceptive simplicity"; "the exquisite balance" with which the author "avoided the propagandistic pitfall"; "the dispassionate way of simply proceeding with the tale, getting on to the tragic denouement, merely stating thus and so is the case, and leaving it at that"; "the full power of its fastidious style and subtleties"; the challenge of never being "quite sure just where and when you [the author] have your tongue in your cheek" so that one can "never trust to one reading"; and finally also the relationship Van Vechten establishes with the audience by placing the burden of comprehension on the reader: "if the reader is a doubting Thomas, let him draw back and be damned to him" (Imes [11 Aug. 1926).[5]

Larsen advances similar aesthetic principles in the more public letter she wrote to Charles Johnson, in which she criticizes a review of Walter White's *Flight* that had appeared in *Opportunity* (Imes, Letter to Charles S. Johnson). In the process of demonstrating that the "reviewer lacked the ability or the range of reading to understand the book which he attacked with so much assurance," Larsen provides invaluable information on the breadth of her own readings and on her aesthetic self-awareness as a writer. Stating that "[i]t is the blindness, not the abuse which annoys me," she focuses on the reviewer's biased and superficial interpretation of the story, and on his "complaints about the author's style," cleverly ridiculing the reviewer's critical pretensions by noticing how he "*grumbles* about 'lack of clarity,' 'confusion of characters,' 'faulty sentence structure'" (emphasis ours). Refuting head-on this generic, and therefore all the more devastating, critique, Larsen challenges its objectivity by foregrounding the reviewer's ignorance of the various possible literary frames of reference for the evaluation of a novel's artistry.[6] Walter White's style may indeed "irritate . . . an admirer of Louis Hémon and Mrs. Wharton," but not someone, like Larsen herself, who judges it "by the present day standards of fiction" and is conversant with authors like "Huysmans, Conrad, Proust, and Thomas Mann." To avoid missing "both its meaning and its charm," White's novel needs to be read in the context of "the Europeans and the American moderns," and Larsen's description of its "more mature artistry" illuminates her own modernist aesthetic: "Actions and words count less and the poetic conception of character, the psychology of the scene more" (160).

Even when Larsen does talk directly about her own work, her letters demand equally close reading, since her often self-disparaging comments and unexpected references to herself as a "poor coloured child who for some reason or other has been feeling blue over that same old book" (Imes, Letter to Van

Vechten [Apr. 1928]) remain "a little flaunting" (Larsen, *Passing* [2007] 143) in the very obviousness of their emphasized humility, as well as in the dialogic complicity created by their assumption of a shared ironic attitude toward prevailing stereotypes of blackness. Both in the letters written before and during the creation of her two published novels, and in the later ones regarding manuscripts that were not published, she discusses her work with the determination of a professional writer who may often disclaim the present quality of her writing but not her potential for writing well. In an oft-quoted passage about *Quicksand*, she notes, "I got awfully tired of it about the middle of the Copenhagen episode. That and the last chapter ought to be longer. I should hate terribly to have to write even one more word for the damned thing, but I suppose I could if I absolutely had to" (Imes, Letter to Van Vechten [7 Dec. 1926]). Balancing self-doubt and self-promotion in discussing a short story she has finished and that she is "not at all sure" may interest *Harper's*, she adds, "I'm inclined to believe that I've squandered an idea that would have made a novel" (Imes, Letter to Van Vechten [29 June 1927]). And in 1931, after reporting a friend's evaluation of one of her manuscripts as "*rotten*" (Larsen's emphasis) she qualifies her acceptance of that critique: "And on re-reading it I came to the conclusion that he was right, though I was sure that there was good stuff in it. Since then I have sweated blood over it. Perhaps that's just as well. I remember you always say that easy writing makes bad reading" (Imes, Letter to Van Vechten [7 Apr. 1931]).

When we ask our students to do close readings of these letters as texts, rather than simply as documents, we are pushing them to examine strategies of indirectness. Instead of quantifying Larsen's epistolary sincerity students thus recover a more analytic sense of her development as professional writer and of the powerful individuality she aimed to preserve. That individuality is maintained even in a close, but nevertheless structurally asymmetrical, relationship with an established white sponsor like Van Vechten, for instance, a personal relationship that in the era of Jim Crow occurred within the kind of racialized and gendered social context that in her fiction she analyzes painstakingly in its multiple societal and personal facets.[7] In her letters, instead, Larsen often uses gossip to reposition herself as an insider/outsider in relation to such context. Gossip (about meetings, people, fellow artists, travels) signals her complicity with Van Vechten, but it also diffuses that intimacy by constantly evoking social events and (absent) others. Gossip is central to the dialogic quality of her letters and also provides a means to negotiate the potential dangers of personal exposure, insofar as her correspondence cultivates the lightness of touch, tongue-in-cheek quality, and semipublic tone of a conversation at a party.

It is illuminating to examine the acute writerly self-awareness in her letters with which she tries to traverse social boundaries through a shared sense of humor, irony, intellectual cultivation, and love of art, in contrast to the brutal force of the stereotyped categorizations that were prevalent in the age of Jim Crow. Her interview with Mary Rennels, which appeared in the *New York Telegram* on 13 April 1929, offers a good illustration of the prevailing racism of her segregationist times. In a letter to Van Vechten, where she describes Rennels's article, Larsen begins by noting "I *am* so upset" (Larsen's emphasis) and then proceeds to explain that in that interview she is "reported to have said that it's perfectly all right to send Negroes around to the back door" and also to have "referred to you [Van Vechten] as a devil." Pointing to the difficulty of finding a space of self-definition among socially predefined gender and racial roles, Larsen not only remarks on how she is misquoted by the interviewer but also on how she is criticized for opposite reasons by her own husband, who, she writes, "rose in the air because he thinks I was 'trying to pose as a silly uplifter of the race'" (Imes [19 Apr. 1929]).

It is through the tone of her letter that she contains and controls her stated "rage and mortification" in ways that reassert her individuality against the segregated social context her interviewer took for granted (Imes [19 Apr. 1929]). The humorous non sequitur of the last lines of her letter ("In fact I see no way out except suicide. Please come to my party anyway. My love to Fania and to you") reestablishes complicity and intimacy, relegating the public discourse of the interview to a distant, alien background. Larsen is so successful in doing so that reading the actual text of the interview comes as a shock, even though her letter should have prepared us for it. Rennels's dehumanizing pseudo-anthropological, classificatory focus on Larsen's skin color (together with her wish to reassure the reader that Larsen "would never pass"); her obtusely stereotyped comments on Larsen's biracial origins ("She doesn't mind being shooed up the employees' entrance in hotels, because her Nordic side waits for such a situation; her negro side understands it"); the unexamined prejudices that seep through her description of Larsen as someone who "selects only amusing and natural people, not too intellectual"; and that she totally misses the irony of Larsen's reference to her own "economic status" in relation to the fact that "[t]he chained and downtrodden negro is a picture that came out of the civil war" throw into sharp relief the elegance of the mind that could transform such obtuseness into the subtle complicity dominating Larsen's own letter about the interview.[8]

It is rewarding to examine this literary metamorphosis in relation to Larsen's use of the limited point of view in *Quicksand*, for instance. In this novel, Helga's inside knowledge of the everyday indignities of segregation and Larsen's focus on the delicacy and the self-protecting mechanisms of her heroine's mind often push into the background the more violent aspects of racial prejudice (such as the preacher's sermon, the ride in the Jim Crow car and the white man spitting in the drinking-water receptacle, job segregation, the commodification of Helga's body). As in her epistolary references to Rennels's interview, this play of (psychological) foreground and (social) background evokes with great historical precision—but also with a stylistic compression that demands keen attention on the part of the reader—a context of pervasive racial oppression that, unless Helga's role as central consciousness is brought forcibly to the attention of students, is too often missed or overshadowed by their irritation at her supposedly excessive fastidiousness. Larsen's letters help foreground how, as McLendon has argued in relation to *Passing*, Larsen is able "to handle both the literary and the sociological implications of her texts seamlessly" ("Double Nature").

As Larsen wrote to Van Vechten, "no subsequent generation can ever recover" the "flying glimpse of the panorama" of one's "own time" (Imes [n.d., 1925] "Thank you"). Yet reading her letters does give us a more vivid sense of her life and times, and a close analysis of her epistolary voice reverberates in illuminating ways on the interpretation of the beauty, force, and timeless quality of her fiction. Much archival work still needs to be done to recover Larsen's correspondence, and this work, to quote one of her contemporaneous European "moderns," "is worth while."[9] As Barbara Christian reminds us, and as we should remind our students, "the unavailability of a text amount[s] to its erasure" (*Black Feminist Criticism* 77). To analyze systematically Larsen's correspondence is a long overdue critical project for scholars of American modernism. To make her correspondence more readily available to students, scholars, and to the general public is an equally long overdue editorial project that will contribute to warding off the "menace of impermanence" that has historically surrounded, and for a long time obscured, the literary career of this brilliant writer (Larsen, *Passing* 229).[10]

NOTES

[1] Larsen, *Passing* [2007] 143. Page references are to the 1986 Rutgers University Press edition.

[2]See also C. Larson.

[3] See also Newman.

[4] McLendon, in *Politics of Color*, writes in greater detail about how Irene and Clare function as doubles.

[5] Along similar lines, in her letter to Charles S. Johnson Larsen writes, "Authors do not supply imaginations, they expect their readers to have their own, and, to use them" (159).

[6] As Fabi has argued in *Passing and the Rise of the African American Novel*, such generic and totalizing aesthetic dismissals are often made in relation to African American writers, especially pre–Harlem Renaissance ones, and their devastating force derives from voicing preexisting widespread assumptions of aesthetic inadequacy. Larsen's cutting critique of how the condescending and prescriptive nature of such comments is often rooted in ignorance of the various coexisting "standards of fiction" and her insistence on the need for wider readings in order to evaluate the work within its literary context remain a valid response to the controversies that have accompanied the redefinition of the American literary canon.

[7] Critics have discussed the complex response to white sponsorship during the Harlem Renaissance also in the case of Zora Neale Hurston and Langston Hughes.

[8] The kind of irony Rennels missed may be found in Larsen's letter to Van Vechten, where she refers to one of the apartments in which she and her husband lived as "Uncle Tom's Cabin" (Imes [1 May 1928]).

[9] These are the closing words of Virginia Woolf's *A Room of One's Own* (112), which was published the same year as *Passing*, in 1929.

[10] The authors of the present essay are currently editing a collection of Larsen's letters and other nonfictional material.

Teaching *Quicksand* in Denmark

Martyn Bone

In the last two decades, a wide range of new scholarship, including no less than three biographies, has reshaped the ways in which teachers and students respond to the life and fiction of Nella Larsen. In this essay, I demonstrate how critical debates and recent revelations about Larsen's links to Denmark transformed my teaching and classroom discussion of *Quicksand* in three different courses at the University of Copenhagen: a postgraduate seminar featuring both Danish and American students, an undergraduate survey course in American literature, and an undergraduate optional course on African American women's fiction. Teaching *Quicksand* in Copenhagen, the Danish capital, which provides the setting for five key chapters of Larsen's novel, generated unique possibilities (and pitfalls) that are unlikely to emerge in university classrooms in the United States. I also draw on student feedback to demonstrate that while my students struggled to connect *Quicksand* to the role of race, slavery, and colonialism in Danish history, they identified telling links between Helga Crane's experiences in early-twentieth-century Copenhagen and the experiences of non-white immigrants to Denmark today.[1]

Until recently, scholars rarely paid serious attention to Larsen's Danish heritage and identity. Especially striking are the views expressed by Larsen's first two biographers. In 1993, Charles Larson asserted that Larsen's "Denmark years are a total fabrication, a fancy embroidery upon the tragedy of her early life" as the apparently abandoned daughter of a white Danish mother (189). In 1994, Thadious Davis downplayed the possibility that Larsen had ever visited Denmark by remarking that "throughout her public life she displayed little intimate or firsthand knowledge of [Denmark], even though she could speak and read Danish" (*Nella Larsen* 68–69)—and, one might add, even though *Quicksand* provides a detailed portrayal of early-twentieth-century Copenhagen. However, in a crucial 1997 essay, "Nella Larsen and the Veil of Race," George Hutchinson proved once and for all that Larsen did visit Denmark, at least twice; moreover, Hutchinson's mammoth 2006 biography demonstrated how Larsen's firsthand experience of Copenhagen between 1908 and 1912 subtly informed *Quicksand*'s depiction of the Danish capital.

In contrast to most Larsen scholars in the United States before Hutchinson, most Danish students of *Quicksand* recognize that Larsen must have known Copenhagen quite intimately. Line, a student in my course on African American women's fiction in spring 2010, remarked that *Quicksand*'s representation of Copenhagen was " convincing to the extent that I don't think anyone could have written it in the beginning of the twentieth century without having actually been here. Where would she get her information? It would certainly demand hours and hours of extensive research for her to be able to describe Copenhagen in such relative detail."[2] Indeed, one of the most rewarding aspects of teaching *Quicksand* to Danish students was working together to locate *Quicksand* with specific reference to the city in which they—like Larsen a century ago—lived, worked, and studied. Having said that, the first time I taught the novel, my pedagogical authority was hampered (even if I did not realize it at the time) by the limitations of both my own reading in Larsen scholarship and the scholarship itself—at least those parts that underestimated Larsen's relation to and representation of Denmark.

In December 2003 I was asked at short notice to come up with a course for Denmark's International Study Program (DIS) that would run the following semester. This course would be aimed primarily at exchange students from the United States, though my department's Danish students would also be eligible. Given the transatlantic class demographic, I decided to offer a course entitled Europe in Twentieth-Century American Fiction. My coteacher, Gregory Stephenson, and I agreed that the course would feature, alongside the usual suspects of the "international theme" (James, Hemingway, Fitzgerald), James Baldwin (*Giovanni's Room*), Don DeLillo (*The Names*), Richard Ford (*Women with Men*), and Larsen. At this point I had read *Quicksand* only once but was intrigued by Larsen's representation of Copenhagen; with a research leave on the horizon, I was already planning to write about *Quicksand*. I figured that teaching the novel would be an opportunity to work through some of my inchoate ideas.

In the first of two ninety-minute classes on Larsen in March 2004, I started by asking whether any of the students—American or Danish—knew of Larsen: none of them did. I ran through some of the standard information about Larsen's relationship to the New Negro movement of the 1920s, but I also emphasized the problem with seeing Larsen only as a novelist of the Harlem Renaissance, especially in the context of a course like this one. I remarked that (and here I quote from the notes for my brief class introduction) "Larsen has tended to be seen as an African American writer, despite her mixed racial heritage, and her fiction has tended to be seen as African American literature, rather than as interracial or international literature. So, when critics assess *Quicksand*, the European dimension receives only limited attention." I proceeded to discuss Paul Gilroy's black Atlantic as a model for conceptualizing the transatlantic dimensions of African American literature and referenced Gilroy's passing suggestion that Larsen was a black Atlantic case study in waiting (18). Finally, I homed in on Larsen's Danish heritage.

At this point, however, my authority was suspect (though neither I nor my students knew it) because my discussion of this Danish heritage drew almost entirely on Davis's biography. So, while Davis's pioneering research helped me convey details of Larsen's matrilineal Danish heritage, it also led me to recapitulate some of Davis's own incredulity about Larsen's claims on a Danish identity. I did qualify that "Davis can seem overly skeptical toward Larsen's Danish credentials; if Larsen did invent her time in Denmark, she went to quite some lengths to do so, and did so consistently. Larsen's portrait of Copenhagen in *Quicksand* does seem remarkably 'authentic,' even down to the local detail—the names of streets, of newspapers, the use of Danish words, and so on." As this quotation from my class introduction indicates, my doubts about some of Davis's arguments derived from my sense that *Quicksand*'s narrative geography mapped convincingly onto the city my students and I knew—something a professor or student based in the United States would be less likely to recognize. What I did not know at the time was that Hutchinson had already proved Larsen's connections to Denmark while charging that "the effect of discounting Larsen's Danish experience and Danish background and her connection to her mother is to subordinate [Larsen's own] mature story of her life to a story that cannot accommodate the possibility of someone being both African American and Danish American" ("Nella Larsen" 339). In my somewhat hasty preparation for the DIS course, I had overlooked Hutchinson's 1997 essay.

As it turned out, *Quicksand*'s representation of Copenhagen and Helga's attempt to claim her Danish heritage did not become central points of discussion in this class. This may have reflected the predominance of exchange students from the United States, who lacked in-depth knowledge of Copenhagen's social history or geography. Like *Giovanni's Room*, *Quicksand* did reveal to the class the presence of the "international theme" in African American literature, and the United States students might not have experienced this so vividly had they been studying the novel at their home universities rather than in Copenhagen itself. Ultimately, though, class discussion was primarily concerned less with the local, historical-material conditions of Copenhagen in the early twentieth century than with broader, more familiar critical tropes such as the contrast between "the prejudiced restrictions of the New World" and "the easy formality of the Old" (96).

By the time I taught *Quicksand* again, in fall 2005, I was rather more familiar with Larsen's life and fiction. I had begun work on a monograph concerned with literary representations of the southern United States in transnational contexts, including a chapter on the depiction of southern United States and Danish folk cultures in *Quicksand*, I had belatedly discovered Hutchinson's 1997 essay and subsequently researched aspects of Danish social history that were relevant to my reading of the novel. I read up on the rural fishwives who came to Copenhagen to sell their wares on Gammel Strand: Helga has a memorable exchange with one such "old countrywoman" (76). Because Helga also encounters "the so-called poor sections" of Copenhagen during her peregrinations (75), I looked into the construction between 1880 and 1910 of new residential districts to accommodate recent migrants from rural Denmark. Finally, I had been focusing on what I had come to regard as a notable lacuna in critical discussions of *Quicksand*: Denmark's history as a slave-trading and colonial power.

Until the abolition of the transatlantic slave trade, both the United States and Denmark were major slave-trading powers. In the list of countries with the dubious distinction of being the world's leading slave-trading nations, Denmark ranks seventh, only one place behind the United States. But whereas the United States developed the peculiar institution within its own borders, the Danish form of racial slavery was confined to three small Caribbean islands: Saint Thomas, Saint Croix, and Saint Jan. Even after the emancipation of slaves in the Danish West Indies in 1846, few "black Danes" traveled to Denmark; when they did, such journeys were usually bound up with Copenhagen's continuing colonial power over the Danish West Indies. Still, as Arne Lunde and Anna Westerstahl Stenport have observed, in the first decade of the twentieth century "it became increasingly common for Copenhagen families to employ African servants and nannies, some from the West Indies, which presumably led to a fairly substantial presence, clearly coded in terms of class, of Danes of color in the city." This history of slavery and colonialism can be said to constitute a "structuring absence" in *Quicksand*'s representation of Copenhagen (232, 229).

In fall 2005 I tried to apply my research focus on Danish (as well as United States) histories of slavery, colonialism, and migration in my undergraduate classes on *Quicksand*. This is not to say that I ignored the rest of the novel. Teaching *Quicksand* as a core text in an American literature survey course at a European university is valuable for a number of reasons. In particular, *Quicksand* helps disrupt students' assumptions that "all black authors write about slavery and oppression; that [they] have all lived the same life" (Skelton 54). Such assumptions may be even more pernicious among Danish students than among (white) Americans, and could conceivably be compounded in an undergraduate survey course where the other African American texts—Frederick Douglass's *Narrative* (1845) and Charles Johnson's *Middle Passage* (1990)—are explicitly "about slavery and oppression."[3] *Quicksand* presents a very different kind of African American experience, and a very different kind of protagonist, to European students.

Still, it was the Copenhagen section of *Quicksand* that had an obvious extra resonance for Danish students in an American literature course at the university where Larsen claimed to have audited classes. I spoke about Nella Larsen, Denmark, and the black Atlantic,[4] telling the students about Larsen's links to Denmark before turning to Denmark's colonial history and trying to indicate how this might relate to Larsen's life and work. It was difficult for me to convey how this history might be relevant, not so much for Larsen's biography—the link to the Danish West Indies through Larsen's father, Peter Walker, is clear enough—but rather in reference to the representation of Denmark and Danish racial attitudes in *Quicksand*. There were a few giggles in the audience when I shifted from English to accented Danish, but once the students began listening to how canonical Danish authors who were contemporaries of Larsen viewed black people, the giggles turned to gasps of astonishment: did Johannes V. Jensen really say *that*?! During the seminar classes, it became apparent that my students generally seemed to know (even) less than I did about Denmark's history of slavery and colonialism. One student, Peter, admitted that he had only a limited understanding of Denmark's colonial history; Peter believed this to be the case with many other Danes, too. As such, whatever I might have expected to gain from local interest in Larsen's links to Denmark was limited to the degree that students were at a loss to see how Larsen's representation of the national capital and colonial center might relate to Denmark's role within the wider black Atlantic world.

Ultimately, students' interest in Helga's Afro-Danish identity derived from another source, and it was here that the unique potential of teaching *Quicksand* to Danish students was most vividly demonstrated. For as it happens, some of the issues that are so important in *Quicksand*—racism, bicultural identity, transnational migration—are profoundly, often disturbingly, resonant in contemporary Danish society. Even though many students were unwilling or unable to talk about Danish colonialism and racial attitudes in the early twentieth century, this had the effect of shifting our focus to Denmark in the early twenty-first century—an increasingly multicultural Denmark that they could debate more easily.

In 1997, Clarice Scott, an African American resident of Denmark, observed in a review of *Quicksand* that the novel seemed "strikingly contemporary" for its depiction of Helga's "mixed cultural heritage, a subject that is more relevant than ever in modern Danish society." In 2005 *Quicksand* seemed even more relevant in a political climate where sections of the mainstream media and certain political parties—in particular, the right-wing populist Danish People's Party, an influential supporter of the ruling center-right coalition—depicted immigrants as a threat to Danish national identity.[5] Some students saw points of comparison between Helga's situation and that of immigrants to Denmark now. Peter observed that Helga's sense of both belonging and not belonging was likely shared today by many immigrants to Denmark. Another student, herself an immigrant, stated that she could relate to Helga's circumstances. Born in Uganda but married to a native Dane, Pamela cited her own experience of "being met by such curiosity both by young and old alike." She further noted how "[h]istory and identity is 'touched' [on] in the novel, and this can be used to reflect on Danish history, especially for a foreign student" like her. If Pamela could empathize with Helga's sense of being hypervisible on the streets of Copenhagen, another student, Anders, invoked his own subject position as a native Dane to identify a national inability to perceive "foreigners," even in central Copenhagen. For Anders, Denmark's status as a small nation with few immigrants meant that native Danes could walk down Stroget, the main thoroughfare through the city center, without really "seeing" foreign-born fellow citizens.

To be sure, there are limits to a comparison between Helga's experiences and those of contemporary immigrants to Denmark. The first and perhaps most obvious point to make here is that Helga's hypervisibility derives from her (supposed) status as the singular "Sorte" ("black person") on the streets of Copenhagen (Larsen 73); by contrast, (nonwhite) immigrants today are far more numerous.[6] Second, unlike most contemporary immigrants, Helga already has a familial link to Denmark and is welcomed into Copenhagen's bourgeois society by her aspirational aunt and uncle, Katrina and Poul Dahl—even if, as Line noted in spring 2010, Helga is also "objectified, orientalized and, to a certain extent, essentialized by her Danish relatives and the people in their social circle." Both Line and Ane, another student in my spring 2010 seminar, contrasted Helga's relatively privileged position in Danish society with the situation of most contemporary immigrants. Ane remarked that "I did not in fact make this connection [between Helga's experience and that of immigrants today] because Helga's situation in the novel is so unusual. . . . She is welcomed because she has a function to her Danish relatives and the way she is treated in every material way seems comfortable and leisurely, which are not exactly terms one would usually use when thinking of immigrants of today." In fall 2005, Maria made an even firmer distinction between Copenhageners' relatively favorable response to Helga and Danish reactions to immigrants today: "Helga Crane is not necessarily perceived in a suspicious or negative manner by her Danish relatives/associates, but rather as someone interesting and exotic because of her appearance and background. Today's immigrants, on the other hand, are often viewed with more suspicion and in a very negative manner—simply because of skin color or religion."

Maria's comment brings me to my third and final qualification: resistance to immigrants in Denmark today is bound up with Islamophobia. This does not mean that religion has trumped race as the primary battleground of national identity: after all, whether Muslim immigrants come from Turkey, Pakistan, Iraq, or Somalia, they are all identifiable as different—as *nydanskere* ("new Danes")—because they are not white. To rework Maria's phrasing, the immigration debate is often (mostly covertly, sometimes overtly) about skin color *and* religion. This shows no sign of abating: even as my two seminar classes discussed *Quicksand* in November 2005, the Muhammad cartoon controversy was simmering before exploding internationally in January 2006. One immediate and telling upshot of the controversy was that applications for membership of the (already thriving) Danish People's Party rose seventeenfold. At the same time, this increasingly global crisis finally alerted at least some sections of the international media that for some years now Denmark "has been moving in the direction of xenophobia and racism—especially towards its Muslim inhabitants" (Day).

When I taught *Quicksand* in my fall 2006 undergraduate seminar Twentieth-Century African American Women's Fiction, discussion turned more explicitly to the ways in which Helga's transnational, biracial subjectivity complicates established notions of not only (African) American but also Danish identity. Patricia, a student of Danish and Malaysian parentage, remarked that "as a biracial person, I do sometime feel that I'm being stared at. I mean, I don't feel like a freak, but more like 'an obscene sore,' to quote [*Quicksand*]." Extrapolating from her own experience as a bicultural individual who is nevertheless Danish by birthright to the situation of those "new Danes" who seek both citizenship and social acceptance, Patricia bluntly observed that "[i]n some ways immigrants appear to be welcome into the Danish society, but there are times where I feel that some Danes have their heads so far stuck up their arses that they can't see the difference between an immigrant and 'an obscene sore.'" However, one student wondered whether the Danish liberal left might be hindering instead of helping the cause of "new Danes." Karoline questioned the tendency for leftist advocates of multiculturalism to fetishize immigrants' difference from ethnic Danes and made an intriguing comparison to the process of exoticization experienced by Helga Crane in an earlier era: "It is perhaps possible . . . to compare the Dahls in *Quicksand* with the sort of present-day Danes named *halal-hippies* by a popular Danish politician of Syrian descent [Naser Khader]. These are the kind of people who, in their eager attempt at being politically correct, loudly praise the cultural benefits of the ethnic idiosyncrasies of immigrants, thus focusing on differences rather than similarities and preventing integration."

Ultimately, my Danish students' responses to *Quicksand* demonstrated how the novel can both illuminate and interrogate fixed categories: not only "black" and "white," but also "American" and "Danish." The strange career of Helga Crane, "moving shuttle-like from continent to continent" (96), helped some students recognize that if society in the United States has been defined by distinctive and stringent racial classifications, race has hardly been absent from Danish history. Like Peter, Maria acknowledged that many Danes remain ignorant about the role of slavery, racism, and colonialism in Danish history. "I think most Danes do not as such consider race and colonialism as aspects of Danish history—certainly not in the same way as race/colonialism are part of . . . U.S. or British history. . . . [W]e Danes rarely consider the fact that our own forefathers played a somewhat significant part in slave trade, but we instantly recognize [the] slave trade as a horribly large part of U.S. history." Moreover, the fact that, as Karoline observed in fall 2006, "race has become a taboo word" in contemporary public discourse suggests that it remains a profoundly sensitive issue in today's tentatively multicultural Denmark.

In such a context, *Quicksand*'s relevance in Danish university classrooms may be stronger than ever, nearly a century after Larsen's last visit to her mother's homeland. In 2015, eighty-seven years after its original publication, *Quicksand* was finally published in a Danish translation; in a surreal twist, two editions of *Kviksand* appeared within a week of each other. In her introduction to *Teaching African American Literature: Theory and Practice*, Maryemma Graham posits that "we want our students to apply what they learn to their everyday lives" (10). For scholars and students of African American literature outside the United States, such everyday relevance is not always apparent, let alone applicable. But reading *Quicksand* in Denmark between 2005 and 2010 impelled me and my students to ask not only, "What does it mean to be an American?"—a question that Katherine Driscoll Coon deems central to the teaching of African American literature (32)—but also, "What does it mean to be a Dane?"

NOTES

[1] This essay is substantially revised and updated from my "African American, Danish American, Black Danish: Teaching Nella Larsen's *Quicksand* in Denmark," in *European Scholars Teaching African American Texts*, ed. Karla Simcikova (Ostrava: Universitats Ostraviensis, 2007. 11–32).

[2] The direct quotations from students featured in this essay come from written responses to email questionnaires that I distributed following the classes on *Quicksand* from the two versions of my Twentieth-Century African American Women's Fiction course that ran in fall 2006 and spring 2010. My thanks to former students Maria Hansen, Karoline Holm, Pamela Birungi Louis, Line Miller, Patricia Rasmussen, and Ane Sjølin for allowing their written feedback to be quoted in this essay.

[3] However, Douglass's *Narrative* recounts how he overcame slavery and oppression, while Johnson's novel gleefully undermines readers' assumptions about the narrative conventions of (African) American literature.

[4] The first seminar on *Quicksand*, focusing on the sections of the novel set in Naxos, Chicago, and Harlem (first time around), was preceded by my lecture on modernism and the Harlem Renaissance.

[5] I made the case for the novel's contemporary relevance in an article published in *Politiken* (the Danish newspaper featured in *Quicksand*) in June 2005 (http://politiken.dk/debat/kroniken/ECE116637/quicksand/). The article was not, however, required reading for the course, and I did not mention it in class.

[6] The question of just why Helga is depicted as the only black resident of Copenhagen (the singular "Sorte") is too complex to address here, but Helga's apparent uniqueness as a black person in the early-twentieth-century Danish capital drew a skeptical response from at least one student in my spring 2010 course. Line pointedly remarked that "Nella Larsen visited Copenhagen at approximately the same time as the Copenhagen Zoo had several exhibitions displaying ['exotic'] people." For Line, it was "quite unbelievable" that Helga "would have been treated . . . relatively indifferently."

Teaching Nella Larsen's *Passing* at an Urban Community College

Zivah Perel Katz

At Queensborough Community College (QCC), the City University of New York, all students are required to take English Composition 2, Introduction to Literature. I routinely teach excerpts from Nella Larsen's *Passing* in this course, and the novel works so well in my classroom because of QCC's demographics, which are common to urban community colleges. It is often the first formal introduction my students have to the concept of passing, although they are familiar with the idea of struggling with one's identity, and I use it as one of the themes that bind together the semester's texts. *Passing* relates to the students personally, and because of this it serves as a unique jumping-off point for their study of literature at the college level.

Queensborough's student population is representative of the population of the borough of Queens, which is one of the most diverse counties in the United States and roughly equal parts African American, Asian Pacific, Caucasian, and Latino. Over half of QCC's students were born in the United States, but a large percentage were born overseas, including many from Jamaica, China, South Korea, and Guyana (Office of Institutional Research and Assessment 13). A large portion of the students born overseas speak languages other than English at home (Martí). QCC's students also vary in age and over twenty-five percent are over twenty-five, well above the age of traditional college students (Office of Institutional Research and Assessment 15). Over seventy percent of first-time, full-time students need remediation of some kind, fifteen percent of whom need triple remediation (reading, writing, and math) (1). These numbers are fairly typical for an urban community college, and keeping this student body in mind is important to teaching successfully at QCC or any other urban community college.

English Composition 2 is one of the few courses that all QCC's students will take and the second in a series of two required writing courses. While many students will go on to take a third English course, for the rest of the students it is the first and last time they will take a literature course at the college level. English Composition 2 is a typical writing course in that it requires six thousand words of writing per semester, including both high- and low-stakes writing, three thousand of which are formally evaluated. At QCC, English Composition 2 addresses general education objective 13: "Students will make informed judgments of the humanities and the arts as aesthetic and intellectual experience." It should include the "major literary genres—fiction, poetry, drama—and may include other genres and media" (*Teaching* 27). The course must serve the dual purposes of addressing the skills young writers need and introducing them to studying literature at the college level.[1]

I divide a typical Introduction to Literature course into several units, each on a different theme. For the last few semesters, those themes have been race, gender, and war. I teach *Passing* near the start of the semester, along with some Harlem Renaissance poetry. Because the pricing of books is so important to my students, I avoid asking them to purchase large anthologies or many texts. One book that has worked well for me is *The Portable Harlem Renaissance Reader*, edited by David Levering Lewis. I teach the Harlem Renaissance poetry to which I refer and *Passing* from the excerpts included in this edition.[2] Although the excerpted passages leave out much of Irene's memories about her childhood, with the introduction of John Bellew's character, and therefore much of the color that shades the climax of the novel, my students are able to extrapolate enough of what they need to know about the characters and their relationships with one another from the excerpts.

While I give my students background information on the Harlem Renaissance period, our primary method of analysis of the novel is not contextual. Rather, since it is the beginning of the semester and the course is the students' first college-level literature course, I focus primarily on close reading and how key passages reflect the larger themes of the text. I also work to connect the text to students' own lives and, in so doing, strive to make the study of literature feel applicable to them.

Although the idea of racial passing is key to Larsen's text and the Harlem Renaissance era, it is passing in a looser form that links the course texts together. Later in the semester, we discuss passing as it relates to gender, social, and political identities.[3] I usually spend two to three class periods (one hour and forty minutes each) on *Passing*, and we spend much of that time close reading selections from the novel.

One of my favorite places to begin with the book is the end; Clare's death provides an opportunity to talk about the difference between the literal and metaphorical. In this way, the excerpts Lewis includes in his volume work well, as they are primarily from the third part of the novel. There is no debate that Clare dies at the end, and what my students are most interested in is how she ends up on the ground below the window. I usually break students up into small discussion groups and ask them to figure out for themselves whether Clare's death is suicide or murder and how the difference might change the meaning of the story. To support their theory, they must provide textual evidence. It is during this discussion that I encourage them to look at the ending of the book beyond the literal and into the figurative.

How Clare dies has serious ramifications for what Larsen tries to do with the novel because each scenario poses different implications about the dangers of passing. When my students have to construct a working theory of Clare's death, what I really am asking them to do is tell me how each scenario plays out metaphorically. For instance, if Clare kills herself, then the book functions as a morality tale against denying one's identity. However, if John Bellew kills

Clare, then the book speaks to the necessity of passing and the danger of African American identity, even during a period of relative enlightenment like the Harlem Renaissance.

Because my students are interested in solving the mystery of Clare's death, they are invested in doing the careful reading necessary to forming a theory. That it is ultimately impossible to argue one cause conclusively also forces them to complicate their thinking to include the multiple implications of her death and the many parties indicted for it. By turning a sensational topic into a source for close reading and argumentation, I am able to engage a student body often resistant to difficult reading. The drama of this murder/suicide is ripe for taking advantage of student interest to push toward a metaphoric reading of Clare's death.

The ambiguity of the ending of the novel and the students' creative thinking about it also helps establish students' feeling of agency as readers since they feel it is up to them to figure out the mystery. This is an important skill for community college students, since they often have struggled academically. Creating a sense of agency empowers students to take command of their reading and learning experience and encourages them to trust their own academic voices.

Discussing the ramifications of passing as described above brings to the fore students' recognition of the shifting role of race during the Harlem Renaissance period. That there was racism in America's recent history is no surprise to any student. However, *Passing* works so well in the classroom because it asks students to examine their own assumptions about race and ethnicity, which they often avoid out of discomfort. These assumptions influence students' readings of Clare's death, and in defending their theories about the end of the book, students begin to unpack the way race has shaped their assumptions about their own lives.

Examining their assumptions encourages students to see the relevance literature from another time period may have to their lives. My students, as do many other college students, typically feel disconnected from literature that they perceive as before their time. When I ask students at the beginning of the semester what their favorite book or movie is, very few if any respond with a text published before their date of birth, and they usually choose something from the last ten years. Convincing students of the value of reading a book written in 1929 is difficult, yet an ability to connect to older texts and to find value in them is a goal of English 102. The key becomes encouraging students not only to recognize the historical relevance of *Passing* (what the novel meant to Larsen when she wrote it and to those who read it in 1929) but also to understand how they can make a text that ostensibly has little to do with their lives relevant to them personally.

Because our discussion of Clare's death leaps into the metaphoric, what we spend much of our class time discussing is the grip our racial identities have on our lives. Although few students have suffered the discrimination regularly felt by the Redfield family, most of my students know what it is to be the other. This otherness can manifest itself in a variety of ways—racial, ethnic, religious, class, age, not to mention that they all feel on the periphery of the American system of higher education—and students feel their differences, regardless of type, with similar intensity. The metaphoric implications of Clare's death then extend further, beyond the book, to students' lives.

Although I typically avoid asking students to write personal narratives since grading them can be fraught, I do ask students to do some informal writing about moments in their lives when they have passed and how they felt about the experience. I ask them to perform a close reading of those moments, just as they did of Clare's death, thinking about the implications for their views of their own identities. Students have the option to share their experience with the class, and they often tell touching stories about feeling like outsiders. The personal narratives are valuable at this particular moment in the semester because they ask students to connect what they are reading to their experiences. (Because it is early in the semester, the narratives also give students a way to relate to one another personally.) By examining the implications of their moments of passing to Clare's, they see how Larsen's novel, albeit dated in their view, can provide insight into their lives.

In "Decoding Essentialism: Cultural Authenticity and the Black Bourgeoisie in Nella Larsen's *Passing*," Candice M. Jenkins notes that the

> ambiguously raced figure is understood as a threat to the physical and psychic boundaries of race. . . . I am interested in how the mulatta unsettles blackness and notions of an internalized black authenticity, particularly in the middle-class community of the New Negro Renaissance that is interrogated in Larsen's work. (133)

What Jenkins addresses here is a kind of essentialism in our conceptions of race. Because QCC's student body is so diverse, the range of experience is vast, and often listening to one another's stories is an eye-opening experience for students who have not yet thought about the experience of those with different racial, ethnic, religious, or other identities. I hope that my students' narratives help them battle the impulse to essentialize racial or other identities in a particular way. Examining their moments of passing and listening to those of their classmates also forces students to come face-to-face with their cultural assumptions of others. Often students are not in touch with what their actions imply about their views. By looking directly at their own identities and then the implications of passing as another, they are forced to examine their cultural assumptions about both.

Nella Larsen's experience as a woman of mixed race resonates for many of my students. I tell them about Larsen's Danish and West Indian background and how her mixed-heritage identity influenced her literary works (McLendon, "Nella Larsen: Overview"). Because of the diversity in my classroom, most students can relate to Larsen's mixed heritage either personally or through someone close to them.

Larsen may draw from her own experiences to inform her work, but she resists making easy judgments about them. Jacquelyn McLendon observes that Larsen contrasts

> black and white worlds within which her protagonists move in their quests for individuality. In recording their responses to a fragmented and often hostile environment, she presents scathing indictments against both black and white society, rarely attempting to inculcate the notion that one is better than the other. This latter impulse in her writing may appear to signal her own racial ambivalence, or it may indicate an attempt at objectivity. In any case, it is one of the primary reasons Larsen remains so hard to grasp, both as a woman and as a writer. ("Nella Larsen: Overview")

Yet it is precisely this refusal to indict either black or white society that makes Larsen so accessible to my students. Her ambivalence makes it easier for students of all backgrounds to relate to her observations and questions.

This ambivalence also breaks the mold of what my students often see as classic tales of African American suffering before the civil rights movement. John Bellew is clearly a villain in the story, but it is really the tension within the African American community about passing that is at the story's core. It would be easy to blame Clare's death on Bellew, but if she was indeed murdered, it was most likely Irene who did it. This takes the central focus of the conflict of the story away from the obvious discrimination faced by the African American people at the hands of whites and instead complicates the conflict as intraracial.

Moreover, Larsen's ambivalence gives my students the opportunity to clarify their views of race and embrace their own ambivalence. Often students feel outside pressure (or pressure themselves) to come up with simple answers, such as racism is bad or African Americans are victims. Larsen gives them tacit permission to resist these simplifications and to create more complex views of race with regard to the text and to extend this complex thought process to their other course work and experiences.

In an introductory-level course, it is particularly important to me to teach students how to perform a close reading, and I focus their attention on aspects of Larsen's writing such as syntax, diction, and imagery. This focus follows a couple of weeks spent at the start of the semester working with students on close reading. I begin an English 102 course in this way because close attention to detail and the analysis of an author's intentions in her writing give students the framework with which to approach all the course texts.

I teach students how to do a close reading by handing out guided questions that help them determine what to pay attention to when reading. I then model it for students during class discussion, using an excerpt near the start of the novel that directly addresses passing for the first time in the excerpts Lewis includes in his volume. We spend some time discussing passing in general and the two positions on passing that Clare and Irene articulate. Their discussion in part 1, chapter 2 works so well for students because each woman represents a different position on passing, providing students with a perspective on both sides. A section of the passage reads:

> Just as she's always had that pale gold hair, which, unsheared still, was drawn up loosely back from a broad brow, partly hidden by the small close hat. Her lips, painted a brilliant geranium red, were sweet and sensitive and a little obstinate. A tempting mouth. The face across the forehead and cheeks was a trifle too wide, but the ivory skin had a peculiar soft lustre. And the eyes were magnificent! dark, sometimes absolutely black, always luminous, and set in, long, black lashes. Arresting eyes, slow and mesmeric, and with, for all their warmth, something withdrawn and secret about them.
>
> Ah! Surely! They were Negro eyes! Mysterious and concealing. And set in that ivory face under that bright hair, there was something about them . . . something exotic. . . .
>
> Into those eyes there came a smile and over Irene the sense of being petted and caressed. She smiled back. (Quicksand *and* Passing 161 [1986])

This passage is generally the first indication students have that Irene may not feel platonically about Clare. We talk about Irene's description of Clare's appearance and how Larsen adds adjectives to the description ("arresting," "mesmeric," "sweet and sensitive") that reveal her feelings, even though she never openly would do so. The description is much more about a person to whom Irene is attracted rather than a friend (or enemy). Students observe that Irene never describes Brian with nearly as much affection or desire as she does Clare.

This scene is indicative of why there is so much at stake for Irene because of Clare's reappearance. For one, it explains why she suspects Brian might be having an affair (who could resist a woman such as Clare?). It also may explain why Irene needs to remove Clare from her world, as her presence would repeatedly remind her of what she sees as her deviant desires. Students see that had they not examined this passage closely, they would be missing important information for interpreting the end of the novel.

The close attention to detail that students need to parse this passage and understand the nuances of Irene's relationship with Clare encourages them to approach their own lives with that same attention. Diction becomes something more than what their professor grades them for but rather a real tool to communicate thoughts and ideas. Larsen's text helps make a concept like diction relevant and practically important for students, who so often struggle with academics.

For my final exam, I ask students to pick five or six course texts and tie them together thematically. Students must use a specific example from each text and explain how they see that example relating to the other texts they chose. Many students write about *Passing*, since it is one of a few texts during the semester that explores the concept of passing. Asking students to make connections among texts encourages them to think creatively about the themes of our course.

One semester, a student wrote that she saw the strongest connection between *Passing* and the film *Brokeback Mountain* (2005), which we watched during our unit on gender. Although set at different times and made in different mediums, the plots of the two stories are strikingly similar. The time we spent discussing passing in terms of Larsen's novel prepared this student to see *Brokeback Mountain* as a story of two men's unsuccessful attempts at passing, a conceptual framework that enhanced the meaning of the film for the student. Once viewed in this context, the student was able to see the issue of gay rights in an entirely new way. By relating it to the struggle for racial equality, one that students unilaterally accept as desirable and necessary, she viewed the struggle for sexual equality in the same way. The novel gave her the means to think about a contemporary issue from a different perspective.

While most of my students have not heard of passing specifically or are not familiar with the term for it, most are familiar with the idea of feeling uncomfortable with one's own racial, ethnic, religious, or other identity. Since so many urban community college students are immigrants and children of immigrants, they have had the experience of trying to balance (or hide) parts of themselves to adapt to American culture. Even those that do not have that background are familiar with the feeling of trying to appear different than they are. Josh Toth's comment in "Deauthenticating Community: The Passing Intrusion of Clare Kendry in Nella Larsen's *Passing*" becomes valuable in explaining why *Passing* works so well in the classroom: "as it is predicated upon the fact that race is performance, the act of passing suggests that all racial categories are arbitrary and ultimately untenable" (57). That racial categories exist is obvious, especially for my students. What they learn from *Passing* is that racial categories, as well as other social categories, are "arbitrary" and "untenable."

This is often a revelation to students, one that helps them begin to see their identities as social constructs that they can manipulate depending on their environment or desire. It also helps them overcome the stigmas they often place on themselves as community college students. I frequently hear from students that coming to QCC feels like a failure to them, that they are there because they could not get into another college. *Passing* encourages them to think of their own identities as more fluid and complex than they themselves have been willing to see. They begin to transcend the struggles common to urban community college students: seeing themselves exclusively as racial minorities, immigrants, students who are older than traditional college age, or as inadequate because of their need for remediation. This hint of liberation is a wonderful place to begin their academic careers.

NOTES

[1] Elaine Showalter's *Teaching Literature* has shaped my pedagogical goals for the literature classes. Her book includes a list of twelve competencies students should be expected to achieve from literature courses. Although achieving all twelve would be too lofty a goal for an introduction to literature course, a few of the competencies from her list stood out to me as consonant with my goals at QCC. These include distinguishing "between literal and metaphorical meaning," identifying the "cultural assumptions" a text makes and using those assumptions to explore one's own, using literature as "cultural references," reading closely, and thinking creatively (26–27).

[2] The following sections of the novel are included in Lewis's volume: portions of part 1, ch. 2; portions of part 3, ch. 1; the entirety of part 3, chs. 2, 3, and 4. My students read all the excerpts from the novel.

[3] Other texts we discuss during the semester that students relate back to *Passing* include Toni Morrison's *Beloved*, Paul Haggis's film *Crash*, Charlotte Perkins Gilman's story "The Yellow Wallpaper," Kate Chopin's "The Storm," Kimberly Peirce's film *Boys Don't Cry*, Tim O'Brien's *The Things They Carried*, and Tony Kushner's play *Angels in America*.

NOTES ON CONTRIBUTORS

Clark Barwick is lecturer of communication at Indiana University, Bloomington. He holds a doctorate in English and American studies from Indiana University, and his dissertation *Obscurity, Blackness, and the Making of the Harlem Renaissance, 1919–Present* considers the racial politics of cultural memory and ongoing African American literary canon formation. He has held fellowships for research at Emory University, Yale University, the New York Public Library's Schomburg Center for Research in Black Culture, and the University of Florida. At Indiana University, he teaches courses on African American literature, American studies, and writing. He was the recipient of the 2013 Indiana University Trustees Teaching Award.

Martyn Bone is associate professor of American literature and coordinator of the Center for Transnational American Studies at the University of Copenhagen. He is the author of *The Postsouthern Sense of Place in Contemporary Fiction*, the editor of *Perspectives on Barry Hannah*, and the coeditor of the three-volume miniseries *Creating Citizenship in the Nineteenth-Century South*, *The American South and the Atlantic World*, and *Creating and Consuming the American South*. His essay on Nella Larsen and Denmark recently appeared in *Afro-Nordic Landscapes: Equality and Race in Northern Europe*. He has also published articles in journals, including *American Literature, Journal of American Studies, Comparative American Studies,* and *CR: New Centennial Review*. His research and teaching interests include United States southern studies, African American literature, transnational American studies, and black Atlantic studies.

Beth Widmaier Capo is professor of English at Illinois College. She is the author of *Textual Contraception: Birth Control and Modern American Fiction* and scholarly essays in anthologies and journals. She teaches courses on nineteenth- and twentieth-century American literature, Japanese literature in translation, young adult literature, gender and women's studies, and composition. Her work in progress focuses on comparative analyses of gendered violence in contemporary Japanese and American fiction.

Martha J. Cutter is professor of English at the University of Connecticut and the former editor of *MELUS: Multi-ethnic Literature of the United States.* She has also edited *The Wadsworth Themes in American Literature Series: 1910–1945.* Other publications include *Lost and Found in Translation: Contemporary Ethnic American Writing and the Politics of Language Diversity*; *Unruly Tongue: Language and Identity in American Women's Writing, 1850–1930*; and essays in anthologies and such journals as *Callaloo*, *Arizona Quarterly*, *American Literary Realism*, *Legacy*, *Literature and Medicine*, *African American Review*, and *MELUS*. She teaches courses on African American literature, post–Civil War American literature, women's literature, and racial passing.

M. Giulia Fabi is associate professor of American literature at the University of Ferrara, Italy. She is the author of *Passing and the Rise of the African American Novel* and coeditor of Barbara Christian's *New Black Feminist Criticism.* She has contributed to *The Oxford Companion to African American Literature* and *The Cambridge Companion* *to the African American Novel* and has published essays in such journals as *The Henry James Review*, *African American Review*, *American Literary Realism*, and *Legacy*. She is the editor of the Penguin Classics edition of W. W. Brown's *Clotel* and of a series of Italian translations of African American novels. Her work in progress is a book on pre-Harlem Renaissance. She is also coediting a collection of Nella Larsen's letters and other nonfiction materials. She teaches courses on African American literature and women's studies.

Cristina Giorcelli is Professor Emerita of American Literature at the University of Rome Three. Her main fields of research are mid- and late-nineteenth-century fiction (Fuller, James, Crane, Wharton, Chopin) and modernist poetry and fiction (W. C. Williams, L. Zukofsky, D. Levertov, W. Cather). She is cofounder (1980) and codirector of the quarterly journal *Letterature d'America*. She edits a series of volumes on clothing and identity (*Abito e Identità*), of which twelve have come out. The University of Minnesota Press has published four volumes from that series under the title *Habits of Being*. She was president of the Italian Association of American Studies (1989–1992) and vice president of the European Association for American Studies (1994–2002).

Lori Harrison-Kahan is associate professor of the practice of English at Boston College. She is the author of *The White Negress: Literature, Minstrelsy, and the Black-Jewish Imaginary*. Other publications include "Inside *Inside Man:* Spike Lee and Post-9/11 Entertainment," as well as scholarly essays and reviews in anthologies and journals. Her research and teaching interests are American literature and culture, gender studies, and comparative race and ethnic studies. She is currently working on a book manuscript titled "It Just Makes Beauty: The Friendship of W. E. B. Du Bois and J. E. Spingarn" and coedited a special issue of *MELUS* for summer 2012.

George Hutchinson is professor of English and Newton C. Farr Professor of American Culture at Cornell University. He is the author of *In Search of Nella Larsen: A Biography of the Color Line*, *The Harlem Renaissance in Black and White*, *The Ecstatic Whiteman: Literary Shamanism and the Crisis of the Union*, and *The Cambridge Companion to the Harlem Renaissance* in addition to scholarly essays in anthologies and journals. He teaches courses on American and African American literature and is currently working on a monograph titled *In a Dark Time: American Literature and Culture in the 1940s*. He has recently published an edition of Anita Reynolds's memoir *American Cocktail: A "Colored Girl" in the World* and coedited with John K. Young *Publishing Blackness: Textual Constructions of Race Since 1850*.

Caresse John is associate professor of English at Belmont University. Her publications include "'Stronger Readers, Stronger People': The Intellectual Challenges of Nella Larsen's Work" and "Strategic Ambivalence: A Feminist Standpoint Theory Reading of Nella Larsen's Novels." She teaches courses on nineteenth- and twentieth-century American literature, literary theory (particularly feminism and narratology), and rhetoric and composition. Her work in progress is a study of the narrative techniques of several American women writers using a feminist-standpoint-theory approach.

Zivah Perel Katz is associate professor of English at Queensborough Community College, the City University of New York. Her publications include "Teaching Tim O'Brien in the Context of War Fiction," "Individuality in Stanley Kubrick's Marine Corps," and

"Transforming the Hero: Reconfiguring Masculine Identity in the 'Secret Sharer.'" She also edited, along with Amy E. Traver, *Service-Learning at the American Community College*. Her research and teaching focus on American war novels and film, interdisciplinarity in teaching, and popular culture. She is working on a book about the influence of the 24-hour news cycle on the novels, memoirs, and films of the two Iraq wars.

Jacquelyn Y. McLendon is a Professor Emerita of English at the College of William and Mary. Her publications include *The Politics of Color in the Fiction of Jessie Fauset and Nella Larsen*; *Phillis Wheatley: Revolutionary Poet*; as well as scholarly essays, reviews, and entries in anthologies and journals. She is also co–series editor of the *Pearson Library of American Literature* database, including several anchor volumes: *American Literature, 1945–Present* and *African American Literature* (vols. 1 and 2). Currently, she is coediting a collection of Nella Larsen's letters and other nonfiction materials. Her work in progress is "Black Expressive Culture and the Ecology of Gardens."

Shealeen A. Meaney is associate professor of American literature and director of women's studies at Russell Sage College. Her publications include "'Sans Clothes and Sans Reproche': Wilderness, Necessity, and Transgression in Post-Suffrage American Women's Travel Narratives," "'In My American Fashion': National Identity, Race, and Gender Tourism," and "'Every head was bobbed': Anti-Tourism, the Identity Market, and Women on the Road in the 1920s." She is guest editor of an issue of *Women Studies* on women and travel. Her research and teaching interests include United States literature and culture of the 1920s, women's travel writing, environmental literature, and intersections of literature and geography. Her work in progress is a book on early-twentieth-century United States women's travel culture.

Gayle M. Murchison is an associate professor of music at the College of William and Mary. Her publications include *The American Stravinsky: The Style and Aesthetics of Copland's New American Music: The Early Works, 1920–1938*, as well as essays on William Grant Still, including "New Paradigms in William Grant Still's *Blue Steel*," and an essay on Mary Lou Williams, "Black Christ / Black Music, Mary Lou Williams, St. Martin de Porres, and Jazz as Sacred Music," as well as other scholarly essays in anthologies and journals. As a historical musicologist, her research and teaching interests are twentieth-century American and African American music, the Harlem Renaissance, music and the civil rights movement, and music and identity. Among her works in progress is a study of the black singer-songwriter and social consciousness.

Suzanne Raitt is professor of English at the College of William and Mary. Her numerous publications include *Virginia Woolf's* To the Lighthouse; *Vita and Virginia: The Work and Friendship of Virginia Woolf and V. Sackville-West*; *May Sinclair: A Modern Victorian*; and *Volcanoes and Pearl Divers: Essays in Lesbian Feminist Studies.* Her research and teaching focus on British modernist women writers, especially biography, history and theory of sexuality, psychoanalytic and cultural theory, lesbian and women's studies. She is coeditor of Virginia Woolf's *Orlando* for the Cambridge edition of Virginia Woolf and is completing a book called *Waste and Efficiency in British Culture, 1864–1922.*

Riché Richardson is associate professor in the Africana Studies and Research Center, Cornell University. She is the author of *Black Masculinity and the U.S. South: From*

Uncle Tom to Gangsta. She is also coeditor of the University of Georgia Press book series The New Southern Studies. Her research and teaching interests include African American literature, American literature, Southern studies, Africana studies, and gender studies. Her book in progress is titled "Black Femininity, Global South: Visualizing the Politics of Race, Reaction, and Revolution."

Beryl Satter is professor of history at Rutgers University, Newark. Among her numerous publications are *Family Properties: Race, Real Estate, and the Exploitation of Black Urban America*; *Each Mind a Kingdom: American Women, Sexual Purity, and the New Thought Movement*; "The Sexual Abuse Paradigm in Historical Perspective: Passivity and Emotion in Mid–Twentieth Century America"; "Cops, Gangs, and Revolutionaries in 1960s Chicago"; and "Marcus Garvey, Father Divine, and the Gender Politics of Race Difference and Race Neutrality." She teaches courses on women's history and urban history in the United States, as well as African American history. Her work-in-progress concerns the history of ShoreBank, a community development bank that attempted to funnel fair credit to urban black communities.

Steven B. Shively is an associate professor of English at Utah State University. He is coeditor of *Willa Cather Newsletter and Review* and a collection of essays titled *Teaching the Works of Willa Cather*. He is also author of "No 'Urbanized Fake Folk Thing': Benjamin Botkin, Sterling Brown, and 'Ma Rainey'"; "Reading the Menuhin Chapter," and "*My Ántonia* and the Parables of Sacrifice," among others. He teaches courses in English education and American literature, as well as courses on multicultural American literature and the Harlem Renaissance. His research and other teaching interests include pedagogy of place, young adult literature, Nebraska writers, and religion in literature.

Lyde Cullen Sizer is professor of United States cultural and intellectual history at Sarah Lawrence College. Her publications include *The Political Work of Northern Women Writers in the American Civil War Era, 1850–1872*; "A Dynamic Process of Remapping: New Work on Women and the Civil War"; "Still Waiting: Intermarriage in White Women's Civil War Novels"; and "Acting Her Part: Northern Women Spies During the American Civil War." She teaches courses on the United States Civil War, United States cultural and intellectual history, and United States women's history.

John K. Young is professor of English at Marshall University. He is the author of *Black Writers, White Publishers: Marketplace Politics in Twentieth-Century African American Literature* and coeditor with George Hutchinson of *Publishing Blackness: Textual Constructions of Race since 1850*. He has also published scholarly articles on Toni Morrison and Oprah's Book Club, Thomas Pynchon and popular magazines, *Passing*'s publishing history, Virginia Woolf as publisher, William Plomer and the Hogarth Press, the Trinidadian novelist Robert Antoni, the Book-of-the-Month Club editions of Richard Wright's *Native Son* and *Black Boy*, and Jean Toomer's publications in the New Orleans magazine *The Double Dealer*. His research and teaching interests include twentieth- and twenty-first-century American, African American, British, and anglophone literature. His *How to Revise a True War Story: Tim O'Brien Processes of Textual Production* is forthcoming from the University of Iowa Press in 2016. He also serves as the executive director of the Society for Textual Scholarship.

SURVEY PARTICIPANTS

Tuzyline Jita Allan, *Baruch College, City University of New York*
Laura Behling, *Gustavus Adolphus College*
Elyse Berube, *Greater Lawrence Technical School*
Jennifer DeVere Brody, *Duke University*
Pamela L. Caughie, *Loyola University Chicago*
Karen A. Chachere, *Independent Scholar*
Katie L. Chiles, *University of Tennessee*
Esperanza Cintron, *Wayne County Community College*
Michael Tavel Clarke, *University of Calgary*
Stephen Criniti, *West Liberty State College*
Amy Cummins, *Fort Hays State University*
Carol Delaney, *Virginia International University*
Ellen Elfstrom, *Florida Keys Community College*
Eva Federmayer, *Eotvos Lorand University, Budapest*
Mar Gallego, *Universidad de Huelva*
Amina Gautier, *Washington University in St. Louis*
Julie Goodspeed-Chadwick, *Indiana University–Purdue University*
Katherine M. Gray, *Lynchburg College*
Kathleen Gyssels, *University of Antwerp*
Stephanie Hankerson, *Albany State University*
Gary Edward Holcomb, *Emporia State University*
Sheila Hassell Hughes, *University of Dayton*
Katharine Ings, *Manchester College*
Adriane Ivey, *Oxford College of Emory University*
Greg Jackson, *Rutgers University, New Brunswick*
Olu Jenzen, *University of Sussex*
A. Yemisi Jimoh, *University of Massachusetts, Amherst*
Catherine Keohane, *Montclair State University*
Meg King, *University of Illinois, Chicago*
Sonia Labrador, *New College of Florida*
Julia Lisella, *Regis College*
Sue Lonoff, *Harvard University Extension School*
Arne Lunde, *University of California, Los Angeles*
Tiffany Magnolia, *North Shore Community College*
Emily Magruder, *California State University, Dominguez Hills*
Devona Mallory, *Albany State University*
Babacar M'Baye, *Kent State University*
Deborah McDowell, *University of Virginia*
Christina Mesa, *Stanford University*
Quentin Miller, *Suffolk University*
Shamika Ann Mitchell, *State University of New York, Rockland Community College*
Joycelyn Moody, *University of Texas, San Antonio*
Tom Morgan, *University of Dayton*

Robert Nowatzki, *Ball State University*
Kofi Owusu, *Carleton College*
Naomi Pabst, *Yale University*
Anita Patterson, *Boston University*
Hiram Perez, *Princeton University*
Kimberley Phillips, *College of William and Mary*
Hermine Pinson, *College of William and Mary*
Lisa Radinovsky, *University of Maryland, University College*
Ben Railton, *Fitchburg State College*
Kya Reaves-Ellis, *Old Dominion University*
Chantae Recasner, *Cincinnati State University*
Elizabeth Rich, *Saginaw Valley State University*
Darcie Rives, *Augustana College*
Jaclyn Rodriguez, *Occidental College*
Rekha Rosha, *Wake Forest University*
Alice Rutkowski, *State University of New York, Geneseo*
Karen Ann Schaller, *University of Sussex*
Jeanne Scheper, *University of California, Irvine*
Michele L. Simms-Burton, *Howard University*
Jeffrey Steele, *University of Wisconsin, Madison*
Anna W. Stenport, *University of Illinois, Urbana*
Dorothy Stringer, *Temple University*
Cammie M. Sublette, *University of Arkansas*
Masami Sugimori, *University of Kansas*
Gina Terry, *Texas A & M University*
Miriam Thaggert, *University of Iowa*
Willie Tolliver, *Agnes Scott College*
Keja Valens, *Salem State College*
Karen R. Veslits, *Independent Scholar*
Linda Wagner-Martin, *University of North Carolina, Chapel Hill*
Sidra Smith Wahaltere, *University of North Carolina, Chapel Hill*
Pricilla Wald, *Duke University*
Cheryl Wall, *Rutgers University, New Brunswick*
Alys Eve Weinbaum, *University of Washington*
Oren Whightsel, *Illinois State University*
Roland L. Williams, Jr., *Temple University*
Kari J. Winter, *University at Buffalo, State University of New York*

WORKS CITED

Abel, Elizabeth, Barbara Christian, and Helene Moglen, eds. *Female Subjects in Black and White: Race, Psychoanalysis, Feminism.* Berkeley: U of California P, 1997. Print.

Aberjhani, and Sandra L. West, eds. *Encyclopedia of the Harlem Renaissance.* New York: Checkmark, 2003. Print.

Ahlin, Lena. *The "New Negro" in the Old World: Culture and Performance in James Weldon Johnson, Jessie Fauset, and Nella Larsen.* Lund: Lund U, 2006. Print.

Alexander, Lally [Lillian A.]. Letter to Elmer S. Imes. 23 Oct. 1926. MS. Box 20, folder 4. Carl Van Vechten Collection. New York Public Lib, New York.

Anderson, Paul Allen. *Deep River: Music and Memory in Harlem Renaissance Thought.* Durham: Duke UP, 2001. Print.

Anderson, Richard. "Gatsby's Long Shadow: Influence and Endurance." *New Essays on* The Great Gatsby. Ed. Matthew J. Bruccoli. Cambridge: Cambridge UP, 1985. 15–40. Print.

Baker, Houston. *Blues, Ideology, and Afro-American Literature: A Vernacular Theory.* Chicago: U of Chicago P, 1984. Print.

———. "Modernism and the Harlem Renaissance." *American Quarterly* 39.1 (1987): 84–97. Print.

———. *Modernism and the Harlem Renaissance.* Chicago: U of Chicago P, 1987. Print.

Baraka, Amiri. "The Changing Same (R&B and New Black Music)." *The LeRoi Jones / Amiri Baraka Reader.* Ed. William J. Harris. New York: Thunder's Mouth, 1991. 186–209. Print.

Barnett, Pamela E. "'My Picture of You Is, after All, the True Helga Crane': Portraiture and Identity in Nella Larsen's *Quicksand.*" *Signs* 20.3 (1995): 575–600. Print.

Bassie, Ashley. *Expressionism.* London: Parkstone, 2008. Print.

Bederman, Gail. *Manliness and Civilization.* Chicago: U of Chicago P, 1995. Print.

"Been in the Storm So Long." Perf. Mary Pinckney. *Classic African American Gospel. Smithsonian Global Sound.* Smithsonian Folkways Recordings, 2008. Web. 18 June 2011.

Behr, Shulamith. *Expressionism.* London: Tate, 2006. Print.

Bennett, Gwendolyn. "The Ebony Flute." *Opportunity* 7 (1928): 153. Print.

Berg, Allison. *Mothering the Race: Women's Narratives of Reproduction, 1890–1930.* Champaign: U of Illinois P, 2002. Print.

Berger, John. *Ways of Seeing.* New York: Viking, 1973. 45–64. Print.

Beuka, Robert. *American Icon: Fitzgerald's* The Great Gatsby *in Critical and Cultural Context.* New York: Camden, 2011. Print.

Blackmer, Corinne. "The Veils of the Law: Race and Sexuality in Nella Larsen's *Passing.*" *Race-ing Representation.* Ed. Kosta Myrsiades and Linda Myrsiades. New York: Rowman, 1998. 98–116. Print.

Blackmore, David L. "'That Unreasonable Restless Feeling': The Homosexual Subtexts of Nella Larsen's *Passing.*" *African American Review* 26.3 (1992): 475–84. Print.

Bloom, Harold. "Elegiac Conclusion." Richter 225–33.

Bone, Robert A. *The Negro Novel in America.* New Haven: Yale UP, 1958. Print.

Bourne, Randolph S. "Trans-national America." 1916. *War and the Intellectuals: Collected Essays, 1915–1919*. Ed. Carl Resek. New York: Harper, 1964. 107–23. Print.

Boys Don't Cry. Dir. Kimberly Pierce. Perf. Hilary Swank, Chloë Sevigny, and Peter Sarsgaard. Fox Searchlight, 1999. DVD.

Brickhouse, Anna. "Nella Larsen and the Intertextual Geography of *Quicksand*." *African American Review* 35.4 (2001): 553–60. Print.

Briggs, Julia. "Between the Texts: Virginia Woolf's Acts of Revision." *Text* 12 (1999): 143–65. Print.

Brody, Jennifer DeVere. "Clare Kendry's 'True' Colors: Race and Class Conflict in Nella Larsen's *Passing*." *Callaloo* 15.4 (1992): 1053–65. Print.

Brokeback Mountain. Dir. Ang Lee. Perf. Jake Gyllenhaal, Heath Ledger, and Michelle Williams. Focus, 2005. DVD.

Bruccoli, Matthew J. *F. Scott Fitzgerald's* The Great Gatsby*: A Literary Life*. New York: Carroll, 2000. Print.

Bryer, Jackson R. "Four Decades of Fitzgerald Studies: The Best and the Brightest." *Twentieth-Century Literature* 26.2 (1980): 247–67. Print.

Buhle, Mari Jo, Teresa Murphy, and Jane Gerhard. *Women and the Making of America*. Upper Saddle River: Pearson–Prentice Hall, 2009. Print.

Burrill, Mary. *They That Sit in Darkness: A One-Act Play of Negro Life*. *Birth Control Review* 3 (Sept. 1919): 5–8. *Life Dynamics*. Web. 9 Sept. 2014. <http://www.lifedynamics.com/library>.

Butler, Judith. *Bodies That Matter*. New York: Routledge, 1993.

———. "Passing, Queering: Nella Larsen's Psychoanalytic Challenge." Abel, Christian, and Moglen, 266–84.

Calvin, Floyd. "Calvin's Weekly Diary of the New York Show World." *Pittsburgh Courier* 6 Nov. 1926, sec. 2: 3. Print.

Capo, Beth Widmaier. *Textual Contraception: Birth Control and Modern American Fiction*. Columbus: Ohio State UP, 2007. Print.

Carby, Hazel V. "It Jus Be's Dat Way Sometime: The Sexual Politics of Women's Blues." *The Jazz Cadence in American Culture*. Ed. Robert G. O'Meally. New York: Columbia UP, 1998. 471–83. Print.

———. "It Jus Be's Dat Way Sometime: The Sexual Politics of Women's Blues." *Unequal Sisters: A Multicultural Reader in U.S. Women's History*. Ed. Ellen C. Du Bois and Vicki Ruiz. London: Routledge, 1990. 238–49. Print.

———. *Race Men*. Cambridge: Harvard UP, 1998. Print.

———. *Reconstructing Womanhood: The Emergence of the Afro-American Woman Novelist*. New York: Oxford UP, 1987. Print.

Carr, Brian. "Paranoid Interpretation, Desire's Nonobject, and Nella Larsen's *Passing*." *PMLA* 119.2 (2004): 282–95. Print.

Caughie, Pamela L. *Passing and Pedagogy: The Dynamics of Responsibility*. Champaign: U of Illinois P, 1999. Print.

Champion, Laurie. *American Women Writers, 1900–1945*. Westport: Greenwood, 2000. Print.

Chandler, Owen. "The Black and Tan Cabaret—America's Most Democratic Institution." *Messenger* (1925): 97+. Print.

Chauncey, George. *Gay New York*. New York: Basic, 1994. Print.

Chinitz, David. "Rejuvenation through Joy: Langston Hughes, Primitivism, and Jazz." *American Literary History* 9.1 (1997): 60–78. Print.

Chopin, Kate. "The Storm." *Great Short Stories b y American Women*. Ed. Candace Ward. New York: Dover, 1996. 89–94. Print.

Christian, Barbara. *Black Feminist Criticism: Perspectives on Black Women Writers*. New York: Teachers Coll. P, 1985. Print.

———. *Black Women Novelists: The Development of a Tradition, 1892–1976*. Westport: Greenwood, 1980. Print.

Clark, William Bedford. "The Letters of Nella Larsen to Carl Van Vechten: A Survey." *Resources for American Literature Study* 8 (1978): 193–99. Print.

Clifford, James. *The Predicament of Culture: Twentieth-Century Ethnography, Literature, and Art*. Cambridge: Harvard UP, 1998. Print.

Coleman, Leon. *Carl Van Vechten and the Harlem Renaissance: A Critical Assessment*. New York: Garland, 1999. Print.

Coon, Katherine Driscoll. "A Rip in the Tent: Teaching (African) American Literature." Graham, Pineault-Burke, and Davis 31–51. Print.

The Cotton Club. Dir. Francis Ford Coppola. Orion, 1984. MGM Home Entertainment, 2001. DVD.

Crash. Dir. Paul Haggis. Perf. Sandra Bullock, Don Cheadle, Matt Dillon, Jennifer Esposito, Brendan Fraser, Terrance Howard, Chris "Ludacris" Bridges, Thandie Newton, Ryan Phillippe, Larenz Tate, and Michael Peña. Lions Gate, 2004. DVD.

Crenshaw, Kimberlé. "Mapping the Margins: Intersectionality, Identity Politics, and Violence against Women of Color." *Stanford Law Review* 43 (1991): 1241–99. Print.

Cutter, Martha J. "As White as Most White Women: Racial Passing in Advertisements for Runaway Slaves and the Origins of a Multivalent Term." *American Studies* 54.4 (2016): 73–97.

———. "Sliding Significations: Passing as a Narrative and Textual Strategy in Nella Larsen's Fiction." *Passing and the Fictions of Identity*. Ed. Elaine K. Ginsberg. Durham: Duke UP, 1996. 75–100. Print.

Davidson, Cathy N., and Linda A. Wagner-Martin, eds. *The Oxford Companion to Women's Writing in the United States*. New York: Oxford UP, 1995. Print.

Davis, Allison. "Our Negro 'Intellectuals.'" *Crisis* 35 (1928): 268+. Print.

Davis, Angela Y. *Blues Legacies and Black Feminism: Gertrude "Ma" Rainey, Bessie Smith, and Billie Holiday*. New York: Pantheon, 1998. Print.

Davis, Arthur. *From the Dark Tower: Afro-American Writers, 1900–1960*. Washington: Howard UP, 1974. Print.

Davis, Thadious. Introduction. Larsen, *Passing* [2002] xi–xvi.

———. *Nella Larsen: Novelist of the Harlem Renaissance: A Woman's Life Unveiled*. Baton Rouge: Louisiana State UP, 1994. Print.

———. "A Note on the Text." Introduction. Larsen, *Passing* [1997] xxxv.

Day, Kiku. "Denmark's New Values." *Guardian*. Guardian News and Media, 15 Feb. 2006. Web. Dec. 2010. <http://www.guardian.co.uk/cartoonprotests/story/0,,1709895,00.html>.

Decker, Jeffrey Louis. "Gatsby's Pristine Dream: The Diminishment of the Self-Made Man in the Tribal Twenties." *Novel: A Forum on Fiction* 28.1 (1994): 52–71. Print.

Dijkstra, Bram. *American Expressionism: Art and Social Change, 1920–1950*. New York: Abrams, 2003. Print.

Dittmar, Linda. "When Privilege Is No Protection: The Woman Artist in *Quicksand* and *The House of Mirth*." *Writing the Woman Artist: Essays on Poetics, Politics, and Portraiture*. Ed. Suzanne W. Jones. Philadelphia: U of Pennsylvania P, 1991. 133-54. Print.

Douglas, Ann. *Terrible Honesty: Mongrel Manhattan in the 1920s*. 1995. New York: Farrar, 1996. Print.

Doyle, Laura. *Freedom's Empire: Race and the Rise of the Novel in Atlantic Modernity, 1640–1940*. Durham: Duke UP, 2008. Print.

Dube, Wolf-Dieter. *The Expressionists*. London: Thames, 1996. Print.

Du Bois, W. E. B. "The Browsing Reader." *Crisis* (1928): 202+. Print.

———. *Dark Princess*. New York: Harcourt, 1928. Print.

———. "Of Our Spiritual Strivings." *The Souls of Black Folk: Writings*. New York: Lib. of America, 1986. 363–71. Print.

———. *The Souls of Black Folk*. 1903. New York: Penguin, 1995. Print.

DuCille, Anne. "Blues Notes on Sexuality: Sex and the Texts of Jessie Fauset and Nella Larsen." *African American Culture and Sexuality*. Spec. issue of *Journal of the History of Sexuality* 3.3 (1994): 418–44. Web. 2 May 2010.

———. *The Coupling Convention: Sex, Text, and Tradition in Black Women's Fiction*. New York: Oxford UP, 1993. Print.

Dumenil, Lynn. *Modern Temper: American Culture and Society in the 1920s*. New York: Hill, 1995. Print.

Durrow, Heidi. "Dear Ms. Larsen, There's a Mirror Looking Back." *Poem/Memoir/Story* 8 (2008): 101–09.

———. "'Passing' across the Color Line in the Jazz Age." *NPR Books*. NPR, 7 Apr. 2010. Web. 30 Jan. 2015.

———. "Three Books to Rescue Nordic Lit from the Dark Side." *NPR Books*. NPR, 22 Feb. 2011. Web. 30 Jan. 2015.

Dvořák, Antonin. *Symphony No. 9 in E Minor "From the New World."* 1893. Perf. New Philharmonia Orchestra. Cond. Riccardo Muti. EMI, 2001.

Eliot, T. S. "Letter to F. Scott Fitzgerald." *F. Scott Fitzgerald Critical Assessments*. Ed. Henry Claridge. East Sussex: Helm, 1991. 173. Print.

———. "The Love Song of J. Alfred Prufrock." *T. S. Eliot: Collected Poems, 1909–1962*. New York: Harcourt, 1991. 3–7. Print.

———. "The Metaphysical Poets." *Selected Essays, 1917–1932*. New York: Harcourt, 1932. 241–50. Print.

Ellis, Havelock, and John Addington Symonds. *Sexual Inversion*. London: Wilson and Macmillan, 1897. Print.

English, Daylanne. "Selecting the Harlem Renaissance." *Critical Inquiry* 25.4 (1999): 807–21. Print.

———. *Unnatural Selections: Eugenics in American Modernism and the Harlem Renaissance*. Chapel Hill: U of North Carolina P, 2004. Print.

"Everybody Gives Me Good Advice." Lyrics by Alfred Bryan. Comp. [James] Kendis, [Herman] Paley. New York: Remick, 1906. *Levy Sheet Music Collection*. Web. 16 June 2011. <https://jscholarship.library.jhu.edu/handle/1774.2/9729>.

"Everybody Gives Me Good Advice." 1906. Perf. Bob Roberts. *Cylinder Preservation and Digitization Project*. Dept. of Special Collections. Donald C. Davidson Lib., U of California, Santa Barbara, n.d. Web. 16 June 2011. 78 rpm disc, Edison Gold Moulded Record.

"Everybody Gives Me Good Advice." 1906. Perf. Bob Roberts. *Cylinder Preservation and Digitization Project*. Dept. of Special Collections. Donald C. Davidson Lib., U of California, Santa Barbara, n.d. Web. Cylinder, Edison Gold Moulded Record.

"Everybody Gives Me Good Advice." 1906. Perf. Bob Roberts. *National Jukebox: Historical Recordings from the Library of Congress*. Lib. of Congress, n.d. Web. 16 June 2011. <www.loc.gov/jukebox>. 78 rpm disc, Victor Records.

Fabi, M. Giulia. *Passing and the Rise of the African American Novel*. Urbana: U of Illinois P, 2005. Print.

———. "'To Fashion the Wonderful Garment': W. E. B. Du Bois's *The Quest of the Silver Fleece* and Nella Larsen's *Quicksand*." *Extravagance and Everyday Wear: Habits of Being IV*. Ed. Cristina Giorcelli and Paula Rabinowitz. Minneapolis: U of Minnesota P, 2015. 202–17. Print.

Fauset, Jessie Redmon. *There Is Confusion*. New York: Boni–Liveright, 1924. Print.

Favor, J. Martin. "A Clash of Birthrights: Nella Larsen, the Feminine, and African American Identity." *Authentic Blackness: The Folk in the New Negro Renaissance*. Durham: Duke UP, 1999. 53–80. Print.

Ferguson, Jeffrey Brown. *The Harlem Renaissance: A Brief History with Documents*. Boston: Bedford–St. Martin's P, 2007. Print.

Ferrall v. Ferrall. 153 NC 174; 69 SE 60; 1910 NC. Supreme Court of North Carolina. *Lexis*. Web. 27 Dec. 2010.

Fisher, Rudolph. "The Caucasian Storms Harlem." *American Mercury* 11 (1927): 393–98. Print.

———. "The City of Refuge." *Atlantic Monthly* 135 (1925): 178–87. Print.

———. *The Walls of Jericho*. New York: Knopf, 1928. Print.

Fitzgerald, F. Scott. *The Great Gatsby*. New York: Scribner's, 1995. Print.

Flohr, Birgitt. "The Relationship between Fiction and Autobiography." *University of Hannover*. N.p., 1–19. Web. 9 Oct. 2015. <www.itp.uni-hannover.de/~flohr/papers/m-american-lit2>. PDF.

Floyd, Samuel A., Jr. *Black Music in the Harlem Renaissance: A Collection of Essays*. New York: Greenwood, 1999. Print.

Foertsch, Jacqueline. "The Right, the Wrong, and the Ugly: Teaching Shelley's Several *Frankensteins*." *College English* 63 (2001): 697–711. Print.

Fordham, Finn. *I Do, I Undo, I Redo: The Textual Genesis of Modernist Selves*. Oxford: Oxford UP, 2010. Print.

Foreman, P. Gabrielle. Introduction, Wilson xxv–lv.

Fuller, Hoyt. Introduction. *Passing*. By Nella Larsen. New York: Collier, 1971. 11–24. Print.

Fusco, Coco, and Brian Wallis. *Only Skin Deep*. New York: Intl. Center of Photography, 2003. Print.

Gabler, Hans Walter. "A Tale of Two Texts; or, How One Might Edit Virginia Woolf's *To the Lighthouse*." *Woolf Studies Annual* 10 (2004): 1–29. Print.

Gates, Henry Louis, Jr., and Evelyn Brooks Higginbotham, eds. *Harlem Renaissance Lives*. New York: Oxford UP, 2009. Print.

Gates, Henry Louis, Jr., and Nelly McKay, gen. eds. *The Norton Anthology of African American Literature*. New York: Norton, 1996. Print.

Genette, Gérard. *Narrative Discourse: An Essay in Method*. 1972. Trans. Jane E. Lewin. Ithaca: Cornell UP, 1980. Print.

———. *Narrative Discourse Revisited.* 1983. Trans. Jane E. Lewin. Ithaca: Cornell UP, 1988. Print.

Giddins, Gary, and Scott DeVeaux. *Jazz.* New York: Norton, 2009. Print.

Gilman, Charlotte Perkins. "The Yellow Wallpaper." *Great American Short Stories.* Ed. 115–29. Paul Negri. Mineola: Dover, 2002. Print.

Gilroy, Paul. *The Black Atlantic: Modernity and Double Consciousness.* London: Verso, 1993. Print.

Giorcelli, Cristina. "Intertextuality in Nella Larsen's *Passing.*" *Letterature d'America: Rivista Trimestrale* 21.86 (2001): 127–47. Print.

Golub, Mark. "*Plessy* as 'Passing': Judicial Responses to Ambiguously Raced Bodies in *Plessy v. Ferguson.*" *Law and Society Review* 39 (2005): 563–600. Print.

Graham, Maryemma. "When Teaching Matters." Introduction. Graham, Pineault-Burke, and Davis 1–11.

Graham, Maryemma, Sharon Pineault-Burke, and Marianna White Davis, eds. *Teaching African American Literature.* New York: Routledge, 1998. Print.

Gray, Jeffrey. "Essence and the Mulatto Traveler: Europe as Embodiment in Nella Larsen's *Quicksand.*" *Novel: A Forum on Fiction.* 27.3 (1994): 257–70. Print.

Green, Amy. "The Critical Reception of *The Great Gatsby.*" *Critical Insights:* The Great Gatsby. Ed. Morris Dickstein. Pasadena: Salem, 2010. 39–45. Print.

Grimké, Angelina Weld. "The Closing Door: A Short Story." *Birth Control Review* 3 (Sept. 1919): 10–14; (Oct. 1919): 8–12. *Life Dynamics.* Web. 11 Sept. 2014. <http://www.lifedynamics.com/library>.

Hamm, Charles. *Yesterdays: Popular Song in America.* New York: Norton, 1983. Print.

"Harlem: Mecca of the New Negro." Spec. issue of *Survey Graphic* 6.6 (1925): 629–724. Print.

Harlem Nights. Dir. Eddie Murphy. Paramount, 1989. Paramount Home Video, 2001. DVD.

Harlem Renaissance: A Gale Critical Companion. Ed. Janet Witalec. Farmington Hills: Gale, 2003. Print.

Harris, Trudier, and Thadious Davis, eds. *Dictionary of Literary Biography: Afro-American Writers from the Harlem Renaissance to 1940.* Vol. 51. Farmington Hills: Gale, 1986. Print.

Harrison, Charles, Francis Frascina, and Gill Perry. *Primitivism, Cubism, Abstraction: The Early Twentieth Century.* New Haven: Yale UP, 1993. Print.

Harrison, Hubert. "Cabaret School of Negro Writers Does Not Represent One-Tenth of Race." *Pittsburgh Courier* 28 May 1927: 3. Print.

———. "Homo Africanus Harlemi." *Amsterdam News* 1 Sept. 1926. Print.

Harrison-Kahan, Lori. "Her 'Nig': Returning the Gaze of Nella Larsen's *Passing.*" *Modern Language Studies* 32.2 (2002): 109–38. Print.

Hart, Jamie. "Who Should Have the Children? Discussions of Birth Control among African-American Intellectuals, 1920–1939." *Journal of Negro History* 79.1 (1994): 71–84. Print.

Haviland, Beverly. "Passing from Paranoia to Plagiarism: The Abject Authorship of Nella Larsen." *Modern Fiction Studies* 43.2 (1998): 295–318. Print.

Heap, Chad. *Slumming: Sexual and Racial Encounters in American Nightlife, 1885–1940.* Chicago: U of Chicago P, 2009. Print.

Herrnstein Smith, Barbara. "Contingencies of Value." Richter 147–53.

Hill, Adelaide Cromwell. Introduction. *Quicksand.* By Nella Larsen. New York: Collier, 1971. Print.

Hine, Darlene Clark, ed. *Black Women in America.* 2nd ed. New York: Oxford UP, 2005. Print.

Hoeller, Hildegard. "Race, Modernism, and Plagiarism: The Case of Nella Larsen's 'Sanctuary.'" *African American Review* 40.3 (2006): 421–37. Print.

The Holy Bible. New York: Ballantine, 1991. Print. King James Vers.

Hostetler, Anne E. "The Aesthetics of Race and Gender in Nella Larsen's *Quicksand.*" *PMLA* 105.1 (1990): 35–46. Print.

Huggins, Nathan Irvin. *Harlem Renaissance.* London: Oxford UP, 1971. Print.

Hughes, Langston. "Cross." 1926. *Selected Poems.* New York: Vintage, 1974. 158. Print.

———. *Fine Clothes to the Jew.* New York: Knopf, 1927. Print.

———. "The Negro Artist and the Racial Mountain." *Nation* 23 June 1926: 692–94. *The Nation.* Web. 11 Mar. 2002. <http://www.thenation.com/article/negro-artist-and-racial-mountain/>.

———. "Those Bad New Negroes: A Critique on Critics." *Pittsburgh Courier* 9 Apr. 1927, sec. 2: 1. Print.

———. *The Voice of the Poet: Langston Hughes.* Random House Audio, 2002. CD.

———. *The Weary Blues.* New York: Knopf, 1926. Print.

Hurston, Zora Neale. "Art and Such." *Reading Black, Reading Feminist: A Critical Anthology.* Ed. Henry Louis Gates, Jr. New York: Meridian, 1990. 21–26. Print.

———. "Characteristics of Negro Expression." 1934. New York: Continuum, 2002. 24–31. Print.

Hutchinson, George. *The Cambridge Companion to the Harlem Renaissance.* Cambridge: Cambridge UP, 2007. Print.

———. "An End to the Family Romance: Nella Larsen, Black Transnationalism, and American Racial Ideology." *Race, Nation, and Empire in American History.* Chapel Hill: U of North Carolina P, 2007. 55–74. Print.

———. *The Harlem Renaissance in Black and White.* Cambridge: Belknap–Harvard UP, 1995. Print.

———. *In Search of Nella Larsen: A Biography of the Color Line.* Cambridge: Harvard UP, 2006. Print.

———. "Nella Larsen and the Veil of Race." *American Literary History* 9.2 (1997): 329–49.

Image Archive on the American Eugenic Movement. Cold Spring Harbor Laboratory, n.d. Web. 20 May 2013.

Illusions. Screenplay by Julie Dash. Dir. Dash. Perf. Lonette McKee, Roseann Katon, Ned Bellamy, and Jack Radar. Women Make Movies, 1983. DVD.

Imes, Nella (*see also* Larsen, Nella). Letter to Charles S. Johnson. Aug. 1926. Larsen, *Passing* [2007] 158–60.

———. Letter to Carl Van Vechten. 7 Dec. 1926. Carl Van Vechten Papers. James Weldon Johnson Collection. Beinecke Rare Book and Manuscript Lib., Yale U., New Haven.

———. Letter to Carl Van Vechten. 11 Aug. 1926, Carl Van Vechten Papers, Manuscripts and Archives Division, Astor, Lenox and Tilden Foundations, New York Public Lib., New York.

———. Letter to Carl Van Vechten. 24 Sept. 1926. Carl Van Vechten Papers. New York Public Lib., New York.

———. Letter to Carl Van Vechten. 7 Mar. 1927. Nella Larsen Papers. James Weldon Johnson Collection. Beinecke Rare Book and Manuscript Lib., Yale U., New Haven.

———. Letter to Carl Van Vechten. 29 June 1927. James Weldon Johnson Collection. Beinecke Rare Book and Manuscript Lib., Yale U., New Haven.

———. Letter to Carl Van Vechten. Apr. 1928. James Weldon Johnson Collection. Beinecke Rare Book and Manuscript Lib., Yale U., New Haven.

———. Letter to Carl Van Vechten. 1 May 1928. Carl Van Vechten Papers. James Weldon Johnson Collection. Beinecke Rare Book and Manuscript Lib., Yale U. New Haven.

———. Letter to Carl Van Vechten. Apr. 1929. James Weldon Johnson Collection. Beinecke Rare Book and Manuscript Lib., Yale U., New Haven.

———. Letter to Carl Van Vechten. 15 Apr. 1929. *Passing.* By Nella Larsen. Ed. Carla Kaplan. New York: Norton, 2007. 168. Print.

———. Letter to Carl Van Vechten. 7 Apr. 1931. James Weldon Johnson Collection. Beinecke Rare Book and Manuscript Lib., Yale U., New Haven.

———. Letter to Carl Van Vechten. 22 Apr. 1931. James Weldon Johnson Collection. Beinecke Rare Book and Manuscript Lib., Yale U., New Haven.

———. Letter to Carl Van Vechten. N.d. [1925]. *Passing.* By Nella Larsen. Ed. Carla Kaplan. New York: Norton, 2007. 158. Print.

Imitation of Life. Dir. John M. Stahl. Perf. Claudette Colbert, Warren Williams, and Louise Beavers. Universal, 1934. Film.

Imitation of Life. Dir. Douglas Sirk. Perf. Lana Turner, Susan Kohner, and Juanita Moore. Universal, 1959. Film.

Jacobson, Matthew Frye. *Whiteness of a Different Color: European Immigrants and the Alchemy of Race*. Cambridge: Harvard UP, 1998. Print.

Jenkins, Candice M. "Decoding Essentialism: Cultural Authenticity and the Black Bourgeoisie in Nella Larsen's *Passing*." *MELUS* 30.3 (2005): 129+. *Literature Resource Center*. Web. 12 Feb. 2010.

"Jesus Knows All About My Troubles." Perf. Moving Star Hall Singers. *Been in the Storm So Long: Spirituals and Shouts, Children's Game Songs, and Folktales*. Prod. Guy Carawan. Folkways Records, 1967. *Music Online: Smithsonian Global Sound*. Web. 16 June 2011. <http://glmu.alexanderstreet.com>.

"Jesus Knows All About My Troubles." Perf. Congregation of the Wesley Methodist Church. *John's Island, South Carolina: Its People and Songs.* Folkways Records, 1973. *Music Online: American Song*. Web. 16 June 2011. <www.folkways.si.edu/johns... /smithsonian>.

Johnson, Barbara. "The Quicksands of the Self: Nella Larsen and Heinz Kohut." *Female Subjects in Black and White: Race, Psychoanalysis, Feminism*, ed. Elizabeth Abel, Barbara Christian, and Helene Moglen. Berkeley: U of California P, 1997. 252–65.

Johnson, James Weldon. Letter to Carl Van Vechten. 10 Sept. 1926. Carl Van Vechten Papers. New York Public Lib., New York.

Kampf, Louis. *On Modernism: The Prospects for Literature and Freedom.* Cambridge: MIT P, 1967. Print.

Kaplan, Carla. "Nella Larsen's Erotics of Race." Introduction. Larsen, *Passing* [2007] vii–xxxii.

Kawash, Samira. *Dislocating the Color Line: Identity, Hybridity, and Singularity in African-American Literature*. Stanford: Stanford UP, 1997. Print.

Kellner, Bruce. *The Harlem Renaissance: A Historical Dictionary for the Era.* Westport: Greenwood, 1984. Print.

Kester-Shelton, Pamela, ed. *Feminist Writers*. New York: St. James, 1996. Print.

Knopf, Marcy. Introduction. *The Sleeper Wakes: Harlem Renaissance Stories by Women*. Ed. Knopf. New Brunswick: Rutgers UP, 1993. xix–xxxvi. Print.

Kraus, Joe. "De-centering the Canon: Understanding *The Great Gatsby* as an Ethnic Novel." *Multiethnic Literature and Canon Debates*. Ed. Mary Jo Bona, Irma Maini, and John Lowe. Albany: State U of New York P, 2006. 127–44. Print.

Kushner, Tony. *Angels in America: A Gay Fantasia on National Themes: Part One: Millennium Approaches*. New York: Theatre Communications, 1993. Print.

Labbé, Jessica. "'Death by Misadventure': Teaching Transgression in/through Larsen's *Passing*." *College Literature* 37.4 (2010): 120–44. Print.

Lacan, Jacques. *Seminar XI: The Four Fundamental Concepts of Psychoanalysis*. Trans. Alan Sheridan. New York: Norton, 1978. Print.

LaCapra, Dominick. *Writing History, Writing Trauma*. Baltimore: Johns Hopkins UP, 2001. Print.

Larsen, Nella (*see also* Imes, Nella). *The Complete Fiction of Nella Larsen: Passing, Quicksand and the Stories*. Ed. Charles Larson. New York: Anchor. 2001. Print.

———. "Freedom." *Young's Realistic Stories* April 1926: 241–43. Print.

———. "New Author Unearthed Right Here in Harlem." Interview by Thelma E. Berlack. *Amsterdam News* 23 May 1928: 16. Print.

———. "Playtime: Danish Fun." *Brownies' Book* July 1920: 219. Print.

———. "Playtime: Three Scandinavian Games." *Brownies' Book* June 1920: 191–92. Print.

———. *Quicksand*. New York: Knopf. 1928. Print.

———. *Quicksand*. Ed. Thadious Davis. New York: Penguin, 2002. Print.

———. *Quicksand*. Gates, Jr., Higginbotham, and McKay 1085–1167.

———. Quicksand *and* Passing. Ed. Deborah E. McDowell. New Brunswick: Rutgers UP, 1986. Print.

———. Quicksand *and* Passing. Ed. Deborah E. McDowell. New Brunswick: Rutgers UP, 1987. Print.

———. Quicksand *and* Passing. Ed. Deborah E. McDowell. New Brunswick: Rutgers UP, 1989. Print.

———. Quicksand *and* Passing. Ed. Deborah E. McDowell. New Brunswick: Rutgers UP, 1994. Print.

———.Quicksand *and* Passing. London: Serpent's Tail, 1995. Print.

———. *Passer la ligne* [*Passing*]. Trans. Jocelyne Rotily. Marseille: ACFA, 2009. Print.

———. *Passing*. New York: Knopf. 1929. Print.

———. *Passing*. Ed. Thadious Davis. New York: Penguin, 1997. Print.

———. *Passing*. Ed. Thadious Davis. New York: Penguin, 2002. Print.

———. *Passing*. Introd. Ntozake Shange. Foreword and notes by Mae Henderson. New York: Modern Lib., 2002. Print.

———. *Passing*. Ed. Carla Kaplan. Critical ed. New York: Norton, 2007. Print.

———. Rev. of *Black Sadie*, by Thomas Bower Campbell. *Opportunity* 7 (1929): 24. Print.

———. Rev. of *Certain People of Importance*, by Kathleen Norris. *Messenger* 5 (1923): 713. Print.

———. *Sabbie Mobili* (*Quicksand*). Ed. M. Giulia Fabi. Trans. Francesca Bilondi. Firenze: Casa Editrice Le Lettere, 1999. Print.

———. "Sanctuary." *Calling the Wind: Twentieth Century African American Short Stories*. Ed. Clarence Major. New York: Harper, 1993. 34–38. Print.

———. *The Short Fiction of Nella Larsen*. Ed. Charles R. Larson. Blacksburg: Wilder, 2010. Print.

———. "To Charles S. Johnson." Larsen, *Passing* [2007] 158–60.

———. "The Wrong Man." *Young's Realistic Stories* Jan. 1926: 243–46. Print.

———. "The Wrong Man." *An Intimation of Things Distant: The Collected Fiction of Nella Larsen*. Ed. Charles R. Larson. New York: Anchor, 1992. Print.

Larson, Charles R. *Invisible Darkness: Jean Toomer and Nella Larsen*. Iowa City: U of Iowa P, 1993. Print.

Larson, Kelli. "Surviving the Taint of Plagiarism: Nella Larsen's 'Sanctuary' and Sheila Kaye-Smith's 'Mrs. Adis.'" *Journal of Modern Literature* 30.4 (2007): 82–104. Print.

Lee, Felicia. "Pushing Boundaries: Mixed-Race Artists Gain Notice." *The New York Times*. New York Times, 5 July 2011. Web. 9 Jan. 2015.

Lemke, Sieglinde. *Primitivist Modernism: Black Culture and the Origins of Transatlantic Modernism*. New York: Oxford UP, 1998. Print.

Levine, June Perry. "An Analysis of the Manuscripts of *A Passage to India*." *PMLA* 85 (1970): 284–94. Print.

Lewis, David Levering, ed. *The Portable Harlem Renaissance Reader*. New York: Penguin, 1995. Print.

———. *When Harlem Was in Vogue*. New York: Penguin, 1997. Print.

Lewis, Earl, and Heidi Ardizzone. *Love on Trial: An American Scandal in Black and White*. New York: Norton, 2001. Print.

The Life and Times of Sara Baartman. Dir. Zola Maseko. Icarus Films, 2008. DVD.

List, George. "The Boundaries of Speech and Song." *Ethnomusicology* 7 (1963): 1–16. *JSTOR*. Web. 2 Dec. 2010. <http://www.jstor.org/stable/924141>.

Locke, Alain, ed. "Harlem Types: Portraits by Winold Reiss." *Survey Graphic* 6 (1925): 51–54. Print.

———. *The New Negro: An Anthology*. 1925. New York: Atheneum, 1968. Print.

Loving v. Virginia. 388 US 1–13. Supreme Court of the US. 1967. *Supreme Court Opinions*. *Findlaw*, n.d. Web. 5 Mar. 2011.

Lunde, Arne, and Anna Westerstahl Stenport. "Helga Crane's Copenhagen: Denmark, Colonialism, and Transnational Identity in Nella Larsen's *Quicksand*." *Comparative Literature* 60.3 (2008): 228–43. Print.

Madigan, Mark. "Miscegenation and 'The Dicta of Race and Class': The Rhinelander Case and Nella Larsen's *Passing*." *Modern Fiction Studies* 36.4 (1990): 524–28.

———. "'Then Everything Was Dark'? The Two Endings of Nella Larsen's *Passing*." *Papers of the Bibliographical Society of America* 83.4 (1989): 521–23. *JSTOR*. Web. 3 Mar. 2016.

Mancini, Olivia. "Vassar's First Black Graduate: She Passed for White." *Journal of Blacks in Higher Education* 34 (2001–02): 108–09. Print.

Margaret Sanger Papers Project. Dept. of History, New York U, 3 May 2010. Web. 20 May 2013.

Martí, Eduardo J. *Welcome to Queensborough!* Queensborough Community Coll., n.d. Web. 5 Jan. 2010.

Martin, Wendy. "'Remembering the Jungle': Josephine Baker and Modernist Parody." *Prehistories of the Future: The Primitivist Project and the Culture of Modernism*. Ed. Elazar Barkan and Ronald Bush. Stanford: Stanford UP, 1995. 310–25. Print.

McCann, Carole R. *Birth Control Politics in the United States, 1916–1945*. Ithaca: Cornell UP, 1994. Print.

McDowell, Deborah E. Introduction. Larsen, Quicksand *and* Passing [1986] ix–xxxviii.

McKay, Claude. *Home to Harlem.* New York: Harper, 1928. Print.

McLendon, Jacquelyn Y. "The Double Nature of Epistolary Discourse in the Fiction of Nella Larsen and E. C. Williams." *Letterature d'America: Rivista Trimestrale* 24.124 (2009): 5–28. Print.

———. "Nella Larsen." *African American Writers.* Ed. Valerie Smith, Lea Baechler, and A. Walton Litz. New York: Scribner's, 1991. *Literature Resource Center.* Web. 11 Jan. 2009.

———. "Nella Larsen: Overview." *Feminist Writers.* Ed. Pamela Kester-Shelton. Detroit: St. James, 1996. *Literature Resource Center.* Web. 8 July 2013.

———. *The Politics of Color in the Fiction of Jessie Fauset and Nella Larsen.* Charlottesville: U of Virginia P, 1995. Print.

———. "(Re)Shaping Content in *Passing*; or, This Text Which Is Not One." McLendon, *Politics* 94–111.

———. "Self-Representation as Art in the Novels of Nella Larsen." *Redefining Autobiography in Twentieth Century Women's Fiction.* Ed. Colette Hall and Janice Morgan. New York: Garland, 1991. Print.

———. "Social Nightmare in Quicksand." Mclendon, *Politics* 71–93. Print.

Mencken, H. L. "As H.L.M. Sees It." *F. Scott Fitzgerald Critical Assessments.* Ed. Henry Claridge. Vol. 2. East Sussex: Helm, 1991. 156–59. Print.

———. "On Being an American." 1920. *The American Scene: A Reader.* Ed. Huntington Cairns. New York: Knopf, 1965. Print.

Michie, Helena. *Sororophobia: Differences among Women in Literature and Culture.* New York: Oxford UP, 1992. Print.

Miller, J. Hillis. *Reading Narrative.* Norman: U of Oklahoma P, 1998. Print.

Monda, Kimberly. "Self-Delusion and Self-Sacrifice in Nella Larsen's *Quicksand.*" *African American Review* 31.1 (1997): 23–39. Print.

Morrison, Toni. *Beloved.* New York: Vintage, 2004. Print.

———. "Black Matters." Richter 310–22.

———. *Jazz.* New York: Vintage, 1992. Print.

Morrissey, Lee. *Debating the Canon: A Reader from Addison to Nafisi.* New York: Palgrave, 2005. Print.

Murfin, Ross, and Supryia M. Ray. *The Bedford Glossary of Critical and Literary Terms.* 3rd ed. Boston: Bedford–St. Martin's, 2009. Print.

"The Negro in Art: How Shall He Be Portrayed: A Symposium." *Crisis* 31.4 (1926): 165; 31.5 (1926): 219–20; 31.6 (1926): 278–80; 32.1 (1926): 35–36; 32.2 (1926): 71–73; 32.4 (1926): 193–94; 32.5 (1926): 238–39; 32.7 (1926): 28–29. Print.

Nelson, Emmanuel S., ed. *African American Authors, 1745–1945.* Westport: Greenwood, 2000. Print.

Newman, Richard. "Two Letters from Nella Larsen." *Biblion: The Bulletin of the New York Public Library* 2.2 (1994): 124–29. Print.

Nielsen, Carl August. *Helios Overture, op. 17.* 1903. Perf. Danish Radio Symphony Orchestra. Cond. Herbert Blomstedt. *Classical Music Library.* EMI Classics, 1997. Web. 16 June 2011. <http://clmu.alexanderstreet.com>.

O'Brien, Tim. *The Things They Carried.* New York: Broadway, 1990. Print.

Office of Institutional Research and Assessment. *Fact Book 2009.* Queensborough Community Coll., n.d. Web. 6 Jan. 2010.

Onwuachi-Willig, Angela. "A Beautiful Lie: Exploring *Rhinelander v. Rhinelander* as a Formative Lesson on Race, Identity, Marriage, and Family." *California Law Review* 95.6 (2007): 2393–2458. *Lexis*. Web. 17 Jan. 2011.

Page, Yolanda Williams, ed. *Encyclopedia of African American Women Writers*. 2 vols. Westport: Greenwood, 2007. Print.

Pascoe, Peggy. *What Comes Naturally: Miscegenation Law and the Making of Race in America*. Oxford: Oxford UP, 2009. Print.

Peretti, Burton W. *Jazz in American Culture*. Chicago: Dee, 1997. Print.

Perkins, Linda M. "The African American Female Elite: The Early History of African American Women in the Seven Sister Colleges, 1880–1960." *Harvard Educational Review* 76 (1997): 718–56. Print.

Perry, Ruth. "Home at Last: Biographical Background to *Pride and Prejudice*." *Approaches to Teaching Austen's* Pride and Prejudice. Ed. Marcia McClintock Folsom. New York: MLA, 1993. 46–56.

Pfeiffer, Kathleen. *Race Passing and American Individualism*. Amherst: U of Massachusetts P, 2003. Print.

Pinky. Dir. Elia Kazan. Perf. Jeanne Crain and Ethel Waters. Twentieth-Century Fox, 1949. Film.

Plessy v. Ferguson. 163 US 537; 16 S. Ct. 1138; 41 L. Ed. 256. Supreme Court of the US. 1896. *Lexis*. Web. 25 Dec. 2010.

Posnock, Ross. *Color and Culture. Black Writers and the Making of the Modern Intellectual*. Cambridge: Harvard UP, 1998. Print.

Prince, Gerald. *A Dictionary of Narratology*. Lincoln: U of Nebraska P, 1987. Print.

Rampersad, Arnold. "Racial Doubt and Racial Shame in the Harlem Renaissance." *Temples for Tomorrow: Looking Back at the Harlem Renaissance*. Ed. Genevieve Fabre and Michel Feith. Bloomington: Indiana UP, 2001. 31–44. Print.

Rennels, Mary. "Behind the Backs of Books and Authors." Larsen, *Passing* [2007] 150–51.

Restuccia, Frances. "'A Cave of My Own': The Sexual Politics of Indeterminacy." *Raritan* 9 (1989): 110–28. Print.

Rhinelander v. Rhinelander. 219 A.D. 189; 219 N.Y.S. 548; 1927 N.Y. App. Div. Supreme Court of New York, Appellate Division, Second Dept., 1927. *Lexis*. Web. 25 Dec. 2010.

Rhodes, Colin. *Primitivism and Modern Art*. London: Thames, 1994. Print.

Richardson, Riché. *Black Masculinity and the U.S. South: From Uncle Tom to Gangsta*. Athens: U of Georgia P, 2007. 118–56. Print.

Richter, David H., ed. *Falling into Theory: Conflicting Views on Reading Literature*. New York: Bedford–St. Martins, 2000. Print.

Roberts, Kimberley. "The Clothes Make the Woman: The Symbolics of Prostitution in Nella Larsen's *Quicksand* and Claude McKay's *Home to Harlem*." *Tulsa Studies in Women's Literature* 16.1 (1997): 107–30. Print.

Robinson, Lillian S. "Treason Our Text: Feminist Challenges to the Literary Canon." Richter. 151–65.

Rogers, J. A. "Jazz at Home." *The New Negro: An Interpretation*. Ed. Alain Locke. 1925. New York: Touchstone, 1997. 216–24. Print.

Ross, Marlon B. "The New Negro Displayed: Self-Ownership, Proprietary Sites/Sights, and the Bonds/Bounds of Race." *Claiming the Stones, Naming the Bones: Cultural Property and the Negotiation of National and Ethnic Identity*. Ed. Elazar Barkan and Ronald Bush. Los Angeles: Getty Research Inst., 2002. 259–301. Print.

Rottenberg, Catherine. "*Passing*: Race, Identification, Desire." *Criticism* 45.4 (2003): 435–52. Print.

Sadie, Stanley, ed. *The New Grove Dictionary of Music and Musicians*. 2nd ed. New York: Grove, 2001. Print.

Said, Edward. "Connecting Empire to Secular Interpretation." Morrissey 221–36.

Sankey, Ira D., James McGranaham, and George C. Stebbins. comp. *Gospel Hymns No. 1 to 6*. Cincinnati: Church; Chicago: Bigelow, 1895. *Internet Archive*. Web. 16 June 2011.

Scar of Shame. Dir. Frank Peregini. Perf. Harry Henderson, and Ann Kennedy. Colored Players Film Corp. of Philadelphia, 1927. Film.

Scheper, Jeanne. "The New Negro Flâneuse in Nella Larsen's *Quicksand*." *African American Review* 42.3–4 (2008): 679–95. Print.

Schuyler, George. "Our Greatest Gift to America." 1927. *Heath Anthology of American Literature*. Ed. Paul Lauter. Vol. 2. Lexington: Heath, 1990. Print.

———. "Views and Reviews." *Pittsburgh Courier* 14 Apr. 1928: A8. Print.

Scott, Clarice. "Black, White, or Somewhere in Between." Rev. of *Quicksand* and *Passing* by Nella Larsen, and *Bulletproof Diva: Tales of Race, Sex and Hair* by Lisa Jones. *Djembe*. N.p., 21 July 1997. Web. Dec. 2010. <http://www.djembe.dk/no/21/32bwosib.html>.

Scruggs, Charles. "Sexual Desire, Modernity, and Modernism in the Fiction of Nella Larsen and Rudolph Fisher." *The Cambridge Companion to the Harlem Renaissance*. Ed. George Hutchinson. Cambridge: Cambridge UP, 2007. 155–69. Print.

Sealts, Merton M., Jr. "Scott Fitzgerald and *The Great Gatsby*: A Reappraisal." *Colorado Review* 25.2 (1998): 137–52. Print.

Serwer, Adam. "In the Mix: Being Biracial in America." *Ebony* May 2011: 86–94. Print.

Shillingsburg, Peter L. *From Gutenberg to Google: Electronic Representations of Literary Texts*. Cambridge: Cambridge UP, 2006. Print.

Showalter, Elaine. *Teaching Literature*. Malden: Blackwell, 2003. Print.

Sim, Jillian A. "Fading to White." 1999. *American Heritage*. American Heritage, 2011. Web. 10 Jan. 2011. <http://www.americanheritage.com/content/fading-white>.

Simmons, Christina. *Making Marriage Modern: Women's Sexuality from the Progressive Era to World War II*. New York: Oxford UP, 2009. Print.

———. "Modern Sexuality and the Myth of Victorian Repression." *Passion and Power: Sexuality in History*. Ed. Simmons and Kathy Peiss, with Robert A. Padgug. Philadelphia: Temple UP, 1989. 157–77. Print.

Singh, Amritjit. *The Novels of the Harlem Renaissance*. University Park: Pennsylvania State UP, 1976. Print.

Skelton, Jane. "Multiple Voices, Multiple Identities: Teaching African American Literature." Graham, Pineault-Burke, and Davis 52–64.

Slonimsky, Nicolas. *Baker's Biographical Dictionary of Musicians*. Centennial ed. New York: Schirmer, 2001. Print.

Smith, Martha Nell. "The Human Touch, Software of the Highest Order: Revisiting Editing as Interpretation." *Textual Cultures* 2 (2007): 1–15. Print.

Smith, Valerie, ed. *African American Writers*. Rev. ed. New York: Scribner's, 2000. Print.

Smith-Pryor, Elizabeth M. *Property Rites: The Rhinelander Trial, Passing, and the Protection of Whiteness*. Chapel Hill: U of North Carolina P, 2009. Print.

Southern, Eileen. *The Music of Black Americans*. 3rd ed. New York: Norton, 1997. Print.

Starkey, Marion L. "Jessie Fauset." *Southern Workman* 61 (May 1932): 217–20. Print.

Stecopoulos, Harry. *Race and the Subject of Masculinities*. Durham: Duke UP, 1997. Print.

Stringer, Dorothy. *"Not Even Past": Race, Historical Trauma, and Subjectivity in Faulkner, Larsen, and Van Vechten*. New York: Fordham UP, 2010. Print.

Sullivan, Neil. "Nella Larsen's *Passing* and the Fading Subject." *African American Review* 32 (1998): 373–86. Print.

Sweeney, Carole. *From Fetish to Subject: Race, Modernism, and Primitivism, 1919–1935*. Westport: Praeger, 2004. Print.

"Swing Low, Sweet Chariot." Perf. Fisk Jubilee Singers. *Fisk Jubilee Singers Vol. 1 (1909–1911). Music Online: American Song [Alexander Street]*. Document Records, 1997. Web. 16 June 2011. <http://amso.alexanderstreet.com>.

"Swing Low, Sweet Chariot." Perf. Paul Robeson. *The Collector's Paul Robeson. Smithsonian Global Sound*. Smithonian Inst., n.d. Web. 16 June 2011.

Talalay, Kathryn. *Composition in Black and White: The Life of Philippa Schuyler*. New York: Oxford UP, 1995. Print.

Tanner, Laura. "Intimate Geography: The Body, Race, and Space in Larsen's *Quicksand*." *Texas Studies in Literature and Language* 51.2 (2009): 179–202. Print.

Tate, Claudia. "Nella Larsen's *Passing*: A Problem of Interpretation." *Black American Literature Forum* 14 (1980): 142–46. Print.

Taylor, Monique M. *Harlem: Between Heaven and Hell*. Minneapolis: U of Minnesota P, 2002. Print.

Teaching First-Year Writing: A QCC Handbook. New York: Queensborough Community Coll. Dept. of English, 2009. Print.

Thaggert, Miriam. "Racial Etiquette: Nella Larsen's *Passing* and the Rhinelander Case." *Meridians* 5 (2005): 1–29. Print.

"There Shall Be Showers of Blessings." Hymn No. 49. *Gospel Hymns No. 5*. Cincinnati: Church; Chicago: Bigelow, 1887. *Internet Archive*. Web. 16 June 2011.

Thurman, Wallace. *The Blacker the Berry*. New York: Macauley, 1929. Print.

———, ed. *Fire!!* 1.1 (1926). Print.

———. "Negro Life in New York's Harlem: A Lively Picture of a Popular and Interesting Section." 1927. *The Collected Writings of Wallace Thurman*. Ed. Amritjit Singh and Daniel M. Scott. New Brunswick: Rutgers UP, 2003. 39–62. Print.

Tolliver, Willie. "The Wings of the Furies: Teaching Nella Larsen and the American Literature Tradition." *Teaching American Literature: A Journal of Theory and Practice* 5.2: (2012): 32–51. Print.

Tompkins, Jane. "'But Is It Any Good?' The Institutionalization of Literary Value." Morrissey 123–30.

Toth, Josh. "Deauthenticating Community: The Passing Intrusion of Clare Kendry in Nella Larsen's *Passing*." *MELUS* 33.1 (2008): 55+. *Literature Resource Center*. Web. 13 Feb. 2010.

Tyson, Lois. "Using Concepts from Feminist Theory to Understand Literature." *Using Critical Theory: How to Read and Write about Literature*. 2nd ed. New York: Routledge, 2011. Print.

Van Houten v. Morse. 162 Mass. 414. 1894. Supreme Judicial Court of Massachusetts. *Lexis*. Web. 25 Dec. 2010.

Van Vechten, Carl. *Nigger Heaven*. New York: Knopf, 1926. Print.

Vogel, Shane. *The Scene of Harlem Cabaret: Race, Sexuality, Performance*. Chicago: U of Chicago P, 2009. Print.

Wacks, Jamie L. "Reading Race, Rhetoric, and the Female Body in the Rhinelander Case." *Interracialism: Black-White Intermarriage in American History, Literature, and Law*. Ed. Werner Sollors. Oxford: Oxford UP, 2000. 162–77. Print.

Walker, Bella August. "Fractured Bonds: Policing Whiteness and Womanhood through Race-Based Marriage Annulments." *De Paul Law Review* 58 (2008): 1–50. Print.

Wall, Cheryl A. "Passing for What? Aspects of Identity in Nella Larsen's Novels." *Black American Literature Forum* 20 (1986): 99–111. Print.

———. *Women of the Harlem Renaissance*. Bloomington: Indiana UP, 1995. Print.

Ware, Susan. *Modern American Women: A Documentary History*. 2nd ed. New York: McGraw, 2001. Print.

Warhol, Robyn R. "Narrative Refusals and Generic Transformation in Austen and James: What Doesn't Happen in *Northanger Abbey* and *The Spoils of Poynton*." *Henry James Review* 28 (2007): 259–68. Print.

Washington, Mary Helen. "Nella Larsen: Mystery Woman of the Harlem Renaissance." *Ms.* Dec. 1980: 50. Print.

Weinstein, Arnold. "Fiction as Greatness: The Case of Gatsby." *Novel* 19.1 (1985): 22–38.

Wentinck, Charles. *Modern and Primitive Art*. Oxford: Phaidon, 1979. Print.

White Like Me. 1975. Saturday Night Live: *The Best of Eddie Murphy*. Dir. Andy Breckman, Claude Kerven, Dave Wilson. Perf. Eddie Murphy. 2004. DVD.

Williams, Bert. "All Going Out and Nothing Coming In." 1901. *National Jukebox: Historical Recordings from the Library of Congress*. Lib. of Congress, n.d. Web. 16 June 2011.

Williams, Erika. "A Lie of Omission: Plagiarism in Nella Larsen's *Quicksand*." *African American Review* 45.1-2 (2012): 205–16. Print.

Wilson, Harriet. *Our Nig; or, Sketches from the Life of a Free Black*. Ed. P. Gabrielle Foreman and Reginald Pitts. New York: Penguin, 2009. Print.

Wintz, Cary D., and Paul Finkelman. *Encyclopedia of the Harlem Renaissance*. 2 vols. New York: Routledge, 2004. Print.

Woolf, Virginia. 21 Dec. 1925. *The Diary of Virginia Woolf*. Ed. Anne Olivier Bell and Andrew McNeillie. Vol. 3. New York: Harcourt, 1980. 51–52. Print.

———. *Orlando*. 1928. New York: Harcourt, 2006. Print.

———. *A Room of One's Own*. 1929. New York: Penguin, 2000. Print.

Yezierska, Anzia. "How I Found America." 1920. *Hungry Hearts and Other Stories*. By Yezierska. New York: Persea, 1985. Print.

Youman, Mary Mabel. "Nella Larsen's *Passing*: A Study in Irony." *CLA Journal* 18 (1974): 235–41. Print.

Young, John K. *Black Writers, White Publishers: Marketplace Politics in Twentieth-Century African American Literature*. Jackson: U of Mississippi P, 2006. Print.

———. "Passing (on) Textual History: The Ends of Nella Larsen's *Passing*." Young, *Black Writers* 37–64.

———. "Pynchon in Popular Magazines." *Critique* 44 (2003): 389–404. Print.

Zimmerman, Bonnie, ed. *Lesbian Histories and Cultures*. New York: Garland, 2000. Print.

INDEX

Modern Language Association of America

Approaches to Teaching World Literature

To purchase MLA publications, visit www.mla.org/bookstore.

Achebe's Things Fall Apart. Ed. Bernth Lindfors. 1991.

Arthurian Tradition. Ed. Maureen Fries and Jeanie Watson. 1992.

Atwood's The Handmaid's Tale *and Other Works*. Ed. Sharon R. Wilson, Thomas B. Friedman, and Shannon Hengen. 1996.

Austen's Emma. Ed. Marcia McClintock Folsom. 2004.

Austen's Mansfield Park. Ed. Marcia McClintock Folsom and John Wiltshire. 2014.

Austen's Pride and Prejudice. Ed. Marcia McClintock Folsom. 1993.

Balzac's Old Goriot. Ed. Michal Peled Ginsburg. 2000.

Baudelaire's Flowers of Evil. Ed. Laurence M. Porter. 2000.

Beckett's Waiting for Godot. Ed. June Schlueter and Enoch Brater. 1991.

Behn's Oroonoko. Ed. Cynthia Richards and Mary Ann O'Donnell. 2014.

Beowulf. Ed. Jess B. Bessinger, Jr., and Robert F. Yeager. 1984.

Blake's Songs of Innocence and of Experience. Ed. Robert F. Gleckner and Mark L. Greenberg. 1989.

Boccaccio's Decameron. Ed. James H. McGregor. 2000.

British Women Poets of the Romantic Period. Ed. Stephen C. Behrendt and Harriet Kramer Linkin. 1997.

Charlotte Brontë's Jane Eyre. Ed. Diane Long Hoeveler and Beth Lau. 1993.

Emily Brontë's Wuthering Heights. Ed. Sue Lonoff and Terri A. Hasseler. 2006.

Byron's Poetry. Ed. Frederick W. Shilstone. 1991.

Works of Italo Calvino. Ed. Franco Ricci. 2013.

Camus's The Plague. Ed. Steven G. Kellman. 1985.

Cather's My Ántonia. Ed. Susan J. Rosowski. 1989.

Cervantes' Don Quixote. First edition. Ed. Richard Bjornson. 1984.

Cervantes's Don Quixote. Second edition. Ed. James A. Parr and Lisa Vollendorf. 2015.

Chaucer's Canterbury Tales. First edition. Ed. Joseph Gibaldi. 1980.

Chaucer's Canterbury Tales. Second edition. Ed. Peter W. Travis and Frank Grady. 2014.

Chaucer's Troilus and Criseyde *and the Shorter Poems*. Ed. Tison Pugh and Angela Jane Weisl. 2006.

Works of Anton Chekhov. Ed. Michael C. Finke and Michael Holquist. 2015.

Chopin's The Awakening. Ed. Bernard Koloski. 1988.

Coetzee's Disgrace *and Other Works*. Ed. Laura Wright, Jane Poyner, and Elleke Boehmer. 2014.

Coleridge's Poetry and Prose. Ed. Richard E. Matlak. 1991.

Collodi's Pinocchio *and Its Adaptations*. Ed. Michael Sherberg. 2006.

Conrad's "Heart of Darkness" and "The Secret Sharer." Ed. Hunt Hawkins and Brian W. Shaffer. 2002.

Dante's Divine Comedy. Ed. Carole Slade. 1982.

Defoe's Robinson Crusoe. Ed. Maximillian E. Novak and Carl Fisher. 2005.

DeLillo's White Noise. Ed. Tim Engles and John N. Duvall. 2006.

Dickens's Bleak House. Ed. John O. Jordan and Gordon Bigelow. 2009.
Dickens's David Copperfield. Ed. Richard J. Dunn. 1984.
Dickinson's Poetry. Ed. Robin Riley Fast and Christine Mack Gordon. 1989.
Narrative of the Life of Frederick Douglass. Ed. James C. Hall. 1999.
Works of John Dryden. Ed. Jayne Lewis and Lisa Zunshine. 2013.
Duras's Ourika. Ed. Mary Ellen Birkett and Christopher Rivers. 2009.
Early Modern Spanish Drama. Ed. Laura R. Bass and Margaret R. Greer. 2006.
Eliot's Middlemarch. Ed. Kathleen Blake. 1990.
Eliot's Poetry and Plays. Ed. Jewel Spears Brooker. 1988.
Shorter Elizabethan Poetry. Ed. Patrick Cheney and Anne Lake Prescott. 2000.
Ellison's Invisible Man. Ed. Susan Resneck Parr and Pancho Savery. 1989.
English Renaissance Drama. Ed. Karen Bamford and Alexander Leggatt. 2002.
Works of Louise Erdrich. Ed. Gregg Sarris, Connie A. Jacobs, and James R. Giles. 2004.
Dramas of Euripides. Ed. Robin Mitchell-Boyask. 2002.
Faulkner's As I Lay Dying. Ed. Patrick O'Donnell and Lynda Zwinger. 2011.
Faulkner's The Sound and the Fury. Ed. Stephen Hahn and Arthur F. Kinney. 1996.
Novels of Henry Fielding. Ed. Jennifer Preston Wilson and Elizabeth Kraft. 2015.
Fitzgerald's The Great Gatsby. Ed. Jackson R. Bryer and Nancy P. VanArsdale. 2009.
Flaubert's Madame Bovary. Ed. Laurence M. Porter and Eugene F. Gray. 1995.
García Márquez's One Hundred Years of Solitude. Ed. María Elena de Valdés and Mario J. Valdés. 1990.
Gilman's "The Yellow Wall-Paper" and Herland. Ed. Denise D. Knight and Cynthia J. Davis. 2003.
Goethe's Faust. Ed. Douglas J. McMillan. 1987.
Gothic Fiction: The British and American Traditions. Ed. Diane Long Hoeveler and Tamar Heller. 2003.
Poetry of John Gower. Ed. R. F. Yeager and Brian W. Gastle. 2011.
Grass's The Tin Drum. Ed. Monika Shafi. 2008.
H.D.'s Poetry and Prose. Ed. Annette Debo and Lara Vetter. 2011.
Hebrew Bible as Literature in Translation. Ed. Barry N. Olshen and Yael S. Feldman. 1989.
Homer's Iliad *and* Odyssey. Ed. Kostas Myrsiades. 1987.
Hurston's Their Eyes Were Watching God *and Other Works*. Ed. John Lowe. 2009.
Ibsen's A Doll House. Ed. Yvonne Shafer. 1985.
Henry James's Daisy Miller *and* The Turn of the Screw. Ed. Kimberly C. Reed and Peter G. Beidler. 2005.
Works of Samuel Johnson. Ed. David R. Anderson and Gwin J. Kolb. 1993.
Joyce's Ulysses. Ed. Kathleen McCormick and Erwin R. Steinberg. 1993.
Works of Sor Juana Inés de la Cruz. Ed. Emilie L. Bergmann and Stacey Schlau. 2007.
Kafka's Short Fiction. Ed. Richard T. Gray. 1995.
Keats's Poetry. Ed. Walter H. Evert and Jack W. Rhodes. 1991.
Kingston's The Woman Warrior. Ed. Shirley Geok-lin Lim. 1991.
Lafayette's The Princess of Clèves. Ed. Faith E. Beasley and Katharine Ann Jensen. 1998.
Novels of Nella Larsen. Ed. Jacquelyn Y. McLendon. 2016.

Writings of Bartolomé de Las Casas. Ed. Santa Arias and Eyda M. Merediz. 2008.
Works of D. H. Lawrence. Ed. M. Elizabeth Sargent and Garry Watson. 2001.
Lazarillo de Tormes *and the Picaresque Tradition.* Ed. Anne J. Cruz. 2009.
Lessing's The Golden Notebook. Ed. Carey Kaplan and Ellen Cronan Rose. 1989.
Works of Primo Levi. Ed. Nicholas Patruno and Roberta Ricci. 2014.
Works of Jack London. Ed. Kenneth K. Brandt and Jeanne Campbell Reesman. 2015.
Works of Naguib Mahfouz. Ed. Waïl S. Hassan and Susan Muaddi Darraj. 2011.
Mann's Death in Venice *and Other Short Fiction.* Ed. Jeffrey B. Berlin. 1992.
Marguerite de Navarre's Heptameron. Ed. Colette H. Winn. 2007.
Works of Carmen Martín Gaite. Ed. Joan L. Brown. 2013.
Medieval English Drama. Ed. Richard K. Emmerson. 1990.
Melville's Moby-Dick. Ed. Martin Bickman. 1985.
Metaphysical Poets. Ed. Sidney Gottlieb. 1990.
Miller's Death of a Salesman. Ed. Matthew C. Roudané. 1995.
Milton's Paradise Lost. First edition. Ed. Galbraith M. Crump. 1986.
Milton's Paradise Lost. Second edition. Ed. Peter C. Herman. 2012.
Milton's Shorter Poetry and Prose. Ed. Peter C. Herman. 2007.
Molière's Tartuffe *and Other Plays.* Ed. James F. Gaines and Michael S. Koppisch. 1995.
Momaday's The Way to Rainy Mountain. Ed. Kenneth M. Roemer. 1988.
Montaigne's Essays. Ed. Patrick Henry. 1994.
Novels of Toni Morrison. Ed. Nellie Y. McKay and Kathryn Earle. 1997.
Murasaki Shikibu's The Tale of Genji. Ed. Edward Kamens. 1993.
Nabokov's Lolita. Ed. Zoran Kuzmanovich and Galya Diment. 2008.
Works of Ngũgĩ wa Thiong'o. Ed. Oliver Lovesey. 2012.
Works of Tim O'Brien. Ed. Alex Vernon and Catherine Calloway. 2010.
Works of Ovid and the Ovidian Tradition. Ed. Barbara Weiden Boyd and Cora Fox. 2010.
Petrarch's Canzoniere *and the Petrarchan Tradition.* Ed. Christopher Kleinhenz and Andrea Dini. 2014.
Poe's Prose and Poetry. Ed. Jeffrey Andrew Weinstock and Tony Magistrale. 2008.
Pope's Poetry. Ed. Wallace Jackson and R. Paul Yoder. 1993.
Proust's Fiction and Criticism. Ed. Elyane Dezon-Jones and Inge Crosman Wimmers. 2003.
Puig's Kiss of the Spider Woman. Ed. Daniel Balderston and Francine Masiello. 2007.
Pynchon's The Crying of Lot 49 *and Other Works.* Ed. Thomas H. Schaub. 2008.
Works of François Rabelais. Ed. Todd W. Reeser and Floyd Gray. 2011.
Novels of Samuel Richardson. Ed. Lisa Zunshine and Jocelyn Harris. 2006.
Rousseau's Confessions *and* Reveries of the Solitary Walker. Ed. John C. O'Neal and Ourida Mostefai. 2003.
Sand's Indiana. Ed. David A. Powell and Pratima Prasad. 2015.
Scott's Waverley Novels. Ed. Evan Gottlieb and Ian Duncan. 2009.
Shakespeare's Hamlet. Ed. Bernice W. Kliman. 2001.
Shakespeare's King Lear. Ed. Robert H. Ray. 1986.
Shakespeare's Othello. Ed. Peter Erickson and Maurice Hunt. 2005.
Shakespeare's Romeo and Juliet. Ed. Maurice Hunt. 2000.

Shakespeare's The Taming of the Shrew. Ed. Margaret Dupuis and Grace Tiffany. 2013.

Shakespeare's The Tempest *and Other Late Romances.* Ed. Maurice Hunt. 1992.

Shelley's Frankenstein. Ed. Stephen C. Behrendt. 1990.

Shelley's Poetry. Ed. Spencer Hall. 1990.

Sir Gawain and the Green Knight. Ed. Miriam Youngerman Miller and Jane Chance. 1986.

Song of Roland. Ed. William W. Kibler and Leslie Zarker Morgan. 2006.

Spenser's Faerie Queene. Ed. David Lee Miller and Alexander Dunlop. 1994.

Stendhal's The Red and the Black. Ed. Dean de la Motte and Stirling Haig. 1999.

Sterne's Tristram Shandy. Ed. Melvyn New. 1989.

Works of Robert Louis Stevenson. Ed. Caroline McCracken-Flesher. 2013.

The Story of the Stone (Dream of the Red Chamber). Ed. Andrew Schonebaum and Tina Lu. 2012.

Stowe's Uncle Tom's Cabin. Ed. Elizabeth Ammons and Susan Belasco. 2000.

Swift's Gulliver's Travels. Ed. Edward J. Rielly. 1988.

Teresa of Ávila and the Spanish Mystics. Ed. Alison Weber. 2009.

Thoreau's Walden *and Other Works*. Ed. Richard J. Schneider. 1996.

Tolkien's The Lord of the Rings *and Other Works*. Ed. Leslie A. Donovan. 2015.

Tolstoy's Anna Karenina. Ed. Liza Knapp and Amy Mandelker. 2003.

Vergil's Aeneid. Ed. William S. Anderson and Lorina N. Quartarone. 2002.

Voltaire's Candide. Ed. Renée Waldinger. 1987.

Whitman's Leaves of Grass. Ed. Donald D. Kummings. 1990.

Wiesel's Night. Ed. Alan Rosen. 2007.

Plays of August Wilson. Ed. Sandra G. Shannon and Sandra L. Richards. 2016.

Works of Oscar Wilde. Ed. Philip E. Smith II. 2008.

Woolf's Mrs. Dalloway. Ed. Eileen Barrett and Ruth O. Saxton. 2009.

Woolf's To the Lighthouse. Ed. Beth Rigel Daugherty and Mary Beth Pringle. 2001.

Wordsworth's Poetry. Ed. Spencer Hall, with Jonathan Ramsey. 1986.

Wright's Native Son. Ed. James A. Miller. 1997.